The Arc of Love

The Arc of Love

How Our Romantic Lives Change over Time

AARON BEN-ZE'EV

The University of Chicago Press
Chicago and London

The University of Chicago Press, Chicago 60637
The University of Chicago Press, Ltd., London
© 2019 by The University of Chicago
All rights reserved. No part of this book may be used or reproduced in any manner
whatsoever without written permission, except in the case of brief quotations in
critical articles and reviews. For more information, contact the University of Chicago
Press, 1427 E. 60th St., Chicago, IL 60637.
Published 2019
Printed in the United States of America

28 27 26 25 24 23 22 21 20 19   1 2 3 4 5

ISBN-13: 978-0-226-63390-9 (cloth)
ISBN-13: 978-0-226-63406-7 (e-book)
DOI: https://doi.org/10.7208/chicago/9780226634067.001.0001

Library of Congress Cataloging-in-Publication Data

Names: Ben-Ze'ev, Aharon, author.
Title: The arc of love : how our romantic lives change over time / Aaron Ben-Ze'ev.
Description: Chicago : The University of Chicago Press, 2019. | Includes
    bibliographical references and index.
Identifiers: LCCN 2018055500 | ISBN 9780226633909 (cloth : alk. paper) |
    ISBN 9780226634067 (e-book)
Subjects: LCSH: Love. | Love—Philosophy.
Classification: LCC BF575.L8 B349 2019 | DDC 306.7—dc23
LC record available at https://lccn.loc.gov/2018055500

♾ This paper meets the requirements of ANSI/NISO Z39.48–1992 (Permanence of Paper).

Contents

Introduction

Love and eggs are best when they are fresh.
RUSSIAN PROVERB

This book is about long-term romantic love and how we go about developing it—or fail to do so. It is about building the foundations for such love and dealing with the difficulties that inevitably emerge in such a challenging and critical construction project. The reader will discover the good news that there is no reason to despair: enduring love *can* be achieved. And, as we shall see, time plays a leading role in this process.

I take an optimistic perspective. Not only is enduring, profound love possible; it is also more common than most of us think. Yet the romantic road is often bumpy and long. Enticing romances encounter many blind alleys. How is the would-be lover to know when such romances are promenades for flourishing love and when they are dead-end streets? In these pages, I provide some helpful signposts along the "freeway of love."

Love is not all you need; but if you have enough of what you need, and love infuses life with joy, your life is more likely to be a many-splendored thing.

The Possibility of Long-Term Romantic Love

There is only one serious question. And that is: . . . how to make love stay?
TOM ROBBINS

.

The first stop on our journey toward the heart of love will consider long-term romantic love.[1] The endurance of romantic love has been debated from time immemorial. Despite this fact, however, we still do not have a handle on how love survives time.

In the field of philosophy, the discussion has centered on the question of whether love is conditional, that is, whether it is dependent on anything. Aristotle, for instance, believed that it is; according to him, love can end if the beloved changes for the worse. Other philosophers, notably Plato and Emmanuel Levinas, considered love to be unconditional; in their view, love can last for a lifetime. In the field of psychology, one also finds conflicting views concerning the possibility of long-term romantic love. In this introductory chapter, I discuss some central issues that have bearing on these questions, such as the role of change and familiarity in love, the basic human drive to yearn for the possible, and the conflict between love and life.

Will You Love Me Tomorrow?

Tonight you're mine, completely . . . but will you love me tomorrow?
CAROLE KING

Carole King asks the burning question of the romantic lover: Will you love me tomorrow? In other words, Will the feeling that I am your beloved last only until the morning sun rises, or will it last for many years? To this question, we might add our own: Must romantic love *endure over time* in order to be considered profound? Can brief romantic affairs be fully satisfied?

As a young boy, I devoured Gustave Flaubert's *Madame Bovary* (1856) and Amos Oz's *My Michael* (1968). These romantic tragedies served as cautionary tales, warning of the consequences to passion withering and love dying. Take the undoing of Emma Bovary, who tries to relieve the banality of her life through a series of adulterous affairs. Ultimately rejected by her lovers and deep in debt, Emma swallows arsenic. Like her, Hannah Gonen (Michael's wife) is drenched in dreams but stunted by her marriage to an unimaginative man. As time goes on, her marriage deteriorates into sadness and depression, and her dreams—along with her sanity—are quashed.

Emma and Hannah appear to be victims of a myth, a dangerous romantic ideology enshrined in both our recordings and our rituals: true love overcomes all obstacles ("There ain't no mountain high enough to keep me from getting to you"); and love lasts forever ("till death us do part"). This seductive notion assumes both the uniqueness of the beloved and a kind of fusion. Soulmates are meant only for each other: lovers form a single entity, and each of the partners is irreplaceable. The lover's attention is focused on nothing but the beloved ("When a man loves a woman, can't keep his mind on nothing else"). Ideal love is total, uncompromising, and unconditional. Hell might be freezing over, but true love will endure.[2]

While such romantic ideology retains its allure, the idea that passion can last a lifetime has lost its luster in modern times. We have all witnessed an increasing gap between the desire for an enduring romantic relationship and the probability of its fulfillment. Breakups, not long-term relationships, are the norm. In many societies, about half of all marriages end in divorce, and many of the remaining half have at some point seriously considered divorce. Love is a trade-off, the prevailing wisdom goes—we can either soar briefly to the highest heights of passion, or we can be content with a meaningful friendship for many years. Is it then fruitless to despair, as do Emma and Hannah, because having both is impossible?

And yet . . . popular culture celebrates long-term love. Moreover, most people, including the current generation of adolescents, continue to believe in the possibility of such love. A survey of young adults (ages 18–29) in the United States revealed that the vast majority holds highly optimistic views about marriage, with 86 percent expecting to have a marriage that lasts a lifetime.[3] However, such love is under attack in contemporary society, where novelty rules, and change is the absolute order of the day. Thus, we are confronted with a paradox: the ideal of love demands that it be endless, lasting until "the sun shines no more," while our lives are littered with crumbling relationships.

Confusing Findings

Nothing in mating remains static. Evolution did not design humans for lifelong matrimonial bliss.

DAVID BUSS

Been with my wife for more than 25 years. We had 2 children together. I love her today
more than I ever have. The thought of growing old with her brings me comfort. Yes,
love can survive and flourish!

CHRIS CURTIS

A large body of research indicates that sexual desire decreases dramatically
over time within relationships. Thus, one's sexual response to a familiar partner will be progressively less intense than such response to a novel partner.
Unsurprisingly, then, the frequency of sexual activity with one's partner tends
to decline steadily as the relationship lengthens. After one year of marriage,
couples tend to be half as sexually active together as they were during their
first month of marriage, with sex declining more gradually thereafter. A similar pattern of decline has also been found among cohabiting heterosexual
couples and among gay and lesbian couples. Hence, enduring romantic love
seems to be uncommon, usually evolving into companionate love in which
sexual desire grows weaker as time passes.[4]

Yet research also suggests that many long-term couples remain deeply in
love. Daniel O'Leary and colleagues asked 274 married individuals: "How in
love are you with your partner?" Forty percent of those married for more
than a decade reported being "very intensely in love." Even more dramatically, among those in marriages of thirty years or more, 40 percent of wives
and 35 percent of husbands reported very intense love for their partner.[5]

Confusing results, indeed. How can we make sense of them? As it turns
out, recent neuroscientific research may have identified the mechanism behind these findings. Bianca Acevedo and colleagues showed ten women and
seven men who had been married for an average of twenty-one years and
reported being intensely in love with their spouses the facial images of their
partners while scanning their brains with fMRI. The scans revealed a significant activation in key reward centers of the brain—much like the pattern
found in people experiencing fresh love, but vastly different from those in
companionate relationships.[6]

Other research has reported cases in which familiarity promotes attraction and others in which it undermines attraction.[7] Christine Proulx and colleagues approached the question from a different perspective. They found
two major trajectories of marital quality: (1) marriages with an initial high,

stable level of marital quality, which are likely to maintain this level in the long term, and (2) marriages that begin with a low level of marital quality, which typically remain at this level or lower. The authors noted that the first trajectory group is quite large.[8]

So, is romantic love by nature short-lived, or not? The jury is still out. In this book, I hope to convince the reader that enduring romantic love is truly possible. While the opposing evidence will certainly still stand, I aim to demonstrate that it does not apply to all cases.

Change and Familiarity

The more I see you, the more I want you. Somehow this feeling just grows and grows. With every sigh, I become more mad about you.

CHRIS MONTEZ

Weirdly, I want the unpleasant situation between me and my husband to change. But then again, I would not have an excuse for a hot lover. Just being honest . . .

A MARRIED WOMAN

People usually experience emotions when *they perceive positive or negative significant changes in their personal situation*—or in that of those related to them. This seems to work against the possibility of enduring romantic love. From an evolutionary point of view, it is advantageous to focus our attention on change rather than on static stimuli. Change indicates that our situation is unstable, and awareness of this may mean the difference between life and death. When we become accustomed to the change, mental activity decreases, as there is no need to waste our time and energy on something to which we have already adapted.

A change cannot persist for an extended period; after a while, we consider the change as normal, and it no longer stimulates us. Like burglar alarms going off when an intruder appears, emotions signal that something needs attention. When no attention is required, the signaling system can be switched off. We respond to the unusual by attending to it.[9] Spinoza stressed this point. In his view, survival is central to any organism. When we undergo marked change, we pass to a greater or lesser perfection, and these changes are expressed in emotions. As we change for the better, we are happy; for the worse, unhappy.[10]

A famous anecdote comes to mind here. Calvin Coolidge, the then-president of the United States, was touring a farm with his wife. They were taken in separate directions. When Mrs. Coolidge passed the chicken pens, she paused to ask the man in charge if the rooster copulated more than once each day. "Dozens of times," was the reply. "Please tell that to the president," Mrs. Coolidge requested. When the president passed the pens and was told about the rooster, he asked: "Same hen every time?" "Oh no, Mr. President, a different one each time." The president nodded slowly, then said, "Please tell that to Mrs. Coolidge." Amusing as it is, this story has a serious side as well. It spawned the scholarly term "the Coolidge Effect" for the phenomenon in which males (and to lesser extent females) in mammalian species exhibit re-newed sexual interest when introduced to new sexual partners.

The central role of change in generating emotions is not obvious, how-ever, and some scholars disagree with it.[11] In order for it to be true, they as-sume, commonly recognized emotional experiences such as long-term love, grief, regret, and hate could no longer be considered "emotions." I will show that some kind of change is also part of enduring emotions.

In addition to the crucial role of change in producing emotions, similar-ity and familiarity have been found to be prompts for emotion. Thus, ro-mantic partners show strong similarity in age and in political and religious attitudes; moderate similarity in education, general intelligence, and values; and little or no similarity in personality characteristics. Only in short-term relationships, where commitment is low, do people prefer dissimilar *partners*. In long-term relationships, which are characterized by high commitment and joint activities, *greater* similarity predicts romantic liking.[12]

Neither repetition nor change alone, however, has been found to produce emotional intensity spikes. It is a particular change—one that happens to a familiar, stable framework—that tends to incite such an intensity increase. In this context, it is worth distinguishing between relational (or localized) novelty and absolute (or global) novelty. Relational novelty has to do with difference within a familiar framework, whereas in absolute novelty, the framework itself changes. A significant emotional change does not necessar-ily mean that something is absolutely novel, though. On the contrary, since absolute novelty, by definition, feels alien to us, it may not take on emotional significance. When it does, negative emotions often follow.

Let's think for a moment about first impressions. Such impressions tend toward the extreme: the new person is often viewed as either strikingly beau-tiful or strikingly ugly. After a while, our impressions begin to moderate, and the very same beautiful individual may be perceived as less beautiful and the ugly one as less ugly. The nineteenth-century English novelist Ouida said it well: "Familiarity is a magician that is cruel to beauty but kind to ugliness." Extreme impressions, which are associated with intense emotional reactions, enable the formation of a quick response toward an unfamiliar figure. When we get to know someone, our extreme response can safely fall away. In fact, moderate perceptions smooth communication. Notably, in contrast to the positive effects of increased levels of attractiveness on new relationships, no significant association has been found between levels of attractiveness and the subsequent quality of marital relationship.[13]

To sum up, while change tends to generate intense, short-term emotion, familiarity tends to produce a more moderate attitude, which can be long-lasting indeed.

Yearning for the Possible

Regret for the things we did can be tempered by time; it is regret for the things we did not do that is inconsolable.
SYDNEY SMITH

People care not only—or even mainly—about the present, but also about the possible. One of humanity's greatest advantages over other animals is our greater capacity to imagine circumstances that differ from our present situation. Imagination is so fundamental to human life that it is impossible to think of living without it. We are hardwired to imagine the possible, so it is humanly impossible to ignore it.

Imagination immeasurably expands our horizons. But the capacity to imagine, which unchains us from the present, also chains us to the possible. Imagination is a double-edged sword: it is a gift, but one that can cut deeply. In the romantic realm, it gives us the wondrous ability to be aware of various romantic possibilities and the chance to develop ourselves accordingly. At the very same time, it can prevent us from enjoying our own romantic lot.

A major dilemma in romantic life is choosing which possibilities to pursue and which to set aside. When should we settle for what we have? It is not easy to decide which romantic doors to leave open and which ones to close; each has its own costs and benefits.

In the romantic arena, people often imagine sweet possibilities while struggling with a painful present. The imagination-driven allure of romantic roads not taken places challenging barriers to being happy with what we have—a feeling that lies at the root of long-lasting love. These moments call for major ammunition: adaptation and compromise. Although these words do not seem sexy in the least, in the course of our journey, we will see how they can take an attractive shape indeed.

Imagination expands our horizons in all temporal dimensions—present, past, and future. In the context of the present, or more precisely, the very near future, we explore what is possible for us to do here and now. This gives us a practical perspective when considering what we currently desire. The horizon directed at the past provides us with a perspective about ourselves and what is meaningful for us. Although we cannot change the past, it influences choices we make in the present and for the future. Of the three temporal horizons, the future-oriented one has the greatest impact on our decision-making. People tend to think more about the future than the past or the present, and many potential events wind up being more pleasurable to imagine than to experience.[14]

Our ability to wander among temporal dimensions, including comparing the past with present and future situations, can prompt a sense of regret. Regret can be understood as a negative attitude toward our past behavior. In the short term, regret often concerns past actions that generated negative consequences; in the long term, however, regret tends to involve inaction—the road not taken—which is seen as responsible for our current limited horizons.[15] Americans, according to one study, express great regret concerning their choices in four fields: education, career, romance, and parenting. Education tops that list, since it functions as a gateway to highly valued options, from higher income to more challenging careers to a diversity of social and romantic contacts. We regret most not extending our horizons. Regret is intimately entwined with opportunity; that is, we are inclined to regret when the prospect of change, growth, and renewal is not fulfilled.[16]

Worry can be thought of as a negative attitude toward our future behavior and circumstances. In the short term, we might worry about specific future events that can harm us; in the long term, worry concerns the future shrinking of our horizons. When we are young, we usually perceive our future horizons as expanding. As we age or become sick, the horizon appears to shrink. Laura Carstensen claims that our motivation in each case is different. When we see our horizons as expanding, we are motivated to broaden our interests and the types of activities we pursue; when we see them as shrinking, we are more likely to focus on the options we already have. This is particularly evident in old age, women's awareness of their "biological clock," and during times of war. Thus, as we grow older, increasingly perceiving time as finite and our horizons as constrained, we reorder our priorities. We attach less importance to long-term considerations and greater significance to goals from which we derive immediate emotional meaning.[17] However, while at a young age, the immediate meaning relates to external (romantic and otherwise) options; at an older age, the immediate meanings tend to be part of our current frame of living.

In the romantic realm, we demonstrate an appreciation of long-term considerations when we nurture our current relationships rather than expend effort on new romantic opportunities. This tending of our own garden encourages a sense of being happy with one's own portion, which in turn decreases the feeling of being romantically compromised and the inclination to look elsewhere. While short-term possibilities tend to take the front burner, it is our long-term horizons that guide our most profound attitudes concerning personal and romantic flourishing.

I Love You, but I Am Leaving You

I'm sorry, I love you, but I have to leave you. You were the right choice, but not my "happy" choice.
HALLIE MANTEGNA

There is love, of course. And then there's life, its enemy.
JEAN ANOUILH

The claim "I love you, but I am leaving you" seems paradoxical. If you love me, why should you leave me? After all, love implies the wish to be with the beloved, and not to leave him. Despite this paradoxical tone, we shall see that there is no paradox in this claim.

Sometimes love and life clash, and we have to make compromises—one such compromise is leaving the one you love.

The Importance of Love in Life

All you need is love.
THE BEATLES

Romantic love adds sweetness to our lives. It does much more than that, however: it enhances health, happiness, and flourishing. It makes us feel alive. Thus, marriages, which are the prevailing framework of long-term love, have been linked to many health advantages, such as lower psychological distress, greater well–being, fewer doctor visits, lower blood pressure, faster healing, and longer life. Love clearly stimulates health, well-being, and (re)productivity. The connection between love (and marriage) and happiness (including flourishing and health) works both ways: it is easier for happy people to fall in love, and it is more likely that those in love will be happy.[18] Hence, those reporting their marriage as "very happy" are among the happiest of people— 57 percent of these couples declared life as a whole to be very happy (compared with 10 percent of those whose marriage is "pretty happy" and 3 percent of those with a "not-too-happy" marriage).[19]

The situation, however, is more complex, as not all marriages are equal: unhappy marriages provide fewer benefits than happy ones. Studies indicate that those not too happy in marriage also had equal or worse health and mortality risk compared to those who were never married, divorced or separated, or widowed. Thus, although being married is associated with better outcomes than not being married, unhappy, poorly functioning marriages may be as harmful to health as happy marriages are beneficial. Marriage is not a panacea; it is beneficial only for those who are pretty happy or very happy in their marriage.[20]

The Importance of Life in Love

Goodbye taught me that people don't always stay and the things that belonged to you today can belong to someone else tomorrow.

RANIA NAIM

We need to love in order to flourish. And it is equally true that profound love craves a flourishing life. Thus, we come to the thorny issue of whether to remain in a romantic relationship that prevents one's personal flourishing. In this regard, the late Princess Diana once quipped, "They say it is better to be poor and happy than rich and miserable, but how about a compromise like moderately rich and just moody?" Similarly, one might claim that it is better to be poor in love than rich without love, but how about a compromise like being moderately rich and just loving (rather being madly in love with) each other?

In romantic compromises, we give up a romantic value, such as passionate love, in exchange for a nonromantic quality-of-life value. Such compromise stems from the awareness that we are limited creatures; we cannot always meet our standards or achieve our ideals. Survival sometimes depends on being flexible, settling for something less—or simply different—than we might have wanted.

Today, the prevailing view is love over life. Time and again, we hear that "love always wins" and "love always finds a way." Life might not be the greatest enemy of love, but it often involves considerations that clash with romantic ones. To admit that in some circumstances life should take precedence over love is to admit the necessity of romantic compromises. As Kierkegaard rightly said, "Life is not a problem to be solved, but a reality to be experienced." And it is a reality that we must take into account.

Despite the importance of love in life and life in love, love and life often clash. This conflict underlies the situation of leaving the person you love. Usually, this conflict can be traced to one of two issues: (1) romantic reasons that have to do with the nature of love between the partners, and (2) reasons concerning the flourishing life of the partners.

I Love You, but Not Strongly Enough

There is a difference between someone who wants you and someone who would do anything to keep you. Actions speak louder than wishes.
UNKNOWN

Romantic love is not an all-or-nothing attitude—it comes in different degrees. Some degrees are good enough for having an affair for a few weeks or months, but not sufficient for sustaining long-term love. Examples of common reasons for loving and leaving in this group are the following:

"I found a new lover."
"In the past, I have loved someone more strongly than I love you."
"I am happy with you in the short term [great romantic intensity], but I do not see prospects for the long term [not much romantic profundity]."
"We are great sexual partners, but not good friends."
"We are profound friends, but not great sexual partners."
"There are major flaws in your behavior preventing me from trusting you and feeling calm with you."
"I cannot give you the love you deserve"; or more bluntly, "My feelings toward you are not strong enough."

The reasons in this group are mainly comparative—indicating a lower level of love or romantic suitability. Here, there is some degree of love, but that degree is not sufficient—at least not when compared to other available options. Choosing life is even clearer when love is not achieved. As one woman said, "I have never really been in love before, so I'm going to go with money."

I Love You but Cannot Live with You

Look, I hate good-byes, too. But sometimes, we need them just to survive.
RACHEL CAINE

If I should stay, I would only be in your way, So I'll go, but I will always love you.
DOLLY PARTON (and later, Whitney Houston)

Long-term romantic relationships should take into account nonromantic factors concerning the living together of the two partners. Loving someone is not always sufficient for deciding to live with someone. Living together and establishing a family together certainly require love—but much more than that. They require the ability to help each other flourish. Examples of common reasons on this basis are the following:

"I love you, but I'm not ready."
"You cannot help me to flourish because you do not bring out the best in me."
"I cannot help you to flourish—on the contrary, being with me blocks your flourishing."
"We are not suitable for building a long-term, thriving life together."
"You are not a good father, husband, or provider (though you may be a great lover)."

In this group of reasons, the degree of love is sufficient for supporting enduring love, but not enduring living together.

People sometimes prefer thriving in life over love—it can be their own thriving or that of their partner. An illustration of the first kind is the case of a married woman who said that she loved her first husband very much, but something was missing in their relationship that made her decide to divorce him: "There was nothing wrong with him," she said, "but nevertheless I felt that self-fulfillment would not be part of my life. He would not block it, but he would not bring out the best in me. With my second husband, I have many fights, but I do feel his profound passion and ability to bring out the best in me." This woman chose losing her first husband over losing herself.

An example of preferring the partner's thriving over love is the case of a partner who, out of profound love, ends a relationship saying that staying together would make his or her beloved miserable in the long term. This is the theme of the above-mentioned song "I Will Always Love You," which many consider the greatest love song of all time. In taking into account this reality, we sometimes hear of a partner, out of profound love, ending a relationship out of concern that staying together would make his or her beloved miserable in the long term. In this case, ending the relationship expresses a genuine interest in the other's profound well-being.

Love, and especially intense love, can make us neglect important aspects of life, thereby hurting ourselves in a way that risks our togetherness. In his memorable song "So Long, Marianne," Leonard Cohen says, "You know that I love to live with you," but adds, "You make me forget so very much, I forget to pray for the angels, And then the angels forget to pray for us"; hence, "So long, Marianne."

Profound love is indeed about the heart's tendencies—but it does not stop there. This kind of love takes the partner and his or her flourishing deeply into account. Profound love involves the desire to live with a partner who is thriving in mutual relationship. Sometimes, when this desire cannot be fulfilled, life wins over love, and one partner might say to the other something along the lines of "1 will always love you, but I do not believe in the future of our love, as we cannot flourish together." Accordingly, profound love is not identical to long-term love. There are couples who divorce despite their profound love.

Profound love cannot remain oblivious to the beloved's thriving—such flourishing is essential for enduring profound love. Bringing out the best in each other, a critical component of lasting love, is impossible in the face of certain extreme challenges, such as when one partner is deeply despondent or when poverty is making life miserable. One might feel that staying together will prevent the partner or both of them from flourishing, or (in the case of a married person) will have a negative impact on any children involved. In such cases, love often takes second place to the need for broader flourishing.

Is Love All We Need?

All you need is love. But a little chocolate now and then doesn't hurt.
CHARLES SCHULZ

We have seen that romantic love has a very positive impact upon one's life. However, people need more than love to flourish. For love to thrive and endure, we need a good-enough living framework. When romantic love thrives, it can contribute to a more general feeling of thriving. Sometimes, however, love and life conflict.

And so, we can find ourselves asking: Which takes precedence, love or life? This can be a hard call. At one extreme, one might sacrifice life for love (let's remember Romeo and Juliet). At the other, one might sacrifice love for life (remaining in a loveless, but otherwise comfortable, marriage, for example). Of course, most of us make romantic decisions that fall somewhere between these harrowing poles. It is the strength of love, the nature of life's demands, and the degree of conflict between them that dictate exactly where we wind up on that continuum.

When intense desire is perceived as the core of romantic love, the conflict between romantic love and life ramps up. Such desire is usually brief and decreases with time. Life, by contrast, tends to last. A lover cannot be blind to life, and love does not always win. In any case, love cannot replace life.

Indeed, in a study on partners in romantic relationships who provided reports on *perceived* changes in their relationship, the participants who continue to be together during the study (four years) *perceived* that their love, commitment, and satisfaction were increasing over time. However, in the case of the couples who experienced breakup, satisfaction was perceived to decrease the most, whereas love was perceived to decrease the least. These results suggest that "people do not end their relationships because of the disappearance of love, but because of a dissatisfaction or unhappiness that develops, which may then cause love to stop growing."[21]

When love and life go head-to-head, love almost always loses, especially when it is based on intense desire. In the long run, it is when lovers nurture the connection between themselves and do things that enable each other to flourish that love is maintained and enhanced. That is how ties to the living framework are tightened.

The claim that "all you need is love" indicates, as Brian Epstein, the Beatles' manager, once said, "a clear message saying that love is everything." Although romantic love is extremely important for our happiness and flourishing, love is neither a necessary, nor a sufficient, condition for a happy and thriving life. As it turns out, love is *not* everything in life, though it is often a central part of it.

If indeed, love is not all we need, then it is certainly reasonable for some people to leave the one they love.

Brief Infatuations and Long Romance

I want both—a long, profound love AND a series of short, intense romantic/sexual experiences. Lust and profound love are both meaningful and satisfying for me.
A WOMAN IN HER THIRTIES

Done with trying to find a woman for life. Much easier to just hook up for a good short time. Avoid all the other personal drama!
FRANK

This book takes the view that long-term, profound love is possible. As we near the end of the introductory chapter, I would like to raise the rather radical question of whether or not this kind of love is a desirable goal. And, even if we decide that the ideal of "endless love" is important and worth pursuing, we can ask if it spells the end of all short-term, intense relationships.

Let's listen to Marianne, a divorced woman and successful businesswoman:

I am happy for people who remain in love with the same partner for a long time. . . . Would I want to be in love with the same man all my life? To be honest with myself, the answer is no. However, while I am intensely in love with a man, I want this love to endure for a long time. I would be happy to feel in love forever with the man I am with now. However, I know that it is impossible and although I am not so young, I am still attracted to excitement. Accordingly, I believe that what I really want, and what actually happens to me, is that I need more than one love in my whole life.

Marianne's attitude rests on a questionable claim—that long-term, profound love is not possible. However, as indicated above, research points to the definite possibility of lifelong love—and to more of this love than many of us ever imagined. Moreover, perceptions of long-term love tend to change over time. As we age, a sense of peacefulness rather than excitement can become the essential element in a marriage.[22]

Marianne's dilemma is genuine—and she is far from alone. Even those who experience profound love can feel this way. Consider the following message from a reader, sent as a comment to a post that I wrote in *Psychology Today*:

I'm a female in my 30s. We cannot know what the future brings, but after many years of seeking the person who is right for me, I am very happy that last year I found the man with whom I want to build a calm and meaningful life and achieve profound love. I love him. The reason I wanted to have this kind of relationship is for stability, calmness, and happiness. However, I have an interesting issue here. . . . Putting all taboos aside and focusing on my true nature, satisfying this long-term need of mine doesn't and didn't suppress my desire for an intense romantic/sexual experience. I am experiencing strong intense sexual desire for another man, besides the man with whom I want to be life partners. If I had never met this other man in my life, perhaps I would not have known how satisfying and meaningful lust and its ups and downs could be. This relationship is a very exciting and meaningful one. But I guess I'm talking about only one sexual partner here, not many; I don't really want short-term/intense relationships with multiple partners. All I need and want is multiple short-term/intense experiences with one man, and a life-long, less intense, more stable and productive relationship with a life partner. So I want both—a long, profound love AND a series of short, intense romantic/sexual experiences. Lust and profound love are both meaningful and satisfying for me, and contribute to my happiness.

In this candid letter, we read how difficult it is for the writer to give up intense sexual activity for the sake of highly desired, long-term love. A single young woman expresses a somewhat similar attitude:

I have three lovers. One of these lovers is married, and it is with him that I have the most profound relationship. Every year, we spend five entire weekends together. My second lover is a "Tuesday person"—we are together in my apartment every Tuesday afternoon for about an hour and a half. The third lover is a kind of fucking friend with whom I have occasional (often, nonstandard) sex. I also have many male friends. I am quite happy with my life, but I would be even happier if I found a man with whom I could combine friendship and sex. He could be my stable and enduring partner, provided that he allowed me (and himself) to have another lover.

The choice people face is between a long and overall high-quality love with moderate excitement and a short and typically overall low-quality love with higher sexual excitement. It seems that for many people the question is not a binary one—not either a long-term profound love or short-term, intense loving relationships, but instead, whether, and how, a combination of the two is possible.

Concluding Remarks

I'm selfish, impatient and a little insecure. I make mistakes, I am out of control and at times hard to handle. But if you can't handle me at my worst, then you sure as hell don't deserve me at my best.

MARILYN MONROE

The romantic road sets high hurdles in our path, but the journey is an intriguing, meaningful, and often pleasurable one. Coping with the complexity of romantic reality is far from simple: sometimes we need to open our eyes and sometimes to close them; sometimes we have to remember and sometimes we need to forget. Ingrid Bergman said it well: "Happiness is good health and a bad memory." The challenge in this society is not that of finding love, as love is always in the air: everywhere you look, every sight and every sound, indicates that love is all around. Unfortunately, the air is often too polluted to enable the development of long-term profound love.

We are condemned to yearn for a constant star while knowing full well that the heart needs steering. As we shall see in this book, balance holds the key. Setting one's mind at rest yet maintaining a certain degree of striving is often a good romantic compromise, one that has the potential to enhance both life and love. It is naïve to believe that love will always win. However, it is usually helpful to maintain the positive illusion that it will.

2

Emotional Experiences

Love is when the other person's happiness is more important than your own.
H. JACKSON BROWN JR.

We continue our tour with a discussion of the nature of emotional and romantic experiences. Here's how things will unfold. The first section describes "acute emotions"; in the section that follows, "extended" and "enduring" emotions are considered. *Acute emotions* are brief, almost instantaneous experiences. *Extended emotions* involve successive repetitions of experiences that are felt to belong to the same emotion. *Enduring emotions* can persist for many years. In light of these distinctions, I further examine the occurrent and dispositional nature of emotions and moods, after which the issue of emotional simplicity and complexity is discussed. The discussion on acute emotions will show their intense and brief nature. This raises the issue of how moderation and balance, which are crucial for lasting happiness and love, can be achieved nevertheless.

Typical Emotions

In vain I have struggled. It will not do. My feelings will not be repressed. You must allow me to tell you how ardently I admire and love you.
JANE AUSTEN, *Pride and Prejudice*

Let's begin with acute emotions. I refer to their typical *cause*, that is, a significant change; the typical *focus of concern*, that is, a personal, comparative concern; the typical *emotional object*, that is, a human being; and the major *characteristics of acute emotions*: instability, great intensity, a partial perspective, and relative brevity.

The typical cause. As we have seen above, emotions typically occur when *we perceive positive or negative significant changes in our personal situation—or* in that of those related to us. A positive or negative significant change substantially interrupts or improves a smoothly flowing situation that is of concern to us.

The typical focus of concern. Emotions emerge when a change is perceived as relevant to our personal concerns. Concerns are matters of interest or importance to us. Emotions serve to monitor and protect our personal concerns. These personal concerns do not make the emotions egoistic, as other people are also included in our emotional environment.[1] This is especially true regarding romantic love.

Emotional meaning is *comparative*. The emotional environment contains not only what is and what will be experienced but also everything that could be or that one hopes will be experienced. We experience such possibilities as simultaneously available and comparable. Comparative concern in emotions is related to the central role of change in generating emotions. An event can be perceived as a significant change only when compared against a certain background or within a certain framework.

While sifting through the possible alternatives and assigning each of them a certain emotional weight, we draw on the mental construction of the *availability of an alternative*.[2] The more available the alternative—that is, the closer the imagined alternative is to reality—the more intense the emotion. Thus, the fate of someone who dies in an airplane crash after switching flights evokes a stronger emotion than that of a traveler who was booked on the flight all along. Greater availability, which increases instability and the possibility that the event could have been prevented, makes the emotional experience more painful. In fact, a crucial element in intense emotions is the imagined condition of "it could have been otherwise."

The typical emotional object. Since emotions express our personal, comparative concerns, and as other people are highly relevant to our well-being, the typical emotional object is another person. As social animals, people are more interesting to us than anything else. The things that people do and say, including the things that we ourselves do and say, are the things that affect us most.[3] Although human emotions are most often directed to situations involving humans and tend to be directed toward a particular person, they can sometimes be generalized, perhaps toward a whole group of people, or even animals and inanimate things. Thus, some people consider a romantic relationship with an artificial being, such as a robot or a sophisticated doll, to be just as meaningful and fulfilling as one with a human being.[4]

The major *emotional characteristics* are instability, intensity, partiality, and brevity.

Instability. Reflecting the fact that change is so fundamental to the production of emotions, instability of the mental and physiological systems is basic to any emotion. Emotions point to a transition in which the preceding context has changed, but adaptation to the new context has not yet taken place. Like storms and fire, unstable states signify agitation. Moreover, they are intense, occasional, and limited in duration. At the basis of an emotional attitude is a kind of caring, which is incompatible with complete indifference.

Intensity. Acute emotions are marked by a great deal of intensity. The lives of people low in emotional intensity show endurance, evenness, and lack of fluctuation. Acute emotions are intense reactions. In such emotions, the mental system has not yet adapted to a given change, and, because of its significance, the change requires the mobilization of many resources. No wonder that acute emotions are associated with urgency and heat. In such emotions, there is no such thing as a minor concern; if the concern is minor, it is not emotional. And emotions magnify: everything looms larger when we are emotional. Thus, it would be insulting to tell one's partner that one loves him a little. Love in such a small measure might refer to liking, but it will not refer to intense love.

Partiality. Emotions are *partial* in two basic senses: (1) a *cognitive* sense— they are focused on a *narrow* target, such as one person or very few people, and (2) an *evaluative* sense—they express a *personal and interested* perspective. Emotions direct and color our attention by selecting what attracts and holds it. They might be compared to heat-seeking missiles, which have no other concern but to find the heat-generating target. Emotions address practical concerns from a personal perspective. We cannot assume an emotional attitude toward everyone or toward those with whom we have no relationship whatsoever. Focusing on fewer objects increases the resources available for each person or concern, hence increasing emotional intensity. Like a laser beam, which focuses on a very narrow area and consequently achieves high intensity, emotions, which express our values and preferences, cannot be indiscriminate.

Brevity. Emotions are usually brief. We cannot mobilize many resources to focus on one event forever. A system cannot remain unstable for a long period and still function normally. A change, or at least an external change, cannot last for long; after a while, the system reads the change as the norm. If emotions were to endure for a long time regardless of what was happening all around, they would not have adaptive value. That acute emotions are temporary states, however, does not mean that their impact is necessarily temporary—a brief emotional state can have an enormous impact on one's life.

The Temporality of Emotional Experiences: Acute, Extended, and Enduring Emotions

> Love doesn't just sit there, like a stone, it has to be made, like bread; remade all the time, made new.
>
> URSULA K. LE GUIN, *The Lathe of Heaven*

Emotions take place in time, last for a specific duration, and often show up again and again. These time-related aspects are especially important in romantic love, where mutuality needs time to develop and deepen. Romantic love does not merely "take" time: it is constituted and shaped by time spent together.[5]

There is a long-standing dispute about how long an emotion can last and still be considered an emotion. Some say that an emotion must be rather brief, a matter of seconds or minutes, and others say that an emotion can last much longer than that. A cross-cultural study found that fear usually lasts for a matter of minutes—in many cases, less than five minutes, and rarely lasts longer than an hour. Anger often lasts more than a few minutes, but rarely for more than a few hours. We feel sadness and happiness, it has been found, often for more than an hour; in fact, in more than half of the cases examined in one study, sadness hung on for longer than a day. Jealousy, grief, and love usually persist even longer. An attitude cannot be regarded as love if it lasts only five seconds; love has to be made and remade again and again. Nor can relief or pleasure in others' misfortune survive for years. Other emotions, however, do not have such temporal constraints and can endure for different amounts of time.[6]

Affective time has four main aspects: location, duration, pace and frequency, and meaningful direction. Temporal *location* refers to when an experience takes place. *Duration* concerns the length of an experience. *Pace* relates to how fast an experience takes place, and *frequency* refers to its repetition, that is, the rate at which the repeating experience, or at least its major features, reoccurs. To these three quantitative aspects, a fourth qualitative aspect can be added: development or deterioration—the *meaningful direction* of an affective experience over time.

As temporal location is common to all types of emotions, we can talk about three major types of emotional experiences: (1) acute emotions, (2) extended emotions, and (3) enduring emotions. *Acute emotions* are brief, almost instantaneous experiences. *Extended emotions* involve successive repetitions of experiences that are felt to belong to the same emotion—for example, being angry or jealous for hours. Compared to acute emotions, extended emotions last longer and occur more frequently. The intensity varies over the period of the episode, and the nature of the emotion can change somewhat. *Enduring emotions* are the longest-lasting of the three and can persist for a lifetime. In addition to their duration and frequency, enduring emotions involve a qualitative meaningful development (and sometimes deterioration), and a dispositional nature that unfolds over time.[7]

An enduring emotion, which includes a series of acute and extended emotions, continuously shapes our attitudes and behavior. A flash of anger might last a few minutes or more, but grief over the loss of a loved one can resonate endlessly, coloring many aspects of our life—our moods, our thriving, and the way we relate to time and space. A person's long-standing love for her spouse sometimes involves acute sexual desire, but it does not involve continuous, acute sexual desire; it also influences her attitudes and behavior toward her spouse and other people. For example, it affects her interest in her spouse's activity, the things she does in his company, her desires toward him and other people, and so on.

Occurrent and Dispositional Emotions and Moods

I hate housework! You make the beds, you do the dishes, and six months later you have to start all over again.

JOAN RIVERS

Intentionality and feeling are two basic mental dimensions. One's intentional perspective can be right or wrong, which is not the case, for example, with a feeling such as toothache. Intentionality, "being about something," involves our ability to separate ourselves from the world and to establish a meaningful subject-object relation. Feeling is a mode of consciousness associated with our own state; it reflects our own state but is not in itself directed at this state or at any other object.

Leaving aside the disputable details of the above distinction, we can say that affective attitudes, the main ones of which are emotions and moods, are a unique combination of intentionality and feeling, consisting of a significant feeling component and a certain (implicit or explicit) evaluative stance (or concern). In complex affective attitudes, such as emotions, intentionality is more specific, and other intentional components are present as well—namely, a significant motivational component (readiness to act) and a cognitive component involving some kind of practical implications. Moods, which have a more general intentionality, may lack these additional intentional components.

We can discuss moods and emotions from several points of view. Let's take three of them: duration, intentionality, and cause. Moods typically last longer than emotions and have a general (if any) intentionality. In this way, they "integrate" us, and we are less likely to experience several moods at the same time. Moreover, moods are less partial than emotions (at least in their focus). Whereas emotions are often caused by specific events that take place at a specific time, moods usually build up from many episodes. Moreover, as compared to emotions, moods tend to be milder, more stable, inclined to linger in the background, and have a looser link to behavior.[8]

In exploring the possibility of enduring affective attitudes, such as long-term love, we need to distinguish between *occurrent* (actual) and *dispositional* (potential) properties. The dispositional emotional background of long-term emotions has a significant impact on our experience of the world. Thus, if we love someone, we are *disposed* to react with fear when that person is threatened.[9]

Dispositional affectivity can be understood in a few senses: (a) having an inherent (built-in) potential to be *repeated* in a somewhat similar manner either within the same affective episode or in a different episode, (b) having an inherent potential to be *actualized* in the sense of moving from the *background* of the affective experience to its *foreground*, and (c) having an inherent potential to *develop*.

We find the first sense of dispositional affectivity in all affective attitudes: every type of emotion and mood can be repeated. People tend to regard repetition, which often generates boredom and damps down human capacities, in a negative light. Yet many capacities, such as playing the piano and dancing, are maintained and enhanced by repeated use. In these cases, repetition yields some degree of joy. Here, the repeated activity is valuable because it contributes to the development of a capacity—thus the old adage "Use it or lose it."

Enduring affective attitudes, such as long-term romantic love or the mood of enduring sadness, are also dispositional in the sense of being able to move from the background of our awareness to the foreground. Even when we do not think about them, they are hiding in the wings of our affective experience—like background music that occasionally moves to the foreground and demands our attention. Even when love or sadness is in the background, it is expressed in our behavior.

Enduring emotional attitudes, such as long-term love, can also be dispositional in the sense of involving the process of their development (or deterioration). This sense has a *normative* aspect in that it leads to behavior that becomes part of oneself. This specific sense of "dispositional" is key for our inquiry into the possibility of long-term profound love.

Emotional Simplicity and Complexity

I like to eat and I love the diversity of foods.
DAVID SOUL

People enjoy talking about how deep or intense their love is, and love songs give this topic a lot of play.[10] But romantic complexity gets much less air time—think, for a moment, of the last time you complained about your lover lacking complexity. However, complexity can make or break romantic relationships.

In an interesting study, researchers discovered that, up to a point, the frequency of listening to a certain kind of music increases the preference for it. Too much familiarity, however, produces boredom, especially if the composition is simple. The more complex the music, the less likely it is that boredom will set in.[11] As with music, so with love. The lovers' emotional complexity strengthens their relationship and weakens the typical decline in intensity. In profound long-term love, the beloved is perceived as a complex human being with whom one can engage in diverse intrinsic experiences.

Keeping in mind the three major intentional components in emotions—cognition, evaluation, and motivation—we can now discuss three related, but different, types of emotional complexity. First, *cognitive* emotional complexity refers to *emotional diversity*—the experience of emotions in a highly differentiated manner; second, *evaluative* emotional complexity refers to *emotional ambivalence*—the simultaneous experience of positive and negative states; and third, *behavioral* (or motivational) emotional complexity refers to our ability to behave in an optimal manner in a complex, diverse emotional environment.

Emotional Diversity

Jordi Quoidbach and colleagues argue that "emodiversity"—that is, the variety and abundance of the emotions that people experience—is an independent predictor of mental and physical health, such as decreased depression and fewer visits to doctors. They further claim that experiencing many different specific emotional states (e.g., anger, shame, and sadness) can have more survival value than experiencing fewer or more global states (e.g., feeling bad). Since the diversity of these specific emotions provides richer information about our environment, the individual is more able to deal with a given emotional situation. Moreover, reporting a wide variety of emotions might also be a sign of self-awareness and authentic life, both of which are linked to health and well-being.[12]

There are different kinds of emotional diversity: here, we'll discuss "sensory diversity" and "affective diversity." Sensory diversity has to do with a range of awareness of sensory content, such as smell, sight, hearing, or taste. Affective diversity has to do with a range of general affective states, such as listening to various types of music, walking in nature, enjoying reading or dancing, or attending a funeral. Up to a point, the greater the diversity in these areas, the more we flourish, as we are satisfied with more things—something likely to endure over time.

We can distinguish between the complexity of our own attitude and the complexity of the object at which our attitude is directed. I am mainly concerned with the complexity of the agent's attitude. There are, of course, also diverse objective degrees of complexity, regardless of one's attitude. For example, a symphony is objectively more diverse than a short song. Nevertheless, in our social environment, the most significant source of complexity is one's own attitude. Thus, in profound romantic love, the lover's attitude is based not only on the partner's external appearance, but on his or her beliefs, achievements, their shared history, and so on.

In love, as in some other emotions, we can discuss two senses of diversity: (1) holistic diversity, as when love is directed at the beloved as a diverse, whole person, and (2) type diversity, as when one person's love is directed at various individuals. The first sense of diversity, which is highly regarded, underlies any type of long-term profound love. The second is more contested. Polyamorous lovers practice this form and maintain that it does not damage, and can even enhance, the intensity and depth of their love overall. Here, I briefly discuss the first sense of diversity, leaving the second to a later discussion on polyamory.

Profound romantic love involves a *comprehensive* attitude that takes into account the rich and complex nature of the beloved.[13] The lover's comprehensive attitude is complex in the sense that it does not focus on simple, narrow aspects of the beloved but considers the beloved as a whole, multifaceted being. Sexual desire or friendship, by contrast, are more limited. In romantic love, we see both the forest and the trees, whereas in sexual desire we often focus on one or several trees.

We can extend the notion of emotional diversity. For example, we can broaden it from what we feel in the here and now to past, present, and future possible and impossible situations. That's how rich our emotional environment is. In fact, the imagined conditions of what could (might/will/or should) be are the bread and butter of our emotional lives. Such broad environmental diversity plays a crucial part in the restless nature of the romantic realm in our society.

Emotional Ambivalence

It seems we are capable of immense love and loyalty, and as capable of deceit and atrocity. It's probably this shocking ambivalence that makes us unique.

JOHN SCOTT

Now let's turn to the *evaluative* type of emotional complexity—namely, emotional ambivalence. In psychology, this is called "emotional dialecticism." Emotional ambivalence refers to experiencing negative and positive emotions at the same time.[14]

Let's consider a reasonably common case of emotional ambivalence. A widow attending the wedding of her daughter feels joy, but also sadness that her late husband, the father of the bride, is not present. Her mixed emotions can last throughout the wedding and even after it. And this is not an irrational experience. In light of the partial nature of emotions, each (partial) perspective is appropriate, while no single perspective expresses an overriding perspective. The same holds for this description of a new lover by a married woman: "Everything in me seems to go soft, to yearn for him, to want to talk with him. It almost hurts. I seem to be sad and glad at the same time." Another common example of emotional ambivalence, which is more common in novel or "forbidden" romantic relationships, is the claim "I love you very much, darling, I almost can't bear it."

Humans come equipped with the ability to hold multiple perspectives at the same time. This is an important survival skill in dealing with our complex reality. The ability allows us to pursue certain values and to compromise others while maintaining a belief in the worth of all of them. This capacity to hold multiple perspectives can produce ambivalence when we notice both positive and negative qualities in someone. Our intellectual system attempts to arrange all these perspectives into one comprehensive viewpoint; it cannot bear the affirmation and negation of the same claim at the same time. Our emotional system, however, can tolerate such ambiguity.[15]

Behavioral Complexity

I do not go searching for erotic affairs, but when something happens, I don't feel I have to say no. It is not at all easy to attract me; affairs did not attract me anyway. My lover does. I have been thinking about him, talking to him, for hours and hours without end. I am not sure what we are allowed to imagine and do now. Even thinking about the various options makes me blush.

A MARRIED WOMAN

The first two types of emotional complexity (the cognitive and the evaluative) have to do with an awareness of our emotional environment. Emotions, however, are not detached from reality: they address a practical concern from a personal perspective. This action readiness is central to the emotions, and some even consider it their most essential element.[16] Emotional complexity, then, should influence our emotional behavior. As we all know, though, being aware of emotional complexity and evaluating it in a certain way do not mean that we will act accordingly. How many times have we heard (or said): "I know this is the right thing to do, but I just can't do it"? In our context, a lover might know that giving his partner more freedom would enhance the quality of their relationship, but jealousy stops him from doing so.

At this point, it's worth differentiating between romantic needs and romantic "wants." People need food, water, and shelter in order to survive and flourish. Romantic needs enable the flourishing of a profound romantic relationship. Romantic needs include sharing valuable activities, caring, reciprocity, and mutual nurturing. A "want," of course, is something you would *like* to have. While getting what we want might contribute to the overall quality of a relationship, the relationship would not topple if we did not get it. Frequent sex, going out for dinner, watching television, gossiping, and telling jokes might fall into the "want" category. Though the distinction between needs and wants is not always clear-cut, we can say that romantic needs are primarily concerned with romantic profundity, whereas romantic wants are mostly concerned with romantic intensity. Both are essential for lifelong loving relationships.

Our relationships are governed by complexity. Emotional complexity often calls for complex behavior (although there are times when a simple course is the best response to complex circumstances). But romantic ideology, like other ideologies, which tend to provoke intense emotions, is simplistic and one-dimensional, allowing little space for complex attitudes and behavior. Thus, romantic ideology tosses out of true lovers' vocabulary terms such as "convenient," "comfortable," "moderation," "hesitation," and "compromise." Pure love is described as involving a boundless desire. This is reflected in sweeping claims such as "Love is all you need" and "Love can conquer all."[17]

The notion of "emotional complexity" is linked to the popular notion of "emotional intelligence." Emotional intelligence is the capacity to process emotional information accurately and efficiently, and accordingly to regulate our own and others' emotions. Like the capacity to experience emotional complexity, emotional intelligence is a kind of sensitivity to certain higher-level stimuli. The two ideas are connected: someone with a great deal of emotional intelligence might be expected to experience emotional complexity, and one needs emotional intelligence to successfully deal with emotional complexity. And, like emotional intelligence, the ability to experience emotional complexity involves not only appraisal and communication but also reappraisal and reflection.

Feeling Good and Flourishing

My old lover makes me feel great and more wonderful than Brad Pitt would. I think beautiful men are like a Prada handbag: women want them to make other women jealous, but in the long run it's not really satisfying.

A MARRIED WOMAN

Aristotle distinguishes between *hedone* (the feeling aspect of happiness) and *eudaimonia* (the more general thriving that supports optimal functioning in life). He is suggesting that we separate the notion of pleasure from that of robust flourishing. Whereas *eudaimonia* has to do with one's overall flourishing of life, *hedone* has to do with feeling good, getting what you want, or enjoying what you are doing. Although feeling good about our situation and being satisfied about our flourishing in life are related phenomena, they are not the same. Grazing animals, for example, experience *hedone*, but people experience both *hedone* and *eudaimonia*. *Hedone* is simpler and easier to measure than *eudaimonia*. Whereas *hedone* refers merely to a subjective state in the here and now, *eudaimonia* connects the present with the past and the future in an individual's virtuous activities, which are expressions of the individual's unique nature and capacities. For Aristotle, intrinsic activities are key to human flourishing, though he also affirms the place of extrinsic (instrumental), goal-oriented activities in such flourishing. Human flourishing, far from a temporary state of superficial pleasure, occurs over time and involves the fulfillment of natural human capacities.

That we are built to thrive over time, however, does not mean that we can't enjoy the moment. After all, we live in the present moment, and it is usually worthwhile to make each moment as pleasurable as possible. But to give priority to the moment over lasting flourishing is to neglect the meaningful role of time in our lives. We live in the present, but also in the past and the future—not to mention the potential dimension. These different dimensions imbue our lives with meaning.

People who live meaningful, thriving lives experience plenty of negative events. These events, of course, reduce happiness. Interestingly, stress and negative life events are two powerful blows to happiness, despite their significant positive association with a meaningful life. Happiness is mainly about getting what one wants and needs, often with the helping hand of others. Meaningful thriving, differently, has to do with doing things that express and reflect the self, and also, doing things that are good for others.[18]

It is in the context of profound love that romantic and personal flourish-ing are most likely to emerge. Flourishing is not built on superficial pleas-ant feelings but on meaningful, ongoing, joint, and intrinsic activities—all of which lay the groundwork for profound love. Although the Aristotelian account of love flourishing presented here is relevant for everyone, it is more appealing as people mature.

Maintaining Moderation and Balance

Are these things really better than the things I already have? Or am I just trained to be dissatisfied with what I have now?

CHUCK PALAHNIUK, *Lullaby*

I never smoke to excess—that is, I smoke in moderation, only one cigar at a time.

MARK TWAIN

Moderation is crucial to flourishing. Yet, when it comes to the emotional realms, balance is problematic, as emotions tend to be intense and volatile. The strong intensity that accompanies acute emotions places the possibility of lasting romantic love at risk. As suggested above, the emotional system can tolerate instability and intensity for only so long before it begins to break down.

What can be done? We need ways to limit the impact of change while moderating emotional intensity. These mechanisms enable the endurance of lasting affective attitudes, such as moods and emotions in general, and ro-mantic love in particular. In this context, I'll discuss three major mechanisms responsible for our emotional balance: (1) *hedonic adaptation*, which dimin-ishes affective intensity; (2) *positive mood offset*, which maintains a moderate level of positive mood; and (3) *enduring moderate dissatisfaction*, which keeps the agent's interest high.[19]

Hedonic adaptation. Related to the major role of change in generating emotions, *hedonic adaptation* reduces the affective intensity of new experi-ences, both pleasant and unpleasant. This is helpful because it prevents us from being excessively happy or utterly miserable. Without such a reduction, we would be overloaded by destructive intensity, thus losing the sensitivity necessary for distinguishing between events of greater and lesser importance.

Thanks to hedonic adaptation, we can stay emotionally stable even in the face of extreme emotional stimuli. With it, we can notice and be affected by external changes while continuing to function well within a stable frame-work. Furthermore, hedonic adaptation helps to generate a long-term, stable attitude—albeit one whose intensity is considerably reduced. The reduced affective intensity associated with hedonic adaptation is particularly evident in positive affective attitudes: hedonic adaptation is faster and more likely to be "complete" in response to positive rather than negative experiences. Thus, it is more a barrier to intense happiness than to abject misery.[20]

Positive mood offset. Hedonic adaptation works to prevent the development of enduring extreme affective attitudes. Luckily, however, it does not block all affective attitudes, as humans need these badly. Positive mood offset helps by making the baseline for adaptation a positive one that is somewhat higher than the neutral point between positive and negative. Partially because of positive mood offset, we tend to feel good in the absence of extreme negative events. Adaptation, then, does not imply the absence of an affective attitude. Furthermore, the positive location of this baseline means that we can enjoy all the advantages of being in a mildly positive mood.

Ed Diener and colleagues have shown that positive mood offset is almost universal, even among those who live in extremely difficult circumstances. People have evolved to react to positive or negative events with intense affective attitudes. At the same time, they are hardwired to be in a mildly positive mood when they are in either positive or neutral circumstances. Diener and colleagues suggest that positive mood offset enables us to behave more effectively when we are in a mildly positive mood. They claim that positive mood offset is an evolutionary adaptation because happier individuals are more likely to do things that promote their survival and reproductive success. Thus, positive moods produce desirable outcomes in several areas: physical health, including fertility and longevity; sociability and supportive social relationships; and coping and resource building, including forethought, planning, and creativity.[21] Good health and flourishing make it easier to maintain an ongoing moderate and positive mood.

Enduring moderate dissatisfaction. Lasting moderate dissatisfaction, a kind of enduring mood, has exceptional evolutionary value: it pushes us to improve our situation. To take a painful example of such absence, those suffering from senility can be continuously content, but this is because they have lost contact with reality. A measure of dissatisfaction is part of being in touch with a reality that is seldom as good as we want it to be. Overcoming obstacles is part of meaningful living. Importantly, it is not only when we do not have much that we experience the enduring mood of being moderately dissatisfied; we experience it pretty much all the time.[22] The moderate measure of dissatisfaction is different from the Rolling Stones' claim, "I can't get no satisfaction." We do get satisfaction, but it is typically blended with dissatisfied tone.

More options do not necessarily translate into more satisfaction. In the romantic realm, this means making romantic compromises and turning aside

from the many alluring romantic roads not traveled. Having a rainbow of options can improve our lives and at the same time leave us with the sense that
we are missing tempting possibilities.[23] Thus, for instance, increased education produces the unpleasant awareness of desirable options that we have to
give up on; dissatisfaction about that reality may well result. However, increased education also increases life satisfaction both in the absolute sense of
providing greater access to better options and in the relative sense of putting
us in a better position compared to other people.[24]

At first glance, enduring dissatisfaction might seem like the opposite of
hedonic adaptation. In hedonic adaptation, we maintain our habits and stability; dissatisfaction, for its part, triggers a restless search for better alternatives. Let's remember, however, that hedonic adaptation is more an obstacle
to intense happiness than to hopeless misery. Thus, the two tendencies act
in the same direction: both prevent us from being too satisfied or too happy.
Similarly, enduring dissatisfaction should be considered in light of positive
mood offset. Being dissatisfied reduces the risk of becoming indifferent while
resting on our laurels. Dissatisfaction, which includes experiencing failures
and unpleasant circumstances, spurs the meaningful development that is the
bedrock of enduring romantic love.

Concluding Remarks

I feel so miserable without you; it's almost like having you here.
STEPHEN BISHOP

Emotions can be understood from the point of view of *cause*—that is, a significant change in our situation—and from the angle of their major *concern*,
which is personal and comparative in nature. Acute emotions are unstable,
intense, partial, and brief. Understanding acute, extended, and enduring emotions enables us to speak about long-term emotions. The dispositional presence of emotions—that is, their potential to be repeated, actualized, and developed—is vital for the possibility of lasting love.

Diverse emotional experiences contribute to the cultivation of complex,
deep, and meaningful love. *Emodiversity* is associated with higher mental and
physical health, as it gives us more room in which to understand and interact
with our romantic environment. This extends to the reciprocal relationship
between partners who experience romantic diversity, when each can appreciate and love the other as a complete person. In long-term profound love, partners acknowledge each other's complexity and intrinsic value. Their romantic
environment is experienced as highly differentiated, thus leaving room for

conflicting emotions or loving different people at the same time and in different ways. It also makes space for activities that promote caring, reciprocity, and nurturing of the beloved and of oneself.

Three major mechanisms responsible for our emotional balance and the feasibility of enduring affective attitudes are hedonic adaptation, positive mood offset, and enduring dissatisfaction.

3

Romantic Experiences

Moving along from our second stop, emotional experiences, we turn down the road to romantic experiences: physical attractiveness and praiseworthy traits and achievements, sex and friendship, romantic intensity and profundity, and the heart-head conflict. We conclude with a discussion of two basic philosophical models of romantic love—caring and sharing.

Attractiveness and Praiseworthiness

Falling in love and staying in love are highly related to (a) *attractiveness*, and (b) *praiseworthiness* of desirable traits and achievements.

Attractiveness is a kind of magnet that draws one person to another. It generates an immediate emotional reaction that triggers a desire to establish a connection. Romantic evaluations of a partner tend to be more positive when the partner is physically attractive. In new romantic relationships, attractiveness almost always plays a starring role. Its importance, however, decreases as the relationship matures. Although physical attractiveness is central in romantic relationships, mainly in the short term, attractiveness is more general, indicating the wish to be with the partner also in the long term. Thus, people with a good sense of humor were rated as more attractive, and viewed as more suitable long-term partners compared to more serious counterparts.[1]

Praiseworthiness involves complex evaluations of the partner's traits and achievements that go beyond the mere wish to spend time together. Praiseworthiness takes into account qualities that we cherish (including those underlying attractiveness). Love is certainly more than mere physical attraction; it includes a general, positive evaluation of the person—the kind that is central to friendship.

Falling in love and staying in love require both attractiveness and praise-worthiness. Everyone has his or her own scale for weighing these aspects, and the scales change depending, for example, upon where one stands in life. But if these two features do not reach a critical weight, a romantic relationship is unlikely to develop. While attractiveness and praiseworthiness are interde-pendent, it is useful to tease out these differences in a romantic attitude. First and foremost, attractiveness pulls for connection: that's why we notice it im-mediately. Admirable traits, by contrast, take more time to identify.

Many of us have had the frustrating experience of unsuccessfully trying to love the "right" person. This common feeling brings home in a powerful way the importance of attractiveness in love. Then, there is the equally familiar experience of being attracted to beautiful people until the moment they open their mouths to speak. This helps us feel deeply the importance of praise-worthy traits in love. A physically attractive woman might want to be loved not merely for her attractiveness but also for her abilities and personal traits. A less attractive woman might wish the reverse: that her beloved values her external appearance as much as he does her kindness or wisdom. She would be offended if her partner said, "You are rather ugly, and I am not sexually attracted to you, but your brilliant brain compensates for everything."

Some people would like to change the relative weight of one of the basic evaluative patterns—not in terms of the beloved's attitude toward it, but re-garding their own attitude. Thus, some people wish that they could attach less significance to physical attraction, recognizing that it is less valuable in the long run. Others might wish the opposite: that their love would be more spontaneous and less calculated; they wish that they could attach more weight to physical attraction. Thus, Nora Ephron said, "In my sex fantasy, nobody ever loves me for my mind."

We mentioned above that these two basic evaluative aspects of love work in tandem. In what ways? Attractiveness has a great impact on the appraisal of our partner's traits. There is much evidence suggesting that attractiveness sig-nificantly influences ratings of intelligence, sociability, and morality. The "at-tractiveness halo" is a common phenomenon in romantic relationships. In this phenomenon, someone perceived as beautiful is assumed to have other good qualities as well. Nancy Etcoff claims that although most people would say they do not believe that "what is beautiful is good," preferential treatment of beautiful people is extremely easy to demonstrate, as is discrimination against the unattractive. Beautiful people are treated better and viewed more posi-tively: they find sexual partners more easily and are more likely to be treated leniently in court and to elicit cooperation from strangers. Conversely, physical unattractiveness leads to major social disadvantages and discrimination.[2] However, as Troy Jollimore has written, "It is rare that anyone ever loves someone else *purely* because she is beautiful, and if there were such a case we would consider that a very shallow love (and a very shallow person)."[3]

The "personality halo" works in a similar manner, but in the opposite direction. In this phenomenon, highly praiseworthy qualities, such as wisdom, caring, kindness, sense of humor, and social status, make people seem more appealing. Consider, for instance, sexual desire, which is mostly based on attractiveness. Having sex appeal is influenced by other qualities relating to the beloved's praiseworthiness—for example, class, race, odor, looks, height, power, resemblance to past lovers, intellect, history of Pavlovian conditioning, risk of AIDS, current mood, and so forth. People who can provide us with social status, such as the rich, the famous, and the powerful, will generate more intense sexual desire and sexual satisfaction. The admiration for these people spills over into the sexual realm and enhances our sexual enjoyment when being with them.

Sexiness and Beauty

> You are so beautiful, to me . . . You're everything I hope for, You're everything I need.
> JOE COCKER

> I think being sexy is far more important for love and sex than beauty; and it is also quickly identifiable. If I see an unsexy pretty man, I can appreciate his looks, but I don't feel sexually attracted to him. This happens often, not just to me, not just to women. I'd like to think of myself as both sexy and good-looking.
> A MARRIED WOMAN

Both sexiness and beauty enhance romantic attraction. Which one is more important? And which one is more positively received? The answer is . . . complicated.

Is Being Sexy More Important Than Being Beautiful?

> She was too beautiful to be kind, Too fine to be good in bed.
> ROGER CICERO

> There is definitely something sexy about a girl with an attitude and a pair of leather pants.
> ELIZA DUSHKU

Most of us are pretty sure that we know "beautiful" when we see it. As a matter of fact, scholars, who like to nail these feelings down in words, talk about beauty as pleasing the senses, especially sight. A colleague of mine once said about beautiful people that they are the ones who, when you walk past them in the street, you stop walking, mutter "Wow," and look back at them. Their beauty calls out for a second glance, almost forcing you to stop and pay attention. As the common expression goes, "I can't take my eyes off you, you are so beautiful."

"Being sexy" has to do with interaction; "being beautiful," however, has to do with the person him/herself. The word "beautiful" has a broader meaning than the word "sexy." It is often used to describe something internal. You might want to spend the night with a sexy woman; you might want to marry a beautiful one. Beautiful is deeper than sexy. Sexy is often associated with being "hot"—that is, the heat is felt by the perceiver. Being beautiful, by contrast, can be associated with being "cold," which implies some distance from the perceiver: one might like to gaze at it but hesitate to touch it and give it a proper place in one's life.

We hear this clearly in Roger Cicero's song, quoted above. There he says that the beautiful woman was too beautiful to be kind and good in bed. She was also too thin to eat much, too chic to watch TV, and too conceited to be a great sport. Being too conceited fits the notion that profound love might stand in need of friendship as its component. Beauty is a cool-minded thing. It is not warmhearted. It does not invite one to settle "without fear and trembling."[4]

Being beautiful is associated with being passive, accepting the situation as it is, and lacking an active wish to improve it. Compatible with this view, it has been found that politicians on the right look more beautiful; indeed, more attractive individuals are more likely to report higher levels of political efficacy, and identify as conservative. A major explanation of this is that good-looking people enjoy preferential treatment, which makes their overall situation better. Hence, there is no reason to actively seek changes in the current situation, which is the main characteristic of being conservative.[5]

Naturally, sexual attraction goes further than just staring, as it prompts the individual to act as well. It increases your action readiness and pushes you toward actual joint interactions. In this sense, being sexy is indeed more conducive to initiating a romantic bond than being beautiful. People are more likely to approach a sexy person than a beautiful one. Being sexy is seen as a kind of invitation, while beauty is distancing. Indeed, Roger Scruton argues that "beauty comes from setting human life, sex included, at the distance from which it can be viewed without disgust or prurience." He further suggests that "our attitude towards beautiful individuals sets them apart from ordinary desires and interests, in the way that sacred things are set apart—as things that can be touched and used only when all the formalities are addressed and completed."[6]

Although sexuality is limited to the romantic realm, being sexy depends upon having other positive characteristics. Thus, it has been claimed that confidence, honesty, talent, brightness, and good manners are all very sexy. This is in accordance with the aforementioned "personality halo," in which praiseworthy qualities boost one's attractiveness.

Nonetheless, beauty is still broader in range than sexiness—it can be related to many areas of life. Thus, we speak about beautiful personalities and beautiful landscapes—and not about sexy personalities or landscapes. People tend to agree more about judgments of beauty, too: sexiness is strongly dependent on personal and cultural differences. Reflecting the greater universality and value placed on beauty, if given the choice, most of us would choose to be thought of as beautiful over being thought of as sexy. Sexiness, however, certainly has its place: it is superb lighter fluid for the romantic flame.

Thirst, Sexual Desire, and Romantic Love

One of the best things for a woman to hear is that she is sexy.
SCARLETT JOHANSSON

Have you ever thought of comparing the desire to drink a glass of water with sexual desire? Scruton has. He argues that in the first case, you are not seeking a specific glass of water—any glass of water will do. Moreover, after you drink the water, your desire is satisfied, and it applies only to the past. Scruton claims that this is the normal nature of our sensuous desires: they are indeterminate (lacking in particularity), directed toward a specific action, satisfied by that action, and brought to an end by it. In his view, sexual desire is a completely different story. It is determinate: there is a particular person whom you want. People are not interchangeable as objects of desire, even if they are equally attractive; and each desire is specific to its object, since it is a desire for that very individual.[7]

I agree with Scruton that sexual desire is different from the desire to drink water. Nonetheless, I would argue that while profound romantic love is indeed completely different from our sensuous desires, sexual desire falls somewhere in between thirst and love on the scale. Profound romantic love is indeed about a particular person: the beloved is not interchangeable, and the loving attitude is specific to the beloved. However, sexual desire differs from both thirst and romantic love. It is determinate in a way that thirst is not, but not in the way that love is. It is not merely that you can satisfy your sexual desire by replacing it with another person, as such a replacement usually increases sexual desire. The objects of sexual desire are not indifferent to the vessel—as is the case with drinking water. Still, there are many people who can satisfy this desire.

The Impact of Time on Being Beautiful and Sexy

Beauty is all very well at first sight; but whoever looks at it when it has been in the house for three days?

GEORGE BERNARD SHAW

As long-term love is an ongoing experience, the relationship requires other types of activities for its enhancement. A crucial kind of attraction in this regard is the *yearning to be with one's lover*. Such yearning makes you think about the beloved even when this person is not with you. This is the kind of attraction that shines in profound love. The first impressions generated by the attraction to beauty, and then by sexual desire, are not sufficient for maintaining this attraction, as both decrease with time. In this sense, their value is more superficial than the desire to be together. Time is a thief, not only of beauty but also of sexual desire. So, we should focus on the more profound aspects that are so relevant for lasting love.

Beauty is a marvelous asset in a romantic relationship. However, if it is not accompanied by the desire for sexual, and other, joint activities, it will be of little romantic value and will remain only in the aesthetic realm. For a lasting loving relationship, the desire to have sex with your partner must develop into a general desire to be together for a lengthy period. Would you prefer to be considered beautiful or sexy? Most people would say, "Both!" When push comes to shove, however, as beautiful is broader and deeper than sexy, most people would choose beautiful. Again, most—but not all.

If the term "beautiful" were limited to physical appearance, many people would prefer to be regarded as sexy, thereby increasing the probability of more dynamic and warmer interactions. Similarly, at the beginning of the relationship, when joint activities are most crucial for creating the romantic bond, most would choose to be seen as sexy. Understanding that sexiness stems from behaviors allows for the possibility of making sexual desire more intense, which is a big plus in romantic relationships. It's less likely that we can somehow become more beautiful. We don't need to fix ourselves to increase our sex appeal; we just need to "fix up" our attitudes and behaviors.

It may, then, be the case that Justin Timberlake was onto something in declaring, "I'm bringing sexy back."

Sex and Friendship

It is not a lack of love, but a lack of friendship that makes unhappy marriages.
FRIEDRICH NIETZSCHE

My mother never breast fed me, she told me she only liked me as a friend.
RODNEY DANGERFIELD

Sex is the icing on the cake of friendship.
UNKNOWN

Friendship is not an emotion but a personal relation that is essential in en-during, romantic flourishing. Friendship, which is based on shared history, often increases over time—unlike sexual desire, whose intensity diminishes over time. Basic features of friendship, such as mutual support, intimacy, and shared activity, all develop over time.[8] Friends care about each other and con-sider the other to have an intrinsic value, though friendship can also have an instrumental value. The intimacy of friendship means that friends will feel closer to each other than colleagues will. Colleagues can meet more often than friends, but it is in a friendship that we reveal ourselves and express commit-ment. We are willing to do more for those within our circle of friends and family than we are willing to do for those outside of it. Love and friendship develop through time spent together and through shared experiences and interactions.[9]

Sexual desire is an acute emotion, not a mere biological drive like hun-ger and thirst. We know that despite their differences, sexual desire and love overlap a great deal in the brain, activating specific, related areas. Along these lines, it has been found that people are reluctant to label their feelings in a romantic relationship as "love" if they do not feel sexual attraction toward the person. Although sexual desire includes both attractiveness and praisewor-thiness, the emphasis is on physical attractiveness. Accordingly, sexual desire calls for less complex capabilities than romantic love does.[10]

The two—romantic love and sex—are often found at opposite poles. Ro-mantic love is considered one of the most sublime human expressions. Sex, for its part, has been associated with vulgarity and disgust, even degrading the partner into a commodity. As one woman put it, "I've always hated know-ing that men wanted to have sex with me without any emotional involvement. I think I trigger sexual desire in almost every man, and it has nothing at all to do with love." Nonetheless, some people fiercely criticize various sexual rela-tionships but still consider sexual exclusivity to be the hallmark of romantic love and see its violation as the ultimate desecration of the romantic bond.

Because of the close relation between romantic love and sexual desire, we cannot be as unromantic about sex as we are about eating. Nonetheless, sometimes sexual desire still has nothing to do with romantic love. Contemporary Western society might equate love and sex, but the excitement of novel changes reduces sexual intensity in lengthy monogamous romantic relationships. As Wednesday Martin quipped, monogamy sounds like monotony, and while we may judge an adulterous woman harshly, we have to admit she is anything but boring.[11]

And here we come to a tricky question: If sex does not lie at the core of romantic love, why do we demand sexual exclusivity in romantic relationships? It seems that from a psychological perspective, the gravest violation of the romantic bond is an affair involving significant intimacy with another person, rather than superficial sexual interaction with someone. However, sexual activities often entail emotional intimacy, which is indeed important for romantic love and can pose a threat to the partner's main relationship. The essence of love is not the sexual activity itself but rather the emotional intimacy, which is sometimes—but not always—associated with it. Although sexual relations do not require love, profound romantic love usually includes sex. When sex is combined with profound romantic love, it is part of the ongoing intrinsic meaningful experience of love that facilitates flourishing.

Of course, there is sex without love. In the case of commercial sex and other purposive sexual relationships, sex is an instrumental activity in which the other is used as a means to satisfy one's sexual desire or to gain wealth, status, or attention. Sex without love can also have an intrinsic value, but this is typically an immediately rewarding, relatively short-lived experience requiring few or no profound human capacities. By itself, this pleasure cannot sustain the individual's flourishing in the long term. This is the difference between a fleeting pleasure and a lasting treasure. We should be careful, however, not to claim that sexual interactions are meaningless. Such interactions increase our well-being in the sense of increasing positive affect and meaning in life, and decreasing negative affect (e.g., having a stress-response dampening effect).[12]

The limited value of sex without love is reflected in the morning-after effect and in the specter of sex addiction. In these cases, superficial pleasurable activities have a negative functional value, since we excessively pursue them instead of engaging in activities that are better for us. However, sometimes sex without love can generate profound love in which sex is part of the ongoing intrinsically valuable experience of love.

Put sex and love together, and you can come out with some very happy people. However, love is a much greater predictor of happiness than sex and different sorts of attachment—including marriage, which is not a good predictor of happiness at all. Yet sex is not the essence of love. There are women who have not experienced an orgasm for many years, even though they love their partner. Some people experience intense sexual pleasure by having casual sex with people other than their partner, whom they love and respect. Love can also reduce sexual intensity, both because some people are too shy to be sexually free with the partner they love and respect and because familiarity can decrease sexual attraction.

The role of sex in romantic love is complex. James McNulty and colleagues, who studied the connection between marital satisfaction, sexual satisfaction, and frequency of sex in the first five years of marriage, found that all three variables declined over time, though the rate of decline in each variable became increasingly less steep. Generally, spouses' own marital and sexual satisfaction were correlated; likewise, spouses' own sexual satisfaction and frequency of sex were positively associated with one another. Yet marital satisfaction did not directly predict changes in frequency of sex or vice versa. These findings suggest that sexual and relationship satisfaction are intricately intertwined.[13]

Sexual desire, and attraction in general, take front-burner status during the initial stage of a romantic connection, when they act as a kind of magnet between the two partners. Indeed, whereas sexual desire declines with time, friendship increases over time. However, sexual activities between the partners generally enhance the romantic relationship, in the sense of drawing them closer to each other.

Long-term profound love, which involves a high degree of both attractiveness and praiseworthiness, also involves a high degree of friendship and sex. Friendship grows deeper as it is a major element in the profound connection between the two that has developed over time. Sexual desire typically diminishes over time; however, in long-term profound love, this decrease is more limited. Thus, a married woman who is having an affair for the first time in her long marriage says, "The best orgasms I get are with my husband, although I can have faster and more orgasms with my lover. There is something unique about sex with my husband; I guess we have had more practice." Oftentimes, novelty increases sexual quantity, while familiarity enhances quality and uniqueness.

The perspective of Zen is noteworthy here. In discussing the importance Zen gives to time and familiarity, Philip Sudo states that no matter how familiar we are with each other, we cannot get bored if we truly pay attention to the complexity of the other. He makes this argument for lovemaking as well, saying there is a level of depth that genuine lovers can only experience after sharing a great deal of time together. They are like musicians, who, having played together for many years, come to know each other very well.[14]

Intensity and Profundity

> We cannot be happy if we expect to live all the time at the highest peak of intensity. Happiness is not a matter of intensity but of balance and order and rhythm and harmony.
> THOMAS MERTON

Something that is profound extends far below the surface and has a lasting effect. Profound emotional experiences have a lingering impact on our life and personality. Profound activities, however, are not necessarily pleasant activities. Some writers and artists—we might think of Vincent van Gogh, for example—experience great agony in the process of creating their works. In such cases, profundity typically involves deep, meaningful satisfaction in overcoming difficulties while using one's most distinctive capacities.

In the romantic realm, we can distinguish between profound and superficial phenomena by paying attention to *romantic intensity*, on the one hand, and *romantic profundity*, on the other. This is a distinction that is frequently overlooked. Romantic intensity is a snapshot of a momentary peak of passionate, often sexual, desire. Romantic profundity goes beyond mere romantic intensity and refers to the lover's broader and more enduring attitude. External change is highly significant in generating romantic intensity; in romantic depth, familiarity, stability, and development are tremendously important. While romantic novelty is useful in *preventing* boredom, romantic familiarity is valuable in *promoting* flourishing.[15]

The profundity of a romantic experience differs from the intensity with which it is felt; profundity involves certain types of activities that take place over time. What the temporal dimension adds to romantic profundity is shared emotional experiences and interactions. In moving from mere romantic intensity to romantic profundity, it is not only time spent together that matters, but also time spent on activities during which the partners flourish. Thus, the joint activities that promote profound love require time to do. If time is available, but the activities are missing, we wind up with an experience that is not profound.

Romantic profundity involves friendship and sexual desire. Friendship takes time to develop and involves mutuality; although we speak of unrequited love, we do not speak of "unrequited friendship." At the beginning of a relationship, romantic intensity depends mainly on physical attractiveness. Over the years, the focus in a romantic relationship shifts from romantic intensity to romantic profundity and from sexual desire to the yearning to be with each other. Romantic profundity is not threatened by a low frequency and intensity of sexual activity but rather by a low quality of shared interactions, mutual support, and intimacy.

Following the intensity-profundity distinction, we can differentiate between fleeting pleasure and lasting satisfaction. Superficial pleasure is an immediately rewarding, relatively short-lived experience requiring few complex human capacities. Superficial experiences affect only the surface and are limited in their scope and impact—although their impact can become rather negative if we engage in them excessively. Profound satisfaction involves optimal functioning, using and developing one's main capacities and attitudes. Part of profound satisfaction is the ability to overcome problems and make progress. While laziness can provide fleeting pleasure, work and activities yield profound satisfaction. Gorging ourselves on consumer goods can give us short-term pleasure, but it is unlikely to make us substantially happier people.

The Development of Sexual Desire

When I first met and sat beside my lover, I felt immediately the urge to touch him, which was strange, as it had never happened to me before.
A MARRIED WOMAN

We have learned that romantic intensity, as typically expressed in sexual desire, is brief, while romantic profundity often grows deeper with time. Time, a frequent enemy of romantic intensity, is a long-standing friend of romantic profundity. Nonetheless, the full picture is complex.

Gurit Birnbaum, who presents a model of the development of sexual desire over time, agrees that sexual desire tends to be strong during the early stages of a romantic relationship before subsiding gradually, with many couples failing to maintain sexual desire in their long-term relationships. However, she also claims that desire is not inevitably doomed to die with the passing of time, and not everyone will eventually lose sexual interest in their partner. Although sexual desire influences the initiation, development, and maintenance of the romantic bonds, its contribution varies over the course of relationship development. Specifically, sexual desire contributes most at the earlier stages of the relationship. Hence, the intensity of sexual desire by itself cannot predict the success of long-term relationships.[16]

Birnbaum argues that sexual desire functions as a gatekeeper in relationship-development processes. Sexual desire also has a relationship-maintaining function—this can be particularly important when other aspects of the relationship fail to reinforce the romantic bond. Unlike in the sports arena, sudden death is unusual in the relationship arena: when relationships end, they generally die over time. Sexual interactions can slow down this process, and in some cases, even prevent it. Engaging in shared sexual activities adds novelty and creates opportunities for development and self-expansion. It seems that sexual profundity is mainly expressed in a greater awareness of the partner's unique needs, as well as a readiness to invest effort in nurturing the partner and fulfilling these needs.[17]

My Heart Has a Mind of Its Own

The heart has its reasons which reason does not understand.
BLAISE PASCAL

I don't think when I make love.
BRIGITTE BARDOT

When the heart and head clash, we are witnessing a conflict between acute emotions—which are personal, partial, and relatively brief—and intellectual considerations—which are broader, more objective, and have longer-term validity. The intellect is concerned with the general and the stable, whereas acute emotions are engaged with the particular and the volatile. With such differences, one might wonder whether the heart and the head could ever be integrated into one single system. The fact is that they *are* integrated, and the interesting question is how it seems to work.

There is a long tradition of degrading the value of emotions. In this tradition, which radically informs our culture today, emotions in general, and romantic love in particular, are seen as obstacles to clear thinking and thus optimal living. The fact is, however, that the emotional response is often the best response. While they are not always practical, emotions are deeply embedded in matters of the heart. We don't do well when we keep emotions under lock and key—but we fare equally badly when we allow emotions to overwhelm us. We should aim at a balance that combines thought and emotion. The popular notion of "emotional intelligence" refers to such an integration.

The heart-head conflict is especially obvious in romantic love, which has often been considered a type of addiction, disease, or, at best, irrational behavior. Despite the crucial weight of the heart in romantic matters, the common and celebrated wish to give complete priority to the heart over the head is often unwise. Following our heart might not always involve acting according to our long-term concerns. Moreover, how can we identify what the genuine expressions of our heart are? Certainly, not all emotional states are genuine expressions of profound love—some of them are superficial experiences that we would not want to endure in the long term. Similarly, being too rational, to the point of neglecting the romantic element, is harmful: it is often irrational to marry for merely intellectual reasons. Considering the larger, long-term picture is indeed rational, but ignoring the immediate, short-term element of passionate love is not rational at all. After all, it is in the immediate present that we actually live.

Commenting on La Rochefoucauld's remark that "the head is always fooled by the heart," Jon Elster asks: Why should the heart bother to fool the head? Can't it just get on with it and do whatever it wants? By way of answer, he suggests that it is important to our self-image to believe we are ruled by reason rather than by passion. Elster terms this tendency "addiction to reason" and rightly points out that it makes those who are so addicted irrational rather than rational. A rational person would know that, under certain conditions, it is better to follow her emotional intuition than to engage in elaborate intellectual gymnastics.[18]

Importantly, the heart-head conflict is not a clear-cut dichotomy. Thus, emotions involve intellectual considerations, and intellectual considerations are influenced by emotional input. Nevertheless, this distinction will help us better understand the two systems.

In the romantic realm, interestingly, we also see the opposite tendency: the heart is sometimes fooled by the head. We can speak of an "addiction to romance" in which people convince themselves that they are staying in their marriages because they still love their partner, while they are really staying because they do not want to pay the cost of leaving. Along these lines, people might choose to marry because of the financial and social status of their partner, as in the case of the "sugar daddy," while convincing themselves that they are marrying out of love. Often, it is considered more meritorious to marry for romantic reasons than for cold, deliberative, and intellectual ones.

Despite current romantic views, then, the head does manage to . . . well . . . stick its head into romantic decisions of the heart. Although romantic love and the intellect seem worlds apart, romantic love is not the irrational beast it has been made out to be. It actually seems to be rather reason-dependent.[19]

Romantic behavior takes place in a world of dead ends and forks in the road, and the head serves as an indispensable GPS. The heart might point to an ideal place, but the head should explore the road ahead, anticipating painful potholes along the way. To make good decisions, we need to engage both the head and the heart. In the romantic realm, the heart should be given considerable leeway, as we love to please our heart, but not exclusive value, as we also love a comfortable life. Even in the choice of romantic partner, which seems to be the exclusive terrain of the heart, the notion of finding the "right" partner implies that the intellectual head should be involved in the search. The romantic heart is often considered to be short-sighted, and its wish for long-term love should be assisted by the head, which is better at taking the long view.

Philosophical Models of Romantic Love: Caring and Sharing

My God, these folks don't know how to love—that's why they love so easily.
D. H. LAWRENCE

Theoretical models of romantic love fill the pages of many books. Some popular models include the "fusion model," in which the two lovers are merged together, and the "self-love model," where the main emphasis is on the lover rather than the beloved. But our journey is toward everyday romantic love. So, we'll narrow our focus to two models that seem most relevant for understanding long-term profound love: the "care model" and the "dialogue model." If we modify the extreme versions of the fusion and self-love models and understand them metaphorically, we can identify them in the care and the dialogue models. Let's see what this means.

The Care Model

I love my house too much to leave my husband.
A MARRIED WOMAN

The care model, which may win the award for the most popular model of love, focuses on the beloved's needs.[20] Without question, caring is central in romantic love. It goes beyond a positive attitude toward, and the wish to be with, the beloved, seeking to enhance the beloved's well-being. Erich Fromm describes love as "the active concern for the life and the growth of that which we love."[21] In this view, genuine love has less to do with the lover's own needs and more to do with a strong concern for the other, accompanied by actual deeds.

The care model is most relevant in loving relationships that involve significant inequality, such as parental love, love of God, or love for someone who is unwell. In such cases, there is nothing wrong with one-sided caring. However, among equals, as in the ideal form of romantic love, one-sided caring (and love) is problematic. This model seems to involve too passive an understanding of love and fails to capture the importance of the interactions between the two lovers that underlie romantic profundity. Caring is an important component in other models of romantic love as well, but in those models, caring is not necessarily the essence of love, and in any case, it is not sufficient for maintaining long-term profound romantic love.

In some extreme versions of this model, reciprocity and the lover's own needs are irrelevant. Thus, Levinas denies the value of reciprocity in love and considers the other to constitute the center and the ultimate preoccupation of the lover's meaningful world. Hence, "the relationship with the other is not symmetrical. . . . At the outset I hardly care what the other is with respect to me, that is his own business; for me, he is above all the one I am responsible for." Love, for Levinas, "is originally without reciprocity, which would risk compromising its gratuitousness or grace or unconditional charity." According to this view, one should even be prepared to sacrifice one's life for the beloved.[22]

In considering the fit of the care model for romantic love, we are not so interested in whether caring is part of love: that is almost always the case. The issue is whether romantic love should be solely defined by reference to caring, or whether other features, such as reciprocity, positive responsivity, joint intrinsic activities, and personal flourishing, are just as important. If this is true, then the care model falls short of fully explaining long-term romantic love.

The Dialogue Model

No man is truly married until he understands every word his wife is NOT saying.
UNKNOWN

This model, whose origins can be traced back to Aristotle, has more recently been advanced by Martin Buber and Angelika Krebs.[23] It considers the shared connection between the partners as the bedrock of love and views shared emotional states and joint activities as the foundational features of the connection. The connection amplifies the flourishing of the lovers as well as the flourishing of their relationship. Krebs further argues that love is not about each partner having the other as his or her object. Rather, love is about what happens between the partners. Thus it is "dialogical." Lovers share what is important in their lives. For Krebs, loving somebody involves being (often enough) deeply satisfied with the experiences and activities you share with her. In loving somebody, you enlarge yourself through closely interacting with and responding to the other person. We do not thrive in isolation: we are social creatures. In shared activities, the participants are integrated into a (psychological) whole, which is more than the sum total of two individual actions. In such activities, both participants contribute (though not necessarily in the same way or to the same extent), and their contributions fit together to actualize the common good.[24]

Unlike the care model, the dialogue model emphasizes the autonomy of lovers and their essential equality in establishing the romantic connection. Sharing can occur when one lover is not autonomous and the relationship is not one of equality. However, such sharing is not deep enough to sustain the development of long-term profound love. The romantic connection expresses the qualities of the romantic partnership that are different and more than the combined value of the lovers' individual characteristics. Robert Nozick argues that romantic love "is *wanting* to form a *we* with that particular person. In a *we*, the two people are not bound physically like Siamese twins."[25]

There is indeed considerable evidence indicating the importance of dialogue in romantic love. In this sense, when it comes to romantic relationships, silence is not golden; couple dialogue and shared activities are the main pillars of a thriving romantic relationship. Thus, research found that shared activities, which are satisfying and stress-free and increased closeness, predicted greater relationship quality concurrently and longitudinally.[26] A substantial body of research has shown that relationship quality tends to be higher among more religious persons and among couples in which partners share common religious affiliations, practices, and beliefs. One study found that couples' in-home family devotional activities and shared religious beliefs are positively linked with reports of relationship quality. As the popular aphorism goes, "Couples who pray together stay together."[27] Moreover, the quality of the shared activities is important as well. It is not enough that you are have more shared activities— the time spent should be quality time. Thus, smartphone use undermines enjoyment, and reduces benefits of face-to-face social interactions.[28]

Comparing the Two Models

It is an extra dividend when you like the girl you've fallen in love with.
CLARK GABLE

It seems that the dialogue model best explains lasting profound love—it is more dynamic and comprehensive than the care model. The care model is useful when considering a central feature of romantic love and some types of nonromantic love, such as parental love.

I compare the two models while examining the following key issues: (a) the possibility of long-term profound love, (b) the possibility of unrequited love, and (c) the issue of where love is.

Long-term profound love. Caring is necessary for long-term profound love—people are less likely to stay together in a lifelong romantic relationship if there is no mutual caring. However, caring is not sufficient for maintaining and enhancing such love. The depth of the romantic connection, expressed in shared emotional experiences and joint intrinsic activities, is essential for long-term profound love. This connection lies at the core of the dialogue, rather than the care, model. Whereas there can be romantic caring without a genuine shared dialogue, romantic dialogue assumes a kind of caring. As dialogical love has more aspects that might facilitate the development of long-term profound romantic love, it seems to be more suitable for explaining such love.

Unrequited love. Romantic love craves reciprocity. For everyone, mutual attraction is a most highly valued characteristic in a potential mate. Lack of reciprocity—that is, the knowledge that you are not loved by your beloved—usually leads to a decrease in the degree of love and ultimately to humiliation and breakup. Even more commonly, we find an unequal romantic involvement between partners, for example, when your partner does not love you as much as you love her. The care model can easily explain unrequited love and unequal romantic involvement, as caring is often unrequited and has various degrees. The dialogue model has a harder time explaining unbalanced love, since genuine dialogue assumes reciprocity and a kind of equality. The dialogue model can still claim the presence of dialogue and reciprocity in at least profound love. Relationships lacking reciprocity are of lower romantic value and are not profound. It takes time to develop profound love, and not all couples are successful in doing so.

Where love is. The centuries-long argument about which organ is responsible for romantic experiences is over: today, we know that it is the brain, not the heart. Nevertheless, the heart is still perceived in popular culture as the center of emotional phenomena in general, and love in particular. An interesting twist in this dispute concerns some versions of the dialogical model that take the shared connection to be not only the focus of love, but its location as well. Does this view make sense?

The view assuming that love is a property of the lover seems to be intuitively true, as love is similar in this regard to other mental attitudes. We attribute to the lover not merely emotions, but other related attitudes, such as feelings and moods. This view, which is compatible with the care model, suggests that caring is indeed a property of the lover.

Proponents of the dialogue model tend to transfer the importance of the romantic connection to the issue of location of love, claiming that love is a property of, and, in some formulations, even resides in, the connection between the two lovers.[29] This claim is problematic. After all, feelings such as pain or enjoyment, which are essential to love, are not a property of the connection between the two lovers. Love is a psychological property of a lover. Accordingly, we would expect that some features of love, such as feelings, evaluations, and action tendencies, are properties of the lover, whereas other features, such as compatibility, resonance, and harmony, are properties of the connection.

Concluding Remarks

Diamonds are a girl's best friend and dogs are a man's best friend. Now you know which sex has more sense.

ZSA ZSA GABOR

In falling and staying in love, both physical attractiveness and praiseworthiness of traits and achievements are important and should be kept in balance. Some level of attraction is necessary, but attraction is not sufficient for the long term if it is not accompanied by positive evaluations of characteristics and accomplishments. Most people would be happy to be regarded as both beautiful and sexy. However, if we must choose, it seems that since beautiful is broader and deeper than sexy, this will be the choice of many, but not all, people. Realizing that sexiness stems from our behaviors enables improving your sexiness in a way that we cannot improve our beauty. Romantic attraction is typically expressed in intense sexual desire and the wish to be with the partner; positive evaluations of traits underlie profound friendship. Both are part of profound love. The intensity-profundity distinction is key to understanding the possibility of enduring love. Romantic intensity decreases over time, while romantic profundity goes in exactly the opposite direction.

The heart-head conflict is as old as the hills, and traditionally the head has been given veto power when decision-making time comes around. Of course, the heart is often given the first vote. The playwright Samuel Beckett had an opinion on the matter: "Dance first. Think later. It is the natural order." This makes sense; after all, the heart responds immediately, while the head takes its own sweet time to work things through. A more difficult question is whether or not the head should be ranking our romantic priorities. Unsurprisingly, the answer depends upon who is asking. We might say, however, that it seems that in matters concerning the loving heart, it is this very heart that ought to be in the driver's seat for making profound decisions.

The two major models of romantic love—the care and the dialogue models—refer to two major aspects in enduring and profound loving relationships. In the care model, we promote our partner's well-being through attentiveness to her needs. In the dialogue model, we focus on our mutual interactions, allowing individual autonomy and mutuality to take center stage.

4

Fostering Enduring Romantic Love

It is easy to hate and it is difficult to love. This is how the whole scheme of things
works. All good things are difficult to achieve; and bad things are very easy to get.
CONFUCIUS

I promised my new married lover that I would not fall for another woman before our
next meeting in a few months.
A MARRIED MAN

Our previous stop gave us a chance to look at the major features and models
of romantic love. At this point in our journey, we can turn down the road to
discuss the different ways long-term romantic love is supported. I begin by
presenting three important distinctions: *preventing* versus *promoting* types
of behavior, *extrinsic (instrumental)* versus *intrinsic* activities, and *external
change* versus *intrinsic development*. After this, I discuss the ideas of *synchrony, positive responsiveness, romantic resonance,* and *romantic consistency*,
all of which underlie the romantic connection.

Preventing and Promoting Behavior

If you are afraid of loneliness, do not marry.
ANTON CHEKHOV

Tory Higgins distinguishes between promotion-focused behavior, which concerns strong ideals related to attaining accomplishments or fulfilling hopes,
and prevention-focused behavior, which concerns felt obligations related to
protection, safety, and responsibility. This distinction highlights the difference between behaviors relating to nurturing and those relating to security.
In the prevention mode, interactions between people occur only when something is going wrong—when some "shoulds" are violated. The promotion
mode is characterized by ongoing activities related to the creation of optimal
conditions for fulfilling strong ideals. In the prevention mode, there is hardly
any sense of development; in the promotion mode, there is a sense of development toward fulfilling shared ideals.[1]

Emotional bonding always involves a delicate balancing act between pro-moting/nurturing and preventing/controlling. We see it clearly in parenting, where there is an obvious need for control, but it is present in romantic love as well. The promotion mode in love focuses on ongoing, nurturing behavior that gradually develops our potential and expands our selves in the direction of fulfilling more of our ideals and hopes. Promoting activities are a matter of degree; they are complex and involve a never-ending process of nurturing our partner and our togetherness. The preventing mode, for its part, focuses on eliminating our personal non-normative romantic behavior.

Romantic relationships involve both ideals and boundaries, and so they require both types of activities. We need to promote various aspects of our loving experiences, and at the same time, we need to remove other aspects. It seems, however, that promoting activities are more significant in improv-ing the quality of romantic relations over time. Spending time together is not sufficient for maintaining and improving a relationship; the type of activity matters as well. Thus, shared activities would boost relationship quality if the shared activities are successful in creating closeness and intimacy. Moreover, the underlying motivation for engaging in shared activities may determine the degree to which shared activities are experienced more positively.[2]

The Negative Bias

Marry a man your own age; as your beauty fades, so will his eyesight.
PHYLLIS DILLER

People spend more time engaging in preventing modes of behavior than they do engaging in promoting modes. This reflects the greater dominance of neg-ative than positive experiences in our emotional environment.

We often see emotions as either "positive" or "negative." As it turns out, negative emotions are more noticeable than positive ones. This fact, which has been called the "negative bias," is found everywhere in life, including in close relationships. Negative emotions, bad parents, and bad feedback have more impact than good ones, and bad information is processed more thor-oughly than good. Accordingly, we are more motivated to avoid bad events than to pursue good ones. In short, from the point of view of our minds, bad is stronger than good.[3]

This negative bias works well for us as a species. We have a better chance of surviving if we notice the lion running after us than the flowers along our path. The likelihood that we'll outlive the attack further increases if we notice how fast the lion is running and in exactly what direction. This is called "differentiation," and it is the reason that negative emotions are more "differentiated" than positive emotions.

Another reason that negative emotions are more noticeable than positive ones has to do with their *temporal* character: we spend much more time thinking about negative events than about positive ones. People ruminate about events inducing strong negative emotions *five times* more often than they do about events inducing strong positive ones. It is no wonder, then, that we recall negative experiences much more readily than positive ones.

At the risk of pushing an image to its limit, potential harm grabs the lion's share of our resources. Potential good, in comparison, is rather undemanding. In a sense, one hardly needs to "cope" with good fortune. Moreover, there are more ways in which a situation can be unpleasant than ways in which it can be pleasant, and there are more ways to destroy something than ways to build it. Furthermore, negative emotions are often experienced when a goal is blocked; this requires the construction of new plans to attain the blocked goal or to compensate for the lost one. In contrast, positive emotions are usually experienced when a goal is achieved. Accordingly, negative emotions require more cognitive resources to be allocated for dealing with the given situation.[4]

What does all this emotional differentiation mean for us? Is noticing negative qualities more important in the romantic realm as well? The answer seems to be yes. Negative qualities can kill a relationship—and in extreme cases, especially those concerning women, can actually kill a person. In a startling claim, John Gottman says that for a relationship to succeed, positive and good interactions must outnumber negative and bad ones *by at least five to one*. If the ratio falls below that level, the relationship is likely to fail. Although the negativity bias is a universal phenomenon, often explained in evolutionary terms as a safeguard survival, when it comes to finding a romantic partner the bias is stronger among women. Why might this be the case? Arguably, it is because a bad partner can prove more harmful to a woman than to a man.[5] Indeed, Peter Jonason and colleagues found that when evaluating potential mates, people weigh negative traits more than positive traits. They claim that although positive traits—dealmakers—reflect characteristics that can improve suitability, the presence of negative traits—dealbreakers—could represent greater suitability costs, causing people to be highly sensitive to mating *cost* information. Over time, however, natural selection probably shaped mate preference mechanisms that are sensitive to both strategies.[6]

Extrinsically and Intrinsically Valuable Activities

Love doesn't make the world go 'round. Love is what makes the ride worthwhile.
ELIZABETH BARRETT BROWNING

Aristotle—and many others—distinguished between extrinsically and intrinsically valuable activities.[7] An extrinsic (or instrumental) activity is a means to an external goal; its value lies in achieving that goal. Goal-oriented activities are assessed on the basis of efficiency—that is, the ratio of benefits to costs. Time is one of the resources that we try to save when engaging in instrumental activities. Examples of such activities are building a house, paying bills, cleaning the house, and being interviewed for a job. We do not value these activities in themselves—in fact, we may even resent performing them. Nevertheless, in the spirit of "Those who sow in tears will reap in pleasure," we engage in such activities when their external goals are beneficial.

With an intrinsically valuable activity, our interest is focused on the activity itself, not its results. Although such an activity has results, it is not performed in order to achieve them; rather, its value is in the activity itself. Reading a book is an example of an intrinsically valuable activity. Unless we are sleep-deprived undergraduates, we read books because we value doing so and not because of a certain external goal (such as passing our courses); accordingly, we do not try to finish reading as quickly as possible. Moral activity, which is accompanied by the pleasure of helping other people—without regard for cost-benefit calculations—is another example of an intrinsically valuable activity. Such activities have a built-in system of reward. Despite the lack of external goals, they are largely responsible for the quality of our lives. As the Roman poet Ovid said, "Nothing is more useful to mankind than those arts which have no utility."

Most human activities can have both intrinsic and instrumental value. Take, for example, dancing, which can be an intrinsically valuable activity if our focus is on the experience itself. Dancing can also be an extrinsically valuable activity whose goal is to find a romantic partner. In this case, our attention is not focused on dancing but on those in the dance hall—here, dancing is a means of achieving an external goal, as quickly as possible.

The combination of *intrinsicality* and *profundity* enables an experience to endure. Thus, if someone considers painting as meaningful for her flourishing, she cannot "be done with" painting. She can merely stop painting from time to time, or she can finish painting a particular picture. Similarly, if we consider deliberative thinking as an essential intrinsic activity for flourishing, we never "finish" such activities; we only stop performing them occasionally.

Profound intrinsic experiences are the stuff of which our flourishing is made. In profound intrinsic activities, time not only seems to pass quickly (this is also true for superficial intrinsic activities), but we also remember profound intrinsic activities for a long time. They have a short-long pattern (short while they last, long in memory) as opposed to superficial intrinsic activities, which have a short-short pattern.[8]

Another related criterion for an intrinsically valuable activity, according to Aristotle, is that it is *complete*, as there is no external goal that it must achieve in order to be fulfilled. In this sense, it is an ongoing activity that does not have an inherent specific target: it is a never-ending process. External circumstances can get in the way of the performance of such activities—hence, their vulnerable nature; however, usually such circumstances cannot stop the activities or their completion.[9]

A profound intrinsic activity is complete in another aspect: while engaging in such activity, our attention is completely absorbed by it. Accordingly, we can, for example, continue the activity for many hours without feeling hungry. In such circumstances, people are sometimes unaware of themselves as separate from their activities.[10] This is because such activities have great significance for the individual's self-identity.

Human flourishing is not a temporary state of superficial pleasure; rather, it refers to a longer period involving the fulfillment of natural human capacities. A relationship in which the partner has no intrinsic value is not genuine love. However, we can speak about love that is not fully intrinsic, in the sense that it is not comprehensive, as it does not refer to all aspects of the partner's flourishing. Thus, a man who loves his wife dearly and has put her on a pedestal can consider his wife's overall flourishing to have intrinsic value, but he might not consider her professional flourishing to have such value, as this flourishing could feel threatening to him. If this is the case, he might object to her going on work-related trips alone or be unhappy when she is promoted.

And now we come to the sticky relationship question of giving full intrinsic value to the beloved in the context of romantic love. It is commonly believed that one's beloved holds this intrinsic value for as long as she is with the loving person—and no longer. The intrinsic value is conditional on the beloved's staying with this person. Do I want my beloved to be happy more than I want her to be with me? The answer from the angle of parental love would be yes, but in romantic love, the case is more complicated.

For many people, love involves the wish for good things to happen to the other person, with no benefit to the one who loves. The lover wishes the other's benefit for its own sake, without calculating whether there is any personal benefit to be drawn. Such love implies that loving someone also means letting her go, if it will increase her happiness and flourishing. In Alice Munro's poignant short story "The Bear Came over the Mountain," Fiona, who has been married to Grant for forty-five years, has been placed in a nursing home because of memory problems. She develops a strong attachment to another resident, Aubrey, who is in an even worse condition. When Aubrey's wife, Marian, removes him from the nursing home, Grant tries to persuade Marian to bring Aubrey back to the home because Fiona and Aubrey's relationship is beneficial for both patients.

To sum up, profound intrinsic activities, and, to a lesser extent, superficial ones, are vital to the development of enduring love. This is true for the following related reasons: (a) the partner is treated as having her own worth and not as a means for achieving the other's ends; (b) such activities are ongoing activities that can endure for a long time, unlike instrumental activities, which end the moment the goal has been achieved; (c) they are complete in the sense that one is satisfied throughout the performance of the activities; (d) they often relate to basic needs rather than to fleeting wants; and (e) they involve deep satisfaction and not merely momentary pleasure. Thus, we can say that if intrinsic activities are an essential part of a romantic relationship and of the lovers' own lives, the prospects of the relationship enduring for a long time and being a part of the lovers' good life are rather good.

External Change and Intrinsic Development

> All change is not growth, as all movement is not forward.
> ELLEN GLASGOW

> During the first year of marriage, put a quarter in a jar each time you make love. Then during the second year, take a quarter out each time you make love. At the end of the second year go to a good restaurant with what's left.
> UNKNOWN

As we all know, over time, things can become boring. With this sense of boredom, emotional intensity can plummet. Change is frequently prescribed as a remedy for boredom. Should we then change our romantic partners in order to fan the romantic flames? In addressing this question, I distinguish between external change and intrinsic development (growth).[11]

Change is commonly taken to mean becoming different, typically without permanently losing one's characteristics or essence. *Development* is a specific type of change that involves a process of improving by expanding or refining. In its full sense, development involves becoming deeper and better. Acute emotions express our sensitivity to immediate change, whose time scale is often seconds or minutes. However, we also need a sensitivity to processes enduring months and years, which are essential for our thriving. In such sensitivity, reasoning, which combines past and present experiences with future development, is crucial.[12]

In this context, Tibor Scitovsky distinguishes between circumstantial changes ("comforts"), such as finding a new place to live or acquiring a new car, and activities that provide new experiences and possibilities, like meeting new people or getting a new job. Whereas circumstantial changes deliver partial and intermittent pleasure, and the individual eventually adapts to the new circumstances, new activities that open our horizons can yield profound satisfaction, challenges, and fulfillment.[13]

The term "development" can be used in a limited sense of being deeper, but not necessarily improving. The process of improving and becoming deeper requires time to know the partner better, thereby taking account of objective reality—that is, the lover's unique personality and circumstances. Such a process of development has a meaningful direction and can be considered an achievement.

The importance of development over time in the romantic realm is expressed in the fact that although profound love at first sight is not possible, intense sexual desire at first sight is. Likewise, stimulation, as one might experience in masturbation, might provide greater sexual intensity than intercourse, but it does not increase romantic profundity. The external change underlying intense love is a one-time, simple event expressed in an acute emotion, or, at most, in an extended one; such a change has a brief impact, since one quickly adapts to it.

The growth underlying profound love is continuous; hence, it is associated with moderate intensity. The process of romantic development leads people to attempt to improve themselves by, for example, increasing their connectedness. We can speak here about an "upward spiral." In romantic love, these circumstances generate the phenomenon of bringing out the best in each other, which is so crucial for long-term profound love.[14]

External changes and intrinsic development operate on different time scales—that of the first is quite short, and that of the second can take years. A significant development on the intrinsic scale could reduce the need for external changes. Whereas the impact of external change depends largely on good timing, intrinsic development is constituted by time. In the case of external change, the individual remains essentially the same, and change is needed to alleviate boredom; in the case of intrinsic, meaningful development, one is continually developing. This means that relying too much on external causes for our romantic satisfaction can upset the balance between our profound and superficial values in a way that we really do not want. Development improves us in a direction that we consider valuable, and, objectively, it is indeed better for us.

Profound love has the potential to nurture growth and improvement and to bring out the best in both lovers. Shared emotional experiences and joint activities are certainly an important aspect of romantic amplification. Moreover, research has demonstrated that when a close romantic partner sees and acts toward you in a manner that matches your ideal self, you move nearer toward that self. This has been colorfully termed "the Michelangelo Phenomenon." Just as Michelangelo saw his process of sculpting as releasing the ideal forms hidden in the marble, our romantic partners "sculpt" us in light of our ideal self. Close partners sculpt one another in a manner that brings each individual closer to his or her ideal self, thus bringing out the best in each other and making both feel good about themselves. In such relationships, we see personal growth and flourishing in statements like "I'm a better person when I am with her."[15]

The process of development is a joint task of the two partners; hence, the changes will likely be reciprocal. Take, for example, the case of an absent-minded man and his super-sensitive wife. The wife might wish to cause a change in her husband that would lead him to be more mindful of her needs and more attentive to their relationship. The husband might want to bring about a change in his partner that would lead her to prioritize differently and attach less importance to every detail of his behavior, thus enabling her to become more tolerant of his "mistakes." One can try to change his or her partner (and self) by taking an interest in what the other enjoys. If you like, say, rap music, trying to help your partner appreciate such music would enhance the quality of your togetherness. Likewise, your partner's desire to share your interest will open up windows onto your world, thereby increasing mutual understanding and sharing.

External change has become the go-to stick for stoking the romantic fire. Think, for instance, of changing a partner, or at least taking an occasional walk on the wild side. Making changes within the couple's relationship, like exploring new places or new activities together, produces less intensity—and at first seems like a kind of pauper's joy. However, when we distinguish between romantic intensity and profundity, these joint interactions go from being a pauper's joy to a millionaire's dream—a powerful engine for the development and enhancement of love. Romantic profundity develops through a gradual ongoing process involving reciprocal intrinsic activities whose value increases with familiarity and use. External changes can increase the intensity of romantic flames, but the heart of the enduring romantic connection lies in its intrinsic development.

Our accelerated cyber society is addicted to external change. Investing time in profound endeavors, including romantic relations, is not our first—or second or third—choice of activity. Yet romantic depth requires serious time investment. Over the past few decades, spouses have spent less and less time together, with work taking more and more of the clock share. And stress, information overload, and multitasking have made the moments that spouses do spend with one another feel less good.[16]

In this book, the term "development" is used in a broad sense that implies becoming both deeper and better. But what about the development of negative relations? In everyday life, we do speak about the development of hatred or envious relationships. This is a narrow sense of development, becoming deeper but not improving. The development involved in negative emotions is often less complex than that which is involved in positive emotions. As we have noted, destroying is far less complicated than building. However, when taking into account the individual coping with the negative situation, as, for example, in grief, we can speak about development also in the broad sense, involving improving as well.[17]

Lack of interaction typically decreases romantic profundity, which is built through joint activities. In hate, the impact is often bidirectional. Lack of interaction can indeed prevent reappraising the individual's negative evaluation, thereby maintaining the hate. Conversely, lack of interaction could make the hated person less central in the individual's emotional environment, thereby decreasing the hate. Greater interaction can decrease hate, as novel, more comprehensive information changes the initial negative evaluation. Yet greater interaction may make the conflict more central, leaving the individual without an escape route. Thus, the Roman historian Tacitus informed his audience that hatred is most violent when it is directed toward family. In such a case, we are unable to distance ourselves from the hated person. Hate "tastes" worst, that is, its negative intensity is highest, when it is fresh. Yet, when hate is not merely a temporary eruption but a constant feature, it distorts the individual's behavior and attitudes. Thus, its moral value worsens with maturity.

Synchrony and Responsiveness

I find that when you open the door toward openness and transparency, a lot of people will follow you through.

KIRSTEN GILLIBRAND

As the tie between two lovers lies at the heart of romantic love, how they interact with each other is one of the building blocks of such love. In this regard,

I distinguish between three phenomena: *synchrony, responsiveness*, and *resonance*. Synchrony, in the sense used here, refers to the coordination of time or rate between two (or more) people. Thus, we can speak about synchrony between a couple when they dance, have sex, or dine together. Responsiveness has to do with partners interacting in ways that include understanding, valuing, and supporting each other in meeting important personal needs and goals. Romantic *resonance* is typically a high-level type of romantic responsiveness that involves an ongoing, dynamic reciprocity. It reinforces or prolongs the romantic connection by a sort of mutual "vibration."

Synchrony can take place between two systems, such as two people, or between different levels within a given system—for example, the neurological and psychological levels, as when brain activities are synchronized with intense sexual desire. My main concern here is with the first type. A primary function of synchrony is to mark and develop similarity with others. Similarity is crucial in the romantic connection, and synchrony is a kind of a dynamic temporal similarity. Synchrony, whose lower level can be just mimicry, constitutes a basic signal by which we interpret similarity, and, consequently, tunes subsequent emotional experiences and behaviors. Thus, synchronized movement increases rapport, liking, and prosocial behavior. Synchrony can be part of higher-level experiences, such as positive responsivity and romantic resonance.

Acting in synchrony with others can foster cooperation and cohesion within groups by generating complementary activities at the appropriate time. This is one reason why religions incorporate synchronous singing and chanting into their rituals. These synchronized joint activities help maintain traditional values and connections, including ongoing romantic bonds. Synchrony is also a partial solution to the free-rider problem, that is, the tendency of some individuals to shoulder less than their fair share in the relation. Piercarlo Valdesolo and colleagues argue that synchrony might not just bring people together, but bring them together to practice the very skills essential for the success of their joint activities. This is also true of romantic relations.[18]

Positive responsiveness is a vital aspect of the romantic connection. If we again reach for our dictionaries, we find that a responsive person reacts *quickly* and *positively*. These two elements of a temporal, built-in, quick response, positive in tone, are indeed central in romantic love. Such responsiveness shows that positivity is a crucial part of the lover's attitude and not a mere add-on. One can have a general positive responsiveness toward people; in romantic love, such responsiveness should also have a unique aspect concerning the beloved.

Harry Reis and Margaret Clark argue that perceived partner responsiveness is fundamental to intimacy. It supports and strengthens both the relationship and its members. For Reis and Clark, responsiveness is the classic example of an interpersonal process that unfolds over time and in which both partners' behavior matters. In this sense, responsiveness is an umbrella construct—a broad principle under which different interactive processes can be organized. They claim that "for both giver and recipient, responsiveness contributes to attraction and liking, trust and commitment, and personal growth. It fosters a sense of security, allowing partners to use their relationships as safe havens in distressing circumstances and as secure bases for exploration."[19]

Birnbaum and colleagues have shown the importance of responsiveness in increasing sexual desire (more strongly so in women); perceived partner responsiveness is intrinsic to the development of intimacy in sexual contexts. They argue that people who perceive their partners as responsive, in the sense that they understand and appreciate their needs, can view sexual interactions as a way to enhance intimate experiences. Accordingly, they might experience greater desire for sexual interaction with them. In contrast, people who perceive their partners as unresponsive might avoid sexual activity with them. Indeed, passion is fueled by cues of rising intimacy.[20]

Furthermore, Birnbaum and colleagues point to the importance of time in the development of romantic responsiveness. In initial encounters, when partners do not know each other well, responsiveness can be interpreted as superficial and negative, a play for quick and more enthusiastic sex. As relationships develop, however, the very same responsiveness may be perceived as profound and genuine. In these circumstances, the individual does not merely express the general positive responsiveness that one usually directs toward all people, but goes beyond such responsiveness, directing it at the partner's particular needs. The partner's recognition of this specific awareness in the individual makes the relationship feel unique. This, in turn, fosters trust and commitment.[21]

Going even further, Birnbaum and colleagues propose a causal connection between partner responsiveness and sexual desire in the long term, too. In particular, partners' expressions of responsiveness outside the bedroom might increase the desire for sex, thereby further promoting the relationship. In contrast, partners' lack of responsiveness could cause a negativity that inhibits sexual desire for both. Though responsiveness is related to intimacy, each can have independent impacts. Hence, couple interactions require responsiveness *plus* intimacy. When partners perceive the other as responsive, they are more likely to experience their relationship as unique and valuable, which in turn can spur desire in a long-term relationship.[22]

The crucial role of responsiveness (as well as synchrony and resonance) in romantic relationships fits quite well with and serves to support the dialogue model. However, as Reis and Clark indicate, caring is also essential in romantic relationships, and responsiveness has a pivotal role in creating and enhancing caring.[23]

Romantic Resonance

You don't love someone for their looks, or their clothes, or for their fancy car, but because they sing a song only you can hear.

OSCAR WILDE

The notion of "resonance" can be traced to antiquity. The term has mystical overtones, as well as elements that artists have sought to evoke in art and architecture. Recently, the word "resonance" has taken on even greater . . . resonance, if you will. Nowadays, we find it everywhere: in physics, music, philosophy, psychology, sociology, and aesthetics.[24]

Resonance refers to the tendency of a system to oscillate with another system at a similar frequency. In physics, it is defined as the "reinforcement or prolongation of sound by reflection from a surface or by the synchronous vibration of a neighboring object."[25]

I suggest considering romantic resonance as involving a high-level responsiveness consisting of an ongoing, synchronous dynamic reciprocity. Most other types of romantic responsiveness are instantaneous, static, and not necessarily reciprocal. Romantic resonance involves reinforcing or prolonging a romantic reciprocity on the causality level. Romantic responsivity may also involve reciprocity, but it is not always present. We can speak about one-directional romantic responsivity, that is, responsivity existing in only one partner. However, one cannot speak about one-directional romantic resonance, as resonance has to do with the connection between two people. If romantic responsivity is to develop into romantic resonance, a dynamic reciprocity on the causal level must be added. Such reciprocity need not be symmetrical at the level of the resulting behavior; it can be, for instance, complementary.[26]

Music may help us here. Scruton compares the aesthetic response to dancing to music, arguing that "dancing is the social activity which stands nearest to the aesthetic response—a way of 'being together'"; the response of the listener to music is "a kind of latent dancing—a sublimated desire to 'move with' the music." He claims that the great triumphs of music "involve this synthesis whereby a musical structure, moving according to its own logic, compels our feelings to move along with it."[27] In this sense, we can say that romantic resonance is a kind of dancing together, a way of "being together"—a sublimated desire to "move with" the partner. During this special dance move, partners will also experience understanding, empathy, sympathy, and sharing.[28]

Thus, romantic resonance is marked by an ongoing, dynamic reciprocity. Additionally, I suggest, it has the following characteristics: (a) shared emotional experiences and joint activities; (b) constitutive similarity; (c) amplification, complementing, damping, and balance; (d) spontaneous response; and (e) autonomous status.

Shared emotional experiences and joint activities. Shared emotional (and other affective) experiences and activities are pivotal to romantic amplification. Aristotle stresses the importance of joint interactions in love, noting that lengthy separation can destroy love.[29] Romantic resonance, involving a suitable coupling, lays the ground for such experiences and activities; it involves movements in which each lover resonates with the other. Romantic resonance is a kind of co-engagement, established by shared experiences and joint activities. In this co-engagement, separate individuals no longer need to bridge any sort of gap between them: the lovers share a romantic space whose foundation is romantic resonance.

Constitutive similarity. Do birds of a feather really flock together? Alternatively, do opposites really attract? In the case of long-lasting profound love, we know the answer: similarity rules the day. Indeed, philosophers from Empedocles, Aristotle, and Cicero to Montaigne and Nietzsche all agree that similarity is the basis of love. We, too, have seen evidence for the significance of similarity. Only in short-term relationships, where commitment is low, do people prefer *dissimilar* partners. When a lover acts in accordance with "constitutive similarity," she acts in an authentic manner that actualizes her own nature. As some Romantics suggest, "The loved one is merely an emotional echo chamber, in which the lover gets to hear his own authentic voice."[30]

Amplification, complementing, damping, and balance. Like other types of resonance, romantic resonance is associated with a kind of interaction that can prolong and *amplify* the romantic experience. The contagious nature of emotions can also amplify romantic resonance. When our loved ones are sad, we are saddened too. And so, too, in the sexual realm: it is easier to achieve orgasm when people know that their partner is enjoying the sexual interaction.

Complementing is a major process associated with romantic resonance. Like resonance, romantic complementing amplifies the value of the connection in forming a whole of a greater value. When complementing goes well, a combination of the two is greater than the sum of their parts. Thus, we say, "A fine wine is a perfect complement to dinner" or "The music complements her voice perfectly." In compromising, we accept something negative and stop pursuing something positive to prevent a greater possible harmful impact on the present situation. Complementing, by contrast, amplifies the positive while bringing out the best in each partner.

Damping refers to losses over time. When damping is small, the resonant frequency is approximately equal to the natural frequency of the system. Resonance can also collapse the system as result of overamplification of its natural frequency. Romantic resonance can be maintained by increasing the intrinsic value of the connection and reducing the negative burden of external circumstances.

Maintaining a *balance* between the various features underlying romantic resonance is an achievement that can preserve a thriving relationship and prevent an overload collapse. Profound love might not always persist in the long term, since significant changes in one partner or in external circumstances can damage love. However, as we are dealing here with constitutive similarity, such similarity is less likely to change; hence, it may help in coping with the negative circumstances. Accordingly, some people say that they never stopped loving their beloved, even when things were going badly. Profound love might end because of external factors, but its long-term survival does not depend only on preventing negative external factors; such survival requires further promoting positive intrinsic factors.

Spontaneous response. Following Spinoza's lead, we can discuss three major cognitive systems: *emotional intuition, deliberative thinking,* and *intuitive reasoning.* Although deliberative thinking generally has more cognitive value than emotional intuition, there is yet another intuitive system, which can be termed "intuitive reasoning," the value of which is generally higher than that of the deliberative system. Expert decision-making leverages such intuitive reasoning.[31] Romantic resonance involves valuable, *spontaneous* intuition. Indeed, spouses' automatic attitudes, not their conscious ones, predict changes in their marital satisfaction, such that, over time, spouses with more positive automatic attitudes were less likely to experience marital dissatisfaction. Implicit spontaneous romantic resonance can bypass self-presentational biases and turn out to be a self-fulfilling prophecy in partner interactions.[32]

Autonomous status. The *autonomous* nature of romantic resonance is expressed in the presence of personal degrees of freedom, through which we cultivate or eliminate a given resonate response. Hartmut Rosa argues that since acceleration is a major problem of modern society, stuffed as it is with so many options, resonance, which limits our freedom, can be a major solution.[33] Resonance revises the prevailing notion of autonomy: it places some limitations on lovers' behavior, since they seek to resonate (but not to fuse) with each other. However, the problem nowadays is mainly not how to find love, but how to keep love once we have found it. Accordingly, the issue of uniqueness is basic to long-term love; resonance, which expresses a unique connection between two individuals, is crucial here. Developing profound love often cultivates romantic resonance; hence, romantic resonance is both an aspect and an achievement of love.

Romantic resonance involves a kind of meaningful responsiveness. Some level of resonance is evident, for example, in flirting, where each partner's emotions are stirred, thereby enabling the two partners to resonate with each other. Resonance is even more obvious in profound love, when the two lovers are in a dynamic, harmonious relationship. The importance of reciprocity and caring in romantic love makes romantic resonance an advantage in such relationships. It can be expressed in the coming together of basic values, including moral, political, and aesthetic ideals. Thus, lovers develop similar preferences—for example, enjoying music to which they were previously indifferent, or even wearing similar colors or clothes. These lovers might say that they know what the other will say before he or she even speaks.

We usually see romantic resonance and other types of positive responsivity in long-term profound love. However, it is possible for profound love to lack resonance—although it is highly unlikely that such love would lack any other type of positive responsivity. Romantic resonance is an achievement that not all profound lovers manage to attain. The caring aspect of romantic love would survive this absence intact, although the dialogical aspect might be impaired.

Romantic Consistency

Dogs love their friends and bite their enemies, quite unlike people, who are incapable of pure love and always have to mix love and hate.
SIGMUND FREUD

Synchrony, responsiveness, and resonance are temporal phenomena that undergird long-term romantic relationships. Yet there is a fourth phenomenon: *consistent behavior*. As the term indicates, this involves acting in a similar way, over time. However, while it is clear that synchrony, responsiveness, and resonance are essential to long-term romantic relationships, the value of consistency in the romantic realm is rather murkier.

There is a basic survival value to consistent behavior—without it, we could not understand and engage in our environment. In personal relationships, consistency helps us to anticipate, and hence to manage, the other's behavior. Consistency is an intellectual demand that has a questionable connection with emotional attitudes. In emotional attitudes, which are generated by change and are context-sensitive, consistency is not at the top of the totem pole of importance. Extreme people, who have a limited awareness of reality, tend to be rigid and consistent, but those who consider the changes around them must be more flexible and, accordingly, seem less consistent.

Moreover, as we have said, our ability to hold multiple opinions can create emotional ambivalence when we perceive both positive and negative values in the same object. Such ambivalence is problematic for the intellectual system, but not for the emotional system. Unlike intellectual deliberations, which seek full understanding, emotional attitudes are partial and hence can deal with different and sometimes even opposing aspects.

Do you ever feel as though you both love and hate someone? If so, you are in awfully good company. But loving and hating the same person at the same time is contradictory. Or is it?

Love and hate: polar opposites. At least, that's how these emotions are normally understood. But let's consider two points. First, love is broader in scope than hate—it takes into account more of what it loves. When we hate someone, we see that person as bad—bad to the bone. In romantic love, though, the lover is viewed in a more "textured" way—as both good and attractive. Second, there are many varieties of emotions (and there are more kinds of love than hate), and each of them cannot be the exact opposite of their counterparts in the other emotion. So, rather than as opposites, love and hate are better described as *distinct* experiences: similar in some ways and different in others.

When people say that they are in a love-hate relationship, they may be referring to different aspects of their attitudes toward the beloved. There are parts of the beloved that the lover admires, and parts that the lover disapproves of and sometimes even hates. Such mixed emotions make sense in a complex love relationship. Yet it is hard when we feel emotions that are both profound and all-encompassing, such as love and hate, toward the same person.

In a love-hate relationships, people change their focus of attention under different conditions; hence, the change in the emotional attitudes. When lovers focus their attention on, say, their partner's sense of humor, they love them dearly. When they think about the humiliation the partner causes them, they hate his or her guts. Thus, people can say: "I hate you, Then I love you . . . Then I hate you, Then I love you more" (Celine Dion); "Sometimes I love you, sometimes I hate you. But when I hate you, it's because I love you" (Nat King Cole). As the songwriters know well, emotional experiences are nothing if not dynamic, and different circumstances can change our emotional attitude toward the same person. This aspect is also nicely illustrated in Charley Pride's song "You're So Good When You're Bad." The protagonist describes his woman as both an angel and a devil, bringing sunshine to his life, but when she reaches out and dims the lights, "I say mmm mmm you're so good when you're bad."

When love turns sour, hate is not far behind. Consider the following testimony of a man convicted of killing his wife: "You don't always kill a woman
or feel jealousy about a woman or shout at a woman because you hate her. No.
Because you love her, that's love." No doubt, love can be extremely dangerous,
and people have committed the most horrific crimes in the name of love.[34]

Alright, you might be saying to yourself. So I can feel love and hate toward
the same person. But toward the same person at the same time? Well, we
might say that we dearly love someone in general but hate his dishonesty. Accordingly, when people say, "I love and hate you at the same time!" they mean
that their profound positive and negative evaluations are directed at different
aspects of the person. In a similar vein, unmarried lovers in an extramarital
relationship might love their married partner deeply, while also hating them
for preferring to maintain the bond with their spouse. Likewise, we might
hate someone because we love them and are unable to free ourselves of our
love for them, or because this love is not reciprocated.

Interestingly, desire for exclusivity arises in romantic love, but not in hate.
On the contrary, in hate, we want to see our negative attitude shared by others. It seems natural that we want to share our negative judgment with others,
while wanting to keep the positive part to ourselves. When we are happy, we
are more open to being attentive to other people, but we might safeguard the
source of our happiness. When we are miserable, we often cut our connections with other people but feel a sense of satisfaction if others are miserable
as well.

To sum up, it is not illogical to hate the one you love. But it certainly
makes life less emotionally comfortable, which in turn can reduce the quality
of the relationship.

Robust Romantic Relationships

I love men. They are intelligent and sensitive, but there's also that hard-edged arrogant
side, which is just so attractive.
RACHEL HUNTER

The distinction between romantic intensity and profundity is associated with
the difference between short-term concerns, which are part of the brief, intense sexual passions, and long-term concerns, which are associated with
profound love. However, we should be careful not to identify profound love
with long-term romantic relationships. There are cases of (1) long-term romantic relationships lacking profound love and (2) separation despite the
presence of profound love. In both cases, there are additional circumstances,

which can be characterized as life and personality circumstances that allow either the endurance of long-term love without romantic profundity, or the free dissolution of a romantic relationship considered by both partners as profound.

The first case is easier to explain. You live with your spouse for a long time, you have joint children and grandchildren, you get used to each other, you have no significant incentive to look for a better option, and living together, even without profound love, is a convenient option. You may or may not supplement it with brief sexual affairs, but overall you are in the marriage to stay.

In the second case there is mutual profound love, but one partner does not want to continue the relation. Although romantic profundity usually is associated with longevity of a relationship, to gauge longevity requires other factors, such as living circumstances and personality, which have some value in deciding whether to live with someone. These are the cases, discussed above, of "I love you, but I am leaving you," and the cases, to be discussed below, in which personal suitability and overall balance are very low. I will discuss this issue in detail later on, so, at this point, an example will be suffice.

Take two romantic relationships. One gets the score of 9 (out of 10) in profundity, and 3 in intensity. The second relationship gets the score of 8 in profundity and 7 in intensity. Which one of them is more likely to endure as a romantic relationship—the first, which has a higher profundity score, or the second, which has a higher intensity score? The winner is the second relationship because it contains a balance of profundity and intensity making it more likely to endure longer. Neither profundity nor intensity alone can effectively predict long-term romantic love. It is the balance between them that makes the difference.

Although romantic profundity usually correlates with longevity of a relationship, we have seen that to gauge longevity it is also necessary to take personal flourishing into account. Since profound love is not identical to long-term love, people divorce despite their profound love.

As factors determining romantic longevity, personal circumstances and flourishing generate what can be characterized as romantic robustness. If you open a dictionary, you will find the word "robust" defined variously as "vigorous," "strong," "healthy," "successful," "unlikely to break," "powerfully built," "active," "dynamic," "working effectively," "marked by richness and fullness," and "sustainable" (in the sense of being capable of continuing for a long time at the same level). Robust romantic relationships have a lot of these characteristics.

Robustness involves striking a balance between intensity and profundity. A high level of each contributes to the robustness of the romantic relationship.

Having a very low level of either intensity or profundity can damage romantic robustness—but this is also the case when one of them is extremely high. Thus, an extreme level of romantic intensity, as we find in infatuation, is likely to reduce the levels of profundity and complexity. It is hard to pay attention to long-term profound considerations or to the subtleties of a complex situation when your heart is on fire and smoke gets in your eyes. Such smoke is unlikely to result in romantic profundity. However, if profundity gets too serious and starts neglecting short-term superficial experiences, then we can say that it is overly profound. But we are not going to find overly robust romantic relationships. Romantic robustness strikes a healthy balance between the many characteristics constituting romantic love and nurtures long-term, vigorous, and successful relationships.

In the following pages, when referring to long-term romantic relationships, I will use also the term "robust" in the sense of including both romantic profundity and intensity. However, because profundity is the major feature in romantic robustness, and indeed romantic profundity is highly correlated with romantic longevity, I will continue to provide running commentary on our tour of profound love.

Concluding Remarks

With my new lover, I feel like I am on a train that is moving so fast that it makes me dizzy. The problem is not that it is the wrong train. It is rather that I hadn't intended to take it as yet. I need more time to tear down the fences, to feel myself into it.
A MARRIED WOMAN

Long-term romantic activities spotlight promoting the beloved's well-being rather than merely preventing harm from coming to him. This includes increasing joint intrinsic activities between the lovers instead of simply sharing instrumental tasks, and creating a process of intrinsic development rather than only being influenced by external changes.

No quality of the beloved is as important as the nature of the connection between the partners. While it can be tempting to give in to preventing behaviors, which often block the heart, these tend to stifle independence and stress criticism. It is more useful to go for promoting behaviors, which aim to cultivate the right environment for nurturing the loving heart. When one views an activity as valuable in and of itself, and that activity is an instance of optimally exercising an essential capacity, then this activity is intrinsically valuable. This is what intrinsic development, as compared to reacting to external changes, is all about. Enduring romantic experiences thrive on a combination of intrinsicality and profundity. Such experiences are deeply meaningful, and they reinforce one's inherent value.

Scratch the surface of enduring romantic experiences and you will likely find synchrony, positive responsiveness, and romantic resonance. Synchrony refers to the coordination in time between two (or more) people. Positive responsiveness is an umbrella term for interactions between lovers that strengthen both the relationship and its partners. Romantic resonance is a high-level type of synchrony and responsivity, which might be described as an ongoing dynamic reciprocity.

Having conflicting emotions toward the beloved, which seems to constitute romantic inconsistency, is natural in complex, partial romantic experiences. A common way to cope with this is to assign different emotions a different level of importance. Thus, we can see our always-tardy partner as wonderful overall but still acknowledge the negativity of a specific quality, such as her lack of punctuality.[35]

The Role of Time in Love

If I could save time in a bottle, the first thing that I'd like to do is to save every day till
eternity passes away just to spend them with you.
JIM CROCE

They say that time heals a broken heart, but time has stood still since we've been apart.
RAY CHARLES

We have logged quite a few miles in our journey toward understanding the
possibility of long-term profound love, and along the way, we have picked up
some handy tools. I will now use these tools to examine various phenomena
that reveal the role of time in romantic behavior. This role is paradoxical.
On the one hand, every moment with the beloved is precious; on the other,
as time passes, romantic intensity tends to decrease. These two perspectives
give rise to two conflicting views: (1) time is a positive and constitutive factor
of profound love; (2) time is either marginal or damaging to intense love. I
begin examining this ambiguity by discussing the difference between *timing*
and *time*, showing that while timing is pivotal for romantic intensity, time is
foundational for romantic profundity.

We see the positive and negative roles of time in love in all temporal
dimensions—past, present, and future. In the *past* dimension, the negative
attitude toward time is evident in the saying "It's no use crying over spilled
milk"; the positive attitude is demonstrated by the yearning for ex-lovers. The
negative attitude toward time in the *present* and future is similar: reducing, if
not abolishing, the value of the future while focusing merely on the present.
This is indicated in expressions such as "It's now or never; tomorrow will be
too late." The positive attitude is evident in the willingness to wait "till the
end of time." The negative attitude toward time in the *future* is articulated in
the proverb "Eat, drink, and be merry, for tomorrow we die"; the positive attitude supports the wish to be with the beloved always and forever. Tellingly,
the musical hit parade broadcasts, without exception, include each of these
attitudes.

Timing Is Not Everything

I married for timing and convenience, I am afraid to say. My spouse will not admit it, but he did as well.

A MARRIED WOMAN

Popular wisdom has it that timing is everything—in life and in love. The issue is more complex. I believe that timing concerning external circumstances, such as the place of meeting, is often decisive in bringing two people together. However, *time*, rather than *timing*, is imperative when it comes to maintaining and enhancing profound love.

External timing refers to a specific point in time that, in retrospect, is thought to have had a good or bad effect on the outcome. Time has a wider reference, including duration, frequency, and development. Timing is of greater importance in finding a partner, while time is more significant in maintaining long-term profound love.

External romantic timing can be related to sheer luck. Two lovers might just happen to meet each other accidently on a train. In this case, the highly likely alternative of not having ever met underlies their feeling of being lucky. However, timing can also involve a sort of skill or aptitude for doing something at the most suitable moment. It can encompass both the luck at being in optimal circumstances at the right time and the skill of being smart enough to recognize such circumstances. In both cases, the individual's actions or responses are short-term, sometimes almost instantaneous.

External timing is key when it comes to generating intense sexual experiences. This is the reason that quickies, makeup sex, and breakup sex are often so intense. The case is typically different with romantic experiences. You can say, "I have a headache at the moment and am not in the mood to have sex with you"; you cannot say, "I have a headache now and am not in the mood to love you." Long-term profound love exists even when one or both lovers are sad; it continues to exist in a dispositional manner even when the lovers are angry with each other or are not thinking about each other. Conversely, sad emotional circumstances are not optimal for sexual interactions, though when the sadness passes, make-up sex can be quite intense.

Today, timing, which is an instantaneous point in time, has become more important than time, in which long-term processes take place. Accordingly, the issue of speed has become central in our society, and many people feel that staying in one place involves compromising and relinquishing the chance of finding a better option. As Meryl Streep said, "Instant gratification is not soon enough" for some people. Nowadays, slow people often fall victim to rapid pace; the fast and often more superficial people seem to have an edge. Credit cards are useful in this regard, as they eliminate the waiting time until the desired object is acquired; accordingly, they have been advertised as "Taking the waiting out of wanting." The internet and various social networks make the connection between people faster and less profound, thereby significantly decreasing the possibility of long-term profound relationships and, unsurprisingly, increasing the problem of loneliness—as loneliness is not generated by lack of social connections, but by lack of meaningful, profound social connections.

When timing takes top priority, lovers are always restless. As optimal timing is often associated with occasional circumstances or sheer luck, lovers continuously worry that they might be missing an alluring opportunity or that an alluring opportunity will ruin their loving relationships. In such circumstances, lovers always need to be on their toes, ready to catch or prevent the temptation of a fleeting opportunity. A constant search prevents many people from achieving long-term profound love, which is characterized by calmness. Romantic love is not a permanent test in which lovers need to prove again and again that they deserve each other and score higher than potential others. Romantic love is accepting the partner as he or she is while trying to bring out the best in each other. No one can always achieve the highest grades. However, each of us is better when not subject to constant testing or comparison.

Restless lovers often go in search of a new partner and need to be clever enough to identify the optimal timing in making first contact with a lonesome soul. Thus, it can be good timing to approach someone when this person is lonely and might be open to a new romantic option. In the graphic words of Carole King, "When my soul was in the lost-and-found, you came along to claim it." When love is all about timing, the lover's role does not go much beyond the technical task of catching the romantic moment, even if this is a brief moment with a low probability of developing into a profound romantic relationship.

The vast number of romantic temptations with which we are continually bombarded have rendered timing rather significant. When there are so many accessible, even superior, alternatives, it seems to make no sense to invest your time and other resources in a current relationship that requires a great deal of work to enhance its profundity. As with many other products and experiences, contemporary love demands instant satisfaction. When romantic satisfaction is a matter of moments, as it were, timing is indeed everything.

With profound love that extends over a long time, however, luck is an expression of ongoing romantic attitudes and activities. Profound love requires

THE ROLE OF TIME IN LOVE

investing in shared activities and emotional experiences. But today, the search for enduring romantic profundity is quickly abandoned, with people satisfying themselves with occasional instant sexual intensity that is dependent on getting the timing just right. While the latter is certainly easier to achieve, at the end of the day it can be exhausting and depressing to rely on such serendipitous and superficial experiences. Many of us, then, are left yearning for romantic profundity, which brings the romantic calmness, stability, and trust that enhance our thriving.

In profound love, lovers carry a lot of responsibility. There are ongoing challenges that are frequently perceived as being against all odds and that often require lovers to stretch to the limit their capacities and resources. Still, despite the burden borne by lovers in profound love, people feel calmer and more secure in such relationships. The realization that they themselves are responsible for enhancing their love makes people calmer than when they are in a series of short, unstable relationships that can quickly end as a result of arbitrary, external circumstances. And calmness is a kind of self-fulfilling prophecy: the calmer you are about the likelihood that your relationship will endure, the greater your willingness to invest in it and the higher the likelihood that it will endure. In addition to profound love, gratitude, compassion, contentment, humility, kindness, and forgiveness do not seem to be high on the list of cherished attitudes in our highly competitive, achievement-oriented society.[1]

To sum up, luck in the sense of good timing can be valuable in finding a romantic partner—many love stories have begun in this way. However, good timing is limited in its scope and is of hardly any value in long-term profound love. Both timing and time are important in different circumstances, as romantic intensity and profundity are both key to romantic love. Understanding the nature of each enables lovers to make the best of their romantic connection.

The Past: Spilled Milk versus Ex-lovers

There is no sense in crying over spilled milk. Why bewail what is done and cannot be recalled?

SOPHOCLES

Some people come into our lives and leave footprints on our hearts and we are never ever the same.

FLAVIA WEEDN

Lovers see the past in opposing ways, and their view of time is constructed in similar opposition. We have the intellectual, negative attitude of "What's done is done," which implies that there is no point crying over spilled milk or trying to save a love that has soured. In contrast, nostalgia and idealization of ex-lovers express the positive attitude toward past experiences.

In a goal-oriented society, the past is of little concern: our gaze is directed at the future. Such a negative attitude toward the past implies that it is not rational to invest resources in past events and that instead we should focus our limited resources on present and future goals. Accordingly, rational, intellectual decision-making involves rejecting the past.

In emotional attitudes in general and romantic love in particular, the past circumstances of the individual are important. Although the past seems to be unchangeable and unfixable, our attitudes toward past events, and hence the impact of the past upon us, mean a great deal for our future relations. Thus, a positive memory bias may be a mechanism of maintaining satisfaction in long-term relationships.[2] William Faulkner went so far as to say, "The past isn't dead. It's not even past."

The importance of the past is nicely expressed in Kobi Oz's witty remark "Do not forget to remember me." Sometimes remembering the past is spontaneous, but sometimes we need to invest some effort and take concrete steps to remember people or experiences from the past. The lover's request of his beloved not to forget to remember him after their separation is reasonable in the sense of not totally erasing a meaningful past—even if that remembering does not lead to any concrete actions.

Sometimes we should cry over spilled milk; otherwise how would we learn to value milk and how would we avoid spilling it again? One of the best ways to take account of the past is to take account of our emotions, as emotions are shaped by, among other things, past events. In the emotional importance of the availability of an alternative, or what might have been, we see the importance of the past for our emotions.[3]

In discussing emotional intensity, I have distinguished between two major groups, one referring to the perceived impact of the *event* eliciting the emotional state and the other to background circumstances of the individual involved in the emotional state. The impact of the event will depend on the *strength*, *reality*, and *relevance* of the event. The individual's background circumstances are made up of her *responsibility* for the emotional change, her *readiness* for the change, and her *deservingness* of the specific emotional change.[4]

Although background circumstances might seem unrelated to a current situation, they can serve to prevent or promote similar experiences in the future. Thus, the more effort we invest in something, the more meaningful it becomes and the stronger the emotion associated with it. As the saying goes, "The more you pay, the more it is worth." The importance of the past in romantic relationships is related to the value of shared activities in a loving relationship. Significant disasters or joys, everyday hardships, and the development of the relationship are integral to the formation of romantic profundity.

However, focusing all of our attention on the romantic past would prevent us from investing in the romantic present and could lead to perceiving the present as a compromise. Although it is unhelpful to ruminate on past failures and successes, neglecting the past can be equally problematic.

Sometimes, it is truly best not to cry over spilled milk. When a loving relationship ends, there is no reason to continue to live in the past. The best route is often to look forward to the next meaningful relationship. The demise of one's love does not mean the death of one's life—not even one's love life. However, our lives would be rather shallow if we were to blot out the past, which is really the groundwork of who we are and what we have experienced and learned.

What factors have an impact on the revival of a past romantic relationship? If love was profound at the time of separation, if the separation was the result of external circumstances that no longer exist, and if the quality of the lovers' current relationships is low, then the chances are very high. However, people usually change after they separate, and this can influence the probability of their reunion. Age and the partners' experiences during the intervening years might have made them more tolerant toward each other, but the opposite might also be true—they might have changed to the point that their love is no longer possible.

In a true love story from the Holocaust, Hedy Weisz, a young Jewish woman, and Tibor Schroedder, a Christian reservist in the Hungarian forces allied with the Nazis, were engaged to be married when World War II erupted. However, after the war, having survived the Auschwitz concentration camp, Hedy, who still loved Tibor very much, refused to meet and marry him. She said that she was now a different person, not the woman whom Tibor had admired and loved. She did not want his admiration and fantasies to be shattered.[5] Similarly, in Henry James's novel *The Wings of the Dove*, after two lovers withhold their love and conceal their engagement, they separate—only to later realize "We shall never be again as we were!"

Books aside, however, people sometimes do not change so much that love cannot flourish again after many years of separation. Romantic love, which involves some degree of idealization of the beloved, also involves the idealization of the past. Thus, when asked whether true love remains forever, one woman answered in the affirmative and cited her first love as an example—despite the fact that she had angrily terminated that relationship six years previously.

Yearning for Ex-lovers

I am very discreet. The only reason I told my ex-lover about my current lover is that I wanted him to see that his chances are zero (at the moment). I am not sure it has worked.

A MARRIED WOMAN

The impact of the past on our romantic life is also expressed in the search to reignite a relationship with a past lover. Today, the positive aspect of the romantic past has given impetus to the search for ex-lovers. Thus, research has found that nearly half of adult daters and cohabiters report a reconciliation (a breakup followed by reunion), and over half of those who break up continue their sexual relationship together ("sex with an ex").[6] This on/off relationship and the appeal of the ex-lover, which reflect considerable instability and uncertainty in adult intimate relationships, have a substantial effect on increasing romantic compromises. The current partner might be considered as a romantic compromise not merely because of future available opportunities but also because the romantic past, which is highly emotional, is not dead—as it is possible to revive old loves. The ability to be happy with your romantic lot is becoming more complex with every touch of the screen.

The renewed searches for past lovers are driven by two factors, a substantial one and a technical one. The substantial factor relates to the value of nostalgia, of which idealization of the past is an essential element. The technical factor is that the information superhighway has made it rather simple to track down ex-lovers.

Nostalgia is a wistful, sentimental longing for the past, often in an idealized form. The term "nostalgia" also has a medical meaning, referring to a form of melancholy. Nostalgia often embroiders upon "the good old days," which become idealized in the current circumstances. It is a longing for circumstances that no longer exist or might never have existed. In fact, it has a utopian dimension due to the considerable role that imagination plays in it. Hence, nostalgia is often about a virtual reality that cannot be actualized. In this sense, nostalgia is not always about the past; it can also be directed toward the future or the present. Nostalgia is a bittersweet longing that combines the pleasurable feeling of the past with the pain of the experience that is now absent. Its content is very positive, but its absence in reality generates pain. Idealization of the past has two opposing consequences. On the one hand, we might feel like we are in an inferior situation compared to our previous one, and idealizing it can leave us feeling sad; on the other hand, we might feel that we have done something meaningful in our life, and this puts us in a better situation.

Lovers who have separated from each other typically feel a sense of longing. They think about their beloveds and suffer because they are not able to be with them. Hence, people like to hear that their lovers long for them, even though it means that the lovers are suffering, as their suffering signals their love for us and their regret at ending the relationship. The gratification we feel when our ex-lovers long for us is less an expression of pleasure in others' misfortune than an awareness of their love for us even when we are not actually together. Of course, it can also be flattering, and therefore pleasurable, to know that you and your lover are still crazy about each other after all these years.

Ex-lovers are popular search subjects these days on the internet and social networks. In a sense, many ex-lovers never disappear from view. It is hard to forget your ex-lover when he is visible on your screen. Indeed, many people have tried to locate an ex-lover in the hopes of rekindling their romantic sentiments. From the distance of time, our memory can enhance our love for our exes, making the relationship seem better than it probably was. We thus feel justified in our romantic search and optimistic about its success. Being familiar with the person for whom we are searching gives the search greater legitimacy and provides us with a kind of cushion in case our current relationship should fail. However, this cushion often prevents us from being happy with the love we already have.

The idealization of the past and the comfort of approaching a familiar person make the notion of reconnecting with previous lovers appealing. However, after the excitement of reunion, the past difficulties can resurface. Change comes hard to us, and the flaws of the past are likely to reemerge in the future. It seems that if the two people were just friends in their youth, the chances of them engaging in a successful romantic relationship in the present are greater. If they shared a committed romantic relationship and separated after not being able to make it work, either because of lack of love or personal incompatibility, the likelihood that they will succeed this time is small. Nonetheless, being older and having gained further romantic experience might change the present circumstances to the extent that a renewed relationship with someone from the past proves more successful than before. Sometimes, the failure of the past relationship was not due to lack of love or to incompatibility but to external circumstances that no longer exist.

People find it easier to have a sexual relationship with an ex-lover than with someone new, as the familiarity and shared history between the former lovers facilitate such activity.[7] In addition, given their previous sexual intimacy, they might perceive it as a more legitimate activity and a lesser sin. In this sense, ex-lovers do indeed constitute a threat and thus often generate greater romantic jealousy in the current partner than someone new on the scene. Reviving past romantic experiences can have a devastating effect on our current relationships.

The Present and the Future: It Is Now or Never versus Loving You Forever

I want to embrace life's every ounce and have great sex and love and experiences and food and wine and massages and swimming in the ocean and poetry and movies before I die!!!!!!
A MARRIED WOMAN

Perhaps there is only one cardinal sin: impatience. Because of impatience we were driven out of Paradise; because of impatience we cannot return.
W. H. AUDEN

Forever and a day, that's how long I'll be loving you.
KELLY ROWLAND

In the present and future dimensions, too, time cuts both ways: only the present is meaningful, while the future is insignificant, or the future is the most meaningful because it is forever. Romantic love often involves impatience, which expresses a narrow temporal perspective. The romantic heart is typically described as impatient: in the words of Elvis Presley, "It's now or never, be mine tonight, . . . tomorrow will be too late." The theme of an impatient heart and the disregard for time is expressed in verses from another Presley song: "One night with you, is what I'm now praying for," as such a night "would make my dreams come true." Indeed, if a single night would enable your dreams to come true, why bother with profound qualities essential for satisfaction through many days and nights? The saying "See Naples and die" carries a similar meaning: It can feel so fulfilling to see the beauty of Naples that once you have done so, you have experienced everything that is truly important in life. Similarly, in the movie *The Hours*, the character of Virginia Woolf says, "A woman's whole life in a single day. Just one day. And in that day her whole life." There are indeed circumstances—such as the day that the two lovers first met—in which one day makes all the difference.

Romantic relationships, however, are not based on a single night; they are about the ongoing development of a couple's flourishing. Sometimes, a one-off or short-term experience can compensate for a long period of suffering, but our main concern should be how to promote the continual enjoyment and thriving of our everyday romantic life. Sexual desire is impatient, while profound love is patient. Sexual desire is partial and brief; it does not last forever, and when it exists, it demands immediate fulfillment. It is hard to be patient when your body is on fire.

We see the conflict between impatient intensity and patient profundity in the way that people (more so women than men) tend to temporarily block fulfilling intense romantic desires in order to achieve greater romantic profundity. Two major ways of doing this are (1) the playing-hard-to-get mode of behavior, and (2) the "in-due-course" policy. In the playing-hard-to-get mode of behavior, the individual hides her genuine interest in order to assess the partner's attitude; in the in-due-course policy, both partners are aware of their love but decide to take the time necessary for their own attitudes to develop and become more profound. In both cases, love must be developed and "earned" and becomes more meaningful over time by enduring the pain of postponing desirable—mainly sexual—interactions. The in-due-course policy is the more serious route of the two. This policy does not necessarily cast doubt on the lover's sincerity, as is often the case in playing hard to get; rather, it involves investing more time so that profundity can be established. The in-due-course policy constitutes a kind of prolonged courtship. Indeed, marital happiness is positively associated with the length of the courtship period.[8]

The heart becomes impatient with matters that appear to have merely superficial, extrinsic value, since in such matters the heart is driven to achieve its goals as fast as possible. In these circumstances, the heart is less willing to invest resources, including time and effort. In profound love, when you are deeply satisfied with your situation, there is no need to rush into anything. The general mood of a patient heart is that of calm, peaceful joy. For the impatient heart, any distance or delay is intolerable. For the patient heart, distance is part of the meaningful togetherness; hence, it can tolerate some types of distance. In the same vein, when love is very intense, toleration is quite difficult. As a married woman said, "I would not call my behavior tolerant, as I was not tolerant toward my lover when he behaved in a wrong way (from my perspective). I love him too much to show tolerance."

Our society has made us impatient—expecting quick rewards for whatever we do. From instant coffee to instant love, we have become trained to demand rapid fulfillment, immediate gratification, and quick results.

In contrast to romantic impatience, which diminishes the role of the future, and generally of time in love, lovers often speak about their patient heart—their readiness to wait for the beloved. Consider the following description by a married man about his feelings while awaiting the arrival of his married lover: "I always came early to our meeting place. Though I was very excited to see her, I felt a kind of calm elation. I had all the patience in the world, as I knew that she would always come, and then I would be in heaven. Sometimes, I even wanted the waiting to last a bit longer, because it felt so good." As profound romantic love takes account of the long term, there is no reason to be impatient while the beloved is absent. When you know that paradise awaits you, you are more likely to feel pleasurable expectation than impatience.

The idealization of waiting for the beloved demonstrates the value of time in romantic relationships, even if this time does not involve shared activities but merely anticipating such activities. Conversely, when the time spent waiting with no shared activities is too long, it can put the relationship itself at risk. Hence, a beautiful song by the Mills Brothers states, "Till then, my darling, please wait for me . . . Some day, I know I'll be back again . . . I know every gain must have a loss, so pray that our loss is nothing but time." Although the loss of time may not necessarily be the loss of a relationship, it is often a significant, painful loss.

The above conflicting attitudes toward the present and the future express the conflict between short-term intense (mainly sexual) experiences and long-term profound love. In the view that foregrounds romantic intensity and relegates romantic profundity to the back burner, the role of the future in romantic love is similarly dismissed. Such intensity calls for immediate actions that will increase the peak of the flame. This attitude is associated with the idea that because life is brief, it is also insignificant. If life is short, and there is nothing that follows, we had better enjoy the brief time given to us by focusing on superficial pleasurable activities. Ironically, however, filling our life with such activities alone can shorten our life and reduce our pleasure. Taking the hedonistic attitude of "Eat, drink, and be merry, for tomorrow we die" can satisfy some immediate sexual desires, but it will prevent profound happiness. It is a superficial means that often worsens one's situation and contributes to ill health and despair.

Limiting ourselves to the immediate romantic present and disregarding the future are impossible, as we live surrounded by possible romantic opportunities. It is hard to act without considering various options—what might be and what could have been. The many alluring possibilities currently available have made love in modern times a rather fluid concept. Accordingly, romantic bonds tend to be frailer than in the past.[9] Such possibilities prevent us from enjoying long-term profound romantic experiences. The superficial, short-term experiences of eating, drinking, and having casual sex are hardly affected in such circumstances, as their brief duration does not exclude other possible superficial pleasurable experiences. It is the profound experiences that we risk losing out on.

Concluding Remarks

Love is hard to find, hard to keep, and hard to forget.
ALYSHA SPEER

The dizzying pace of modern society poses a threat to love in that timing is often emphasized over time. It is the latter, though, that lends itself to profound love. Our tendency to choose superficial future possibilities can spoil our ability to reach romantic profundity. In consuming ourselves with immediate and ever-changing superficial possibilities, we tend to neglect the more stable and profound aspects of the present and the long-term future. Time is also relevant when considering a return to a past lover. However, the idealization of the past can contribute to a mistaken expectation that things will somehow be different or better than the first time around. Whether it is considering a return to a past lover or establishing a new connection entirely, the quest for profound love requires a patient heart and an awareness of the impact of time.

The role of time in romantic love has both positive and negative aspects. This is so because time is a positive and constitutive factor of profound love, whereas time is either marginal or at worst destructive to intense love. In long-term robust love, there is an overall optimal balance between the various aspects of time.

6

The Romantic Connection

I love you—I am at rest with you—I have come home.
DOROTHY L. SAYERS

At the heart of romantic love lies the connection between the lovers. What is the nature of this connection? We have seen that both caring and sharing, as well as responsivity and resonance, are central to this bond. Yet there is more. I begin by considering the basic human need for such a connection, or more specifically, the need to belong to someone. Next, I discuss the connection of love to marriage, which is still the prevailing form of long-term, committed relationships. I then examine the possibility of having a "perfect" loving relationship, the replaceability of the beloved, the question of whether cohabitation before marriage leads to more divorces, and the role of inequality and envy in romantic relationships. I also explore relationships in which the one you love doesn't love you (as much).

The Need to Belong

You belong to me.
JO STAFFORD (AND MORE THAN SEVENTY OTHER SINGERS)

You don't own me. Don't say I can't go with other boys.
LESLEY GORE

Belonging is a main feature of the romantic connection. Despite its political incorrectness, lovers still commonly inform one another, "You belong to me." Of course, each of us is autonomous, and no one can actually belong to another person. But belonging in a psychological sense is very real. The term "belonging" has to do with "possession" and "being a natural part." Belonging in its literal sense of *possession* is obviously inappropriate in any relationship, including a romantic one—possessing your partner implies ownership and control. However, in the sense of being *accepted as a natural part*, it makes sense. Belongingness here expresses the creation of something from nothing, as it is the result of this unique romantic bond. This belongingness is even felt strongly at the cutting of the connection, sometimes to the extent of an actual feeling of an amputated arm.

Roy Baumeister and Mark Leary argue that the need to belong stems from the fundamental human need to form and maintain a minimum number of lasting, positive, and significant interpersonal relationships. Satisfying this need requires (a) frequent, positive interactions with the same individuals and (b) engaging in these interactions within a framework of long-term stable care and concern.[1]

The imperative for stable, caring interactions with a limited number of people can even override the excitement of changing romantic partners. For Baumeister and Leary, people are "naturally driven toward establishing and sustaining belongingness." Hence, "people should generally be at least as reluctant to break social bonds as they are eager to form them in the first place." They further argue that we are even hesitant to dissolve destructive relationships. The need to belong goes beyond the need for superficial social ties or sexual interactions; it is a drive for meaningful, profound bonding. Our very well-being seems to hinge on a sense of belongingness. Without it, we are less healthy and happy. People who lack belongingness suffer higher levels of mental and physical illness and are more prone to a broad range of behavioral problems, ranging from traffic accidents to criminality to suicide.[2]

You Belong to Me, Darling

All the lonely people, where do they all belong?
THE BEATLES

As soon as you set foot on a yacht you belong to some man, not to yourself, and you die of boredom.
COCO CHANEL

If our health and well-being depend on belonging, then the statement "You belong to me" is more than so much romantic nonsense. Such belongingness is actively created by lovers, through meaningful joint activities. This is the positive side—and there is a negative one as well—to the negative attitude toward a violation of belongingness, often expressed as jealousy. The fear of losing something that in some sense belongs to you is as significant as the hope of gaining some kind of meaningful togetherness.

And belongingness goes further in the journey toward romantic love. According to Baumeister and Leary, it fuels mutuality. People prefer relationships in which both parties give and receive care—mutuality strengthens the romantic relationship. Unequal involvement is a strong predictor of romantic breakup. When both partners are equally involved in the relationship, the likelihood of their future togetherness increases. Studies comparing people who received love without giving it and people who gave love without receiving it found that neither group was happy with the relationship. Baumeister and Leary conclude that apparently "love is highly satisfying and desirable only if it is mutual." Hence, when love "arises without belongingness, as in unrequited love, the result is typically distress and disappointment."[3]

The starring role belongingness plays in romantic love works well with the dialogical model of love. Love, for Krebs, is not about each partner serving as the object of the other; rather, love is what happens *between* the partners. Loving somebody involves the meaningful enjoyment of their togetherness, which is constituted by the sense of meaningful belongingness.[4] Importantly, we are not talking about an unhealthy fusing of the lovers' identities—quite the contrary. Fusion, a kind of conjoined-twins model, implies not merely a loss of freedom but also a loss of each partner's identity. Neither loss works well with the meaningful belonging underlying profound love, which provides optimal circumstances for the personal flourishing of two independent individuals.

To sum up, it is not wrong for a lover to feel that the beloved belongs to her, so long as the belonging is limited to the psychological sphere and the sense of belongingness is mutual. Social life and romantic love come with a built-in need to belong, leaving room for jealousy to materialize. Doubts can arise, not about the importance of mutual belonging, but about how it should work itself out in reality. There is no romantic life without a sense of meaningful belonging, but such belonging comes with a price: it limits the number of romantic partners we can have—after all, belongingness involves commitments and the allocation of scarce resources. Profound lovers, however, tend to take this limitation in stride.

Love and Marriage

Love and marriage, love and marriage, go together like a horse and carriage . . . You can't have one without the other.

FRANK SINATRA

Romantic love and personal fulfillment are newcomers to the drama of marriage: most marriages looked rather different for most of history. However, once romantic love and personal fulfillment arrived on the scene, they became crucial to both the length and the quality of marriages.

Types of Marriages

Being a couple is not merely about love and sex; it is also about mutual support, which is one of the most sublime expressions of love. Mutual support is not as colorful as flowers, not as mysterious as the glow of a candle, not as exciting as a personal letter and not as awesome as good sex; and yet, it is very distinct. It has a kind of romantic magic. Mutual support is the simple lackluster soldier of love. And the moment this simple soldier goes AWOL (Absent Without Official Leave), perhaps it is time to consider the bitter end of love.

AVINOAM BEN-ZE'EV

For most of human history, marriage was a practical arrangement designed to enable the couple to meet their basic survival and social needs. Passionate love had precious little to do with it. Stephanie Coontz shows that this ideal emerged only about 200 years ago: "People have always fallen in love, and throughout the ages many couples have loved each other deeply. But only rarely in history has love been seen as the main reason for getting married." She observes that "in many cultures, love has been seen as a desirable outcome of marriage, but not as a good reason for getting married in the first place."[5] Pascal Bruckner argues aptly that in the past, marriage was sacred, and love, if it existed at all, was a kind of bonus; now, love is sacred and marriage is secondary. Accordingly, the number of marriages has been declining, while divorces, cohabitation, and single-parent families are increasing. It seems that "love has triumphed over marriage, but now it is destroying it from inside."[6]

To the aforementioned marriage types—pragmatic and loved-based—Eli Finkel adds a third type: personal fulfillment ("self-expressive") marriage, which in his view developed in the United States around 1965. Finkel argues that during the pragmatic era, the primary functions of marriage revolved around the fulfillment of lower needs (such as water, food, and physical, psychological, and economic security); during the love-based era, it centered on midlevel needs (such as romantic love), while the self-expressive era emphasized higher needs (such as self-actualization).[7]

Among the various features that Finkel attributes to self-fulfilling marriages, the following are the most relevant: (a) reciprocal self-fulfillment, (b) authenticity, (c) time, which is crucial for development and survival, and (d) lack of shame about pursuing a good-enough marriage.

In self-fulfilling marriages, we do not merely want our spouses to meet our needs, but we want to meet their needs as well. Mutual support is crucial in love and marriage. In such marriages, our spouses develop deep understanding of our authentic selves. Accordingly, they often perceive us as better than we really are. Indeed, we are happiest when our partner views us with a blend of accuracy and idealization. As emphasized in this book, time plays a crucial role in thriving through marriage (and other committed relationships). Finally, there is no shame in pursuing a "good-enough marriage." We may aim high in our ideal marriage, but we should have the ability to be satisfied with a less-than-perfect marriage. Constant comparison is lethal to thriving marriages.[8]

We shall discuss these claims further in the following pages, but one implication is already obvious: thriving committed relationships should enjoy a great deal of flexibility and balance.

Marital Quality over Time

> I never knew what real happiness was until I got married. And by then it was too late.
> MAX KAUFFMAN

> My husband said it was him or the cat. I miss him sometimes.
> ZSA ZSA GABOR

Marital quality over the life course has been explained in two main ways: (1) a U-shaped course, with high quality in the early (honeymoon or preparental) years of marriage, declining during the child-rearing phase, and increasing in the later years when children leave the home; (2) a linear course, with marital quality declining over time. These two views of marital quality have been challenged by more recent studies using multiple trajectories over time. The aim of the standard growth curve modeling is to obtain a single average curve describing all married couples while accounting for the variance around the curve. In contrast, a group-based trajectory model considers major differences in marital quality as multiple distinct trajectories instead of a single mean curve.[9]

There is evidence that early in relationships partners develop attitudes concerning the relationships, and they carry these into the marriage. Similarly, it has been found that husbands and wives fit into distinct marital-happiness trajectory groups, characterized by either high/stable marital happiness over time or moderate-to-low happiness that declined over time. It was also found that most couples report moderate-to-high marital happiness over time. An additional interesting phenomenon, called "the honeymoon-as-ceiling effect," refers to the findings that marital quality rarely increases beyond its initial point of marriage, or prior to it. This effect does not suggest that marriages cannot improve, but that they normally improve after a marital decline, and they rarely rebound to initial levels.[10]

The above findings are compatible with Finkel's views on marriage in contemporary society. Finkel identifies two major trends in our society—the increased emphasis on fulfilling higher-level needs through marriage, and the reduced investment of time and other psychological resources in marriages. The negative consequence of these trends is that the proportion of spouses whose marriages fall short of expectations has grown. The positive result is that the benefits of having a marriage that meets our expectations have grown. Hence, Finkel claims, "as marriage has become both more fragile and more important, its quality—the extent to which we experience it as fulfilling—has become an increasingly important predictor of our overall happiness with life."[11] Such research supports the idea, central to this book, that long-term profound love is not only possible, but also common.

In romantic flourishing, it is not merely the connection between the partners that flourishes, but each partner flourishes as well. Personal flourishing does not contradict marital flourishing, but rather enhances it.

Perfect Love with an Imperfect Person

If you look for perfection, you'll never be content.
LEO TOLSTOY, *Anna Karenina*

What happens when perfection isn't good enough?
SCOTT WESTERFELD

We dream of finding the "perfect" person with whom to establish a "perfect" romantic relationship. More often than not, however, we are rudely awakened from such dreams. Toward understanding this situation, I shall here introduce some different possible aspects of the lover's attitude toward the beloved: (a) the beloved can be considered perfect in the sense of being flawless or being the most suitable partner, (b) the lover can discover the beloved's virtuous properties or bestow them upon the beloved, and (c) the beloved's most significant properties can be either nonrelational or relational. The comparative approach is central to the attitude that the perfect beloved is flawless and that her perceived major cherished attributes are discovered and nonrelational. The uniqueness approach is central to the attitude that the beloved is the most suitable partner and her significant attributes are mainly relational and bestowed. An awareness of these differences is crucial for building a perfect (i.e., most suitable) relationship with an imperfect partner (i.e., a partner who is not flawless).

The Possibility of Perfect Love

I am far from perfect, so expecting a perfect partner would be unrealistic. Imperfection
is perfect for me. Growth comes from imperfection!

JUNE BRADSELL

In romantic ideology, the only acceptable love is the "perfect" one. In a related
respect, it has been claimed that love can conquer all, and that all you need is
love. All of these notions have in common a disregard for reality, which is often
not as good as it is in our brightest dreams. In this view, love is perfect (in the
sense of having no faults), uncompromising (as being able to conquer all), and
unconditional (as being all you need). This ideology, which insists on our search
for the perfect partner and nothing short of it, shares with other ideologies the
flaws of being simplistic and one-dimensional. In general, ideology allows little
room for the intricacy necessary to cope with the complexities of life.[12]

Iddo Landau rejects the perfectionist notion that meaningful lives must
show some perfection or excellence, some rare or difficult achievement. In
this view, to be meaningful, one's life must transcend the common and the
mundane. For Landau, perfectionists are so busy searching for the perfect
that they neglect to notice and find satisfaction in the good.[13]

Landau's view can be usefully applied to the romantic realm—but with
caution. Let's begin. Our trusty dictionary defines "perfect" as (a) *flawless*: being entirely without fault or defect; and (b) most *suitable* (or optimal): being as
good or correct as it is possible to be, and completely appropriate for someone.
While the first meaning focuses on the negative aspect, the second meaning
centers on the positive one.

The search for the flawless person is an exercise in utter futility. However,
looking for the *most suitable person in the given circumstances*, with whom
you can build a "perfect" intimate connection, could yield a flourishing and
harmonious partnership.

Discovering and Bestowing

Sometimes I look at my boyfriend and think . . . Damn, he is one lucky man.

UNKNOWN

Do we love our beloved because she is kind, wise, and beautiful? Perhaps we
think that she is kind, wise, and beautiful because we love her. The first account
claims that love essentially involves *discovering* (or detecting) the beloved's objective attributes. In the second account, the value *bestowed* upon the beloved
is the effect of our loving her. These two approaches have been described as the

"appraisal account" and the "bestowal account." But this is confusing, because both accounts involve appraisal. Less confusing, and more accurate, would be to say that the two accounts differ in their view of the main activity: discovering or bestowing.[14]

A simplistic version of the discovering and bestowing accounts raises doubts about the possibility of long-term romantic love. The first account raises the problem of the replaceability of the beloved. If love is indeed all about discovering the person with the best properties, then there is no reason to stay with your beloved if you can find a person with better properties. As it is easy to compare these properties in different people, in this view, one's beloved would be in constant peril of being replaced by a person with better properties.

In a simplistic version of the bestowing account, we *attribute* to the beloved her most significant properties. This approach can generate illusions stemming from our intense desire toward her. As the old love song runs, "When your heart is on fire, You must realize, Smoke gets in your eyes." These illusions about the beloved's virtues are likely over time to be found to be misleading, thereby placing into jeopardy a lasting romantic relationship.

We need *both* accounts to make sense of the lover's attitude. To be sure, one's traits trigger love. We do not fall in love with a shadow. Yet, we also view the world—and our beloved—through our evaluative glasses, as a constructed, interpreted figure.

Profound love combines the two accounts. Unlike in romantic ideology, lovers should be sensitive to reality and not wander in the wonder world. They should assign the appropriate weight to the beloved's various characteristics, without distorting reality too much. Take, for example, someone whose partner is not particularly intelligent. This person can say that her partner's kindness is much more important than his intelligence, and perhaps that he is not the least intelligent person she has ever met. At a certain point, she will become very familiar with the limits of his intelligence. However, she may think of him as "not brilliant," rather than as "stupid." It is not helpful to pretend that every frog will turn into a prince, but you can be generous in evaluating your partner's positive traits.

The Comparative and Uniqueness Approaches

If you have an old habit of competing and comparing yourself with others, then you are still living your life like a sperm. GROW UP!!
SAURABH SHARMA

I love you more than coffee, but please don't make me prove it.
ELIZABETH EVANS

The view that regards the beloved as the perfect person, in the sense of being without faults, has a strong comparative push; it considers the beloved's main characteristics to be flawless, nonrelational (in the sense of standing on their own, regardless of the relation to the partner), and easily discoverable (by others as well). This comparative approach takes a static view of romantic love in which love is essentially fixed, while occasionally moving from one point of comparison to another.

The view that considers the beloved to be a perfect partner in the sense of being most suitable emphasizes the uniqueness of the relationship; it sees the beloved's most important qualities as relational and sees confirmation of many of them during interactions. The uniqueness approach offers a dynamic kind of romantic love over time. Such love involves intrinsic development that includes bringing out the best in each other.

Both the comparative and uniqueness approaches describe important aspects of long-term robust love; it seems, however, that the odds of establishing such love are better in the second of these.

Landau distinguishes between two meaningful attitudes toward life: (1) aspiring to be the best and (2) aspiring to improve. He criticizes the first attitude, which is often associated with overcompetitiveness, involving an endless, unproductive search for "the best," and praises the second, which is associated with meaningful development.[15]

This distinction is also captured by the difference between the comparative and uniqueness approaches to romantic love. Being romantically meaningful in the first sense depends on comparison with factors that are external to the connection between the two lovers. In the second sense, love depends mainly on the activities of the two lovers. Improving the connection between the two lovers, rather than finding the person with the best nonrelational properties, is the most meaningful task of romantic profundity. If romantic meaning mainly concerns achieving the best, lovers will always be restless, consumed with concern about missing the perfect person, or perhaps the younger, the richer, or the more beautiful one. If, however, romantic flourishing mainly involves improvement, achieving it lies much more in the hands of the couple.

Being married to someone who is not perfect but is still a caring and loving partner is not necessarily a compromise. In fact, that partner might be the optimal choice. We can have an (almost) perfect loving relationship with an imperfect lover. Many people even view their partners' imperfections with compassion and amusement and consider these negligible compared to his or her profound virtues and their own flaws. This takes us back to the ambivalent nature of emotional complexity. The ability to notice and cope with both negative and positive aspects of the beloved expresses emotional complexity and is valuable for profound love.

For many people, the quest for the perfect *person*, instead of the perfect (in the sense of most suitable) *partner*, is a major obstacle to an enduring, profound, loving relationship. Since life is dynamic and people change their attitudes, priorities, and wishes over time, achieving such romantic compatibility is not a onetime accomplishment but an ongoing process. In a crucial and perhaps little-understood switch, perfect compatibility is not necessarily a precondition for love; it is love and time that create a couple's compatibility.

To sum up, the distinction between two senses of "perfect"—flawless and most suitable—can help us understand the comparative and uniqueness approaches to the nature of the beloved. In the comparative approach, the perfect beloved is flawless, her most relevant traits are discovered, and her major cherished characteristics score very high in comparison to other people. In the uniqueness approach, the perfect beloved is the most suitable partner, and her most significant romantic traits are mainly relational and "bestowed." Both approaches are common, and both contribute to the task of choosing a romantic partner.

The Replaceability of the Beloved

I have good-looking kids. Thank goodness my wife cheats on me.
RODNEY DANGERFIELD

Profound love is based on a strong romantic connection. And sometimes strong connections fracture. The most painful rupture occurs when the beloved is replaced by another person. This is closely connected to the issue of the lover's commitment.

The Lover's Commitment

A girl must marry for love, and keep on marrying until she finds it.
ZSA ZSA GABOR

Romantic commitment is not something that shatters without cause—there should be good reasons to breach a romantic commitment. Such commitment mainly stems from the relationship with our partner and not from comparing the partner to other people. Shared history is highly relevant to the issue of commitment, which is enhanced with time. Our commitment to someone we have been with for ten years is far greater than to the one we are with for merely ten minutes. This does not mean that lovers should be blind to other people or that comparison and replacement are immoral. It just emphasizes the obvious: shared history and commitment carry great weight when considering a partner replacement.

Jollimore discusses the role of the *connection* in love. He claims that there is something in the romantic connection that is nonuniversalizable and non-assessable in which both parties play crucial, irreducible roles in the relation. Such roles, which are largely responsible for the uniqueness of the interactions, underlie any personal commitment. It is evident that lovers have some commitment toward their beloveds and that this makes the transfer of love from one person to another very hard.[16] This does not mean that partner replacement is never justified. There are extreme circumstances, the obvious being that of domestic violence, where such replacement is highly justified. There are opposite extreme cases, such as those where profound love is replaced by short-term superficial excitements, in which the replacement is usually unjust. The hardest cases are those that fall in between. Commitment should be respected, but not at any price; excitement, development, diversity, and complexity should also be appreciated—but again, not at any price.

The lover's actual attitude toward the beloved falls along a behavioral continuum reflecting the actualization of the lover's attitude. Three major types of such actualization are (1) a mere *wish*, which cannot, or is not intended to be, translated into actual behavior; (2) a want or *desire*, which is not manifested in actual behavior because of external constraints; and (3) a *full-fledged desire*, which is also expressed in actual behavior. Love, for example, typically includes full-fledged desires expressed in characteristic activities: caring, yearning, caressing, cuddling, fulfilling the needs and wishes of the beloved, and so on. Not all of these have to be manifest at all times. However, the total absence of such behavior might suggest that love is absent as well.[17]

A mere wish is one that actually cannot be fulfilled in the present circumstances, such as "Fly me to the moon, let me play among the stars." A mere wish can also be one that in principle can be fulfilled, but you really do not want to actualize it even if you could—for example, killing the partner of your beloved. A want, such as the desire to run away with your lover, can, in principle, be fulfilled, but you do not do it because you do not want to get divorced. A full-fledged loving attitude includes various actual joint romantic, sexual, and caring activities. You do what a loving relationship is all about—having many joint activities and experiences.

These kinds of connections between a loving attitude and its behavioral implementation are indications of the lover's commitment. The least degree of a commitment breach is feeling the temptation as a mere wish that is not intended to be implemented in actual behavior. A greater "sin" is to consider implementing the temptation, but not doing so because of external concerns related, for example, to the personal cost it involves or the harm to the primary partner. The greatest violation of one's commitment, in this regard, is acting on the temptation.

The Mate-Switching Phenomenon

Why have you left the one you left me for?
CRYSTAL GAYLE

Despite all good intentions, lovers separate and replace each other. Love is risky, as lovers are vulnerable to profound frustrations, unexpected misfortune, or dishonest behavior. These risky circumstances often generate the stressful situation of having to switch mates.

David Buss and colleagues argue that the romantic fantasy of long-lasting, committed mating rarely materializes in reality. The prevailing circumstances include a gradual inattentiveness to each other's needs, a steady decline in sexual satisfaction, the exciting lure of infidelity, and the wonder about whether the humdrum grayness of married existence is really all life has to offer. They further claim that in the context of the struggles against this situation, the major strategy is that of long-term, committed pair-bonding. However, as nothing in mating remains static, and since "evolution did not design humans for lifelong matrimonial bliss," people should prepare themselves for the possible situation of marriage dissolution. This issue is of particular concern in women's mate-switching behavior, as the risk women face in switching mates seems to be higher and their gain less apparent.[18]

People try to take precautions aimed at easing the painful nature of this switch. Three such major strategies are (1) *positive coping* by enhancing the quality and the commitment of the current relationship; (2) *giving up romance* by initiating a breakup, living alone, or at least being in a nonpassionate, committed relationship; and (3) *fighting* under the shadow of a possible switch. The first strategy is the focus of the current book; this strategy's success would somewhat reduce romantic loneliness. The second strategy, of giving up on romantic love and focusing on life or other types of love (such as friendship or parental love), is of some value in certain circumstances, especially those in which the search for romantic love is proving more harmful than a nurturing life of living without such love. The third strategy can be acted on in various ways that mainly involve having multiple relationships simultaneously. Two major subtypes of this strategy are (1) having extramarital affairs and (2) cultivating backup mates. I will discuss the issue of affairs later in the book; at this point, I focus on the backup strategy.

The Backup Strategy

Save a boyfriend for a *rainy day*—and another, in case it doesn't rain.
M A E   W E S T

One major strategy for preparing to switch mates is to lay the groundwork for a kind of preemptive strike by cultivating backup mates—that is, potential replacements for the current mate, should the relationship implode. Buss and colleagues show that people of both sexes report having an average of three potential backup mates. People also indicate that they would be upset if their backup mates became seriously involved romantically with someone else. Women are more likely than men to report that they would be upset if their backup person entered a long-term relationship or fell in love with someone else.[19] Despite such difficulties, some people prefer being vicarious partners to their married lovers to not being together at all.

The backup strategy is present in both dating and committed relationships. This is most evident on romantic dating sites, which offer a dazzling display of prospective partners. People have a long backup list, sometimes consisting of a few dozen candidates, and if one date is not going well, they turn to the next person on the list. Such an abundance of replacements decreases a person's incentive to focus on a worthwhile partner and invest in deepening their connection. The backup list creates problems associated with "more is less" and "too much of a good thing" and reduces the likelihood of establishing a committed, profound romantic relationship.

The backup strategy, which is a kind of insurance policy against getting hurt, dumped, or bored with current love, is often harmful within a committed relationship, as it damages the individual's commitment to the current relationship, thereby making the strategy a self-fulfilling prophecy. While having a backup list of romantic partners might well reduce the cost of separation, it often increases the likelihood of such separation. The negative impact of such a strategy is particularly evident in low- and medium-satisfied relationships, where the existing commitment is already not high.

Romantic backup activities are like window-shopping. You do not intend to purchase anything now, but if you find something attractive, you might purchase it at a more convenient time. Like window-shopping, romantic backup activities can be pleasant, involving intrinsically valuable activities such as enjoyable flirting. Many people would assume that there is nothing wrong with such romantic window-shopping, as long as it does not become an alternative about which the shopper ruminates and which she actually considers acquiring.

The backup strategy is wasteful in terms of resources. Nowadays, we do not lack romantic options: we have too many of them. The problem today is not finding love but maintaining and enhancing love over time. So, investing effort and resources in cultivating further options seems to be unwise. It might have been of some benefit for our ancestors, who did not enjoy as many romantic options as we do, but these days, it is unnecessary, unwise, and wasteful.

It can be argued that while one does not need any backups in brief sexual encounters, backups are useful in longer relationships, which require time to develop. This claim makes some sense, and indeed people in longer relationships tend to nurture a few backup alternatives. Nevertheless, the lack of ongoing profound interactions with such backup people reduces the ability to fully examine and nurture the relationship with them. This reduces the value of the backup strategy, especially in light of the high cost it inflicts on the current relationship. Like positive illusions, backup behavior can lead to self-fulfilling prophecies. However, while in the case of backup behavior a self-fulfilling prophecy often destroys the possibility of profound love, positive illusions tend to maintain and enhance such love.

At first glance, it might seem that the romantic backup strategy is more important than positive illusions, as it is more sensitive to objective reality. But is this really the case? In my opinion, it is not. Sometimes, it can be advantageous to disregard the unpleasant aspects of reality, as it increases our chances of fulfilling our positive attitudes. The promise of everlasting love prompts lovers to believe in the possibility of such love. Positive illusions also lead to higher motivation, greater persistence in tasks, more effective performance, and ultimately greater success. Thus, a positive view of the self typically leads a person to work harder and longer on tasks. The same goes for optimism, including unrealistic optimism, which can become a self-fulfilling prophecy. However, the unrealistic nature of positive illusions can also be harmful in that it impedes our ability to cope with the real problems that arise in intimate relationships.

Romantic connections do not come with a guarantee. When you let love lead the way, a concern for security takes something of a back seat. Although backup plans can be helpful, their value is doubtful in the case of profound romantic love, mainly because the potential cost far exceeds its future benefits. Using this strategy is likely to prevent you from establishing profound love. Not only can no lover promise you a rose garden; certain activities can poison the whole garden.

Why Try to Change Me Now?

You know I'll love you, Till the moon is upside down. Don't you remember, I was always your clown. Why try to change me now?
FRANK SINATRA, BOB DYLAN, FIONA APPLE, and many others

Partner replacement is strongly connected to another aspect of romantic relationships—the desire to change the partner's negative traits. Although in trying to regulate our partner's behavior we are often attempting to improve the relationship, this plan usually fails. This is because such attempts are likely to increase awareness of the gap between the idealized lover and the partner, and they are also likely to communicate a lack of acceptance of the partner. Attempts to change the partner are powerful signals that he or she is failing to meet expectations. Thus, the greater the amount of attempted regulation to which people are subjected, the less they feel they match their partner's ideal standards. Accordingly, regulatory efforts tend to backfire, and both people become even unhappier with their relationship. Moreover, any changes in the partner would be minor and would not make her much closer to your ideal lover.

The type of change we should seek in our romantic partner and in ourselves is that which develops the romantic connection, by bringing out the best in both of us. The wish to change your partner should not indicate that there is something wrong with your partner, but rather that growing together requires greater compatibility. The likelihood of a successful process of development is greater when both partners realize that such a process requires ongoing adaptation to each other, rather than changing each other. In such relationships, personal growth and flourishing are evident. Retaining each partner's identity and autonomy is crucial in such a process, as it is in many other circumstances.

Romantic Drifting: Does Cohabitation Lead to More Divorces?

Only dead fish swim with the stream.
MALCOLM MUGGERIDGE

Many people's long-term romantic behavior is similar to dead fish floating with the current, slowly drifting with the stream. Is such behavior damaging? Not always, as it turns out.

Decision-Making Mechanisms

As he read, I fell in love the way you fall asleep: slowly, and then all at once.
JOHN GREEN, The Fault in Our Stars

Deliberative thinking and intuitive knowledge are two major decision-making mechanisms. The deliberative mechanism typically involves slow and conscious processes, which are largely under voluntary control, and it usually utilizes verbally accessible information and operates in a largely linear, serial mode. The intuitive mechanism involves spontaneous responses that rely more on tacit and elementary evaluations. Intuitive activity is often fast, automatic, and accompanied by little awareness. It is based on ready-made patterns that have been set during evolution and through both social and personal development; in this sense, history and personal development are embodied in these patterns. We may speak here of "learned spontaneity." Since intuitive patterns are part of our psychological makeup, we do not need time to activate them; they are available to us when the appropriate circumstances show up.[20]

Drifting is another decision-making mechanism. More accurately, it is an avoidance mechanism involving either not deciding or deciding not to decide. Drifting involves lack of control. In some languages the word "drifting" denotes both slow and fast movement. Love at first sight is an example of fast drifting. I focus here on slow drifting.

Many of us experience slow drifting. From a subjective perspective, such drifting is convenient: it demands a minimal investment of resources, and, in the case of failure, one's responsibility is correspondingly minimal. From an objective perspective, drifting is a gradual process that takes reality into account. There are no rushed decisions; choices are left to simmer on low heat until they are "well cooked." Drifting can get us into trouble because it favors short-term considerations that maintain the status quo rather than long-term activities that actively advance our situation. Accordingly, drifting often inflates the eventual cost of changing the status quo and disproportionately reduces the weight of improvement. This helps to avoid immediate conflicts, but increases the likelihood of profound, long-term calamities.

Slow Romantic Drifting

Continents drift, and so do hearts.
JOHN MARK GREEN

Slow romantic drifting facilitates a gradual shift from one romantic state to another, without one's full awareness or deliberate choice. Slow romantic drifting, during which love is eroded or developed, is a long process, though the realization that one does not love one's spouse or that one has fallen in love with one's friend can be abrupt and instantaneous. Although the drifting process can be long, the realization of its import often comes in an instant, taking one by surprise. Thus, Bertrand Russell claimed that he was happily married until one day, while riding his bicycle, he suddenly realized that he no longer loved his wife.[21] Drifting is characterized by habituation and the lack of strong emotional intensity. Everything occurs in small incremental steps, and nothing constitutes a change that is significant enough to generate great emotional intensity, as is typically the case in acute emotions.

Romantic drifting might appear to be a reason-less, choice-less, action-less process of which we are unaware, but this is not entirely correct. Drifting is *not reason-less*; it is just not characterized by the more familiar method of conscious thinking. Although drifting does not involve a deliberative choice in which all options are considered, one does, in fact, *make some choices* without being coerced. While we are less aware of the drifting process than we are of our deliberative thinking, we are *partially aware* of some aspects of drifting. Thus, partners who are drifting apart can be aware of their marital difficulties but might not be fully aware that these difficulties have gradually worsened, or that they are indicative of romantic erosion. Drifting is also *not entirely action-less*. Although people who are drifting seem similar to dead fish floating with the stream, (unlike the fish) they always have an alternative they can take. Often, they do not take this alternative because it is regarded as having little value, or as being risky, unpleasant, or embarrassing. The individual's responsibility in romantic drifting stems from not investing more effort in exploring the implicit, partial information they have. In some cases, such efforts could change the situation.[22]

Given that slow drifting takes place over a relatively long time, it reflects some stable features of reality. Thus, romantic drifting apart reveals the sad reality of the deteriorating relationship. In the slow, incremental process of drifting apart, partners lose their romantic attachment over time and become increasingly less passionate toward each other. When people feel that something inside has died and it's too late to change, hide, or fake it, then all doubts disappear, and separating becomes the natural step to take.

When a couple is aware of this but continues to live within the loveless framework into which they drifted, they are romantically compromising. Not infrequently, this compromise can be traced to fears that a search for ideal love elsewhere will be unsuccessful, to heartbreaks experienced in previous searches for love, or to the sense that the risks of such a quest outweigh its advantages. Drifting out of love genuinely discloses the way people feel toward each other when the situation seems to be one of no return. However, if lovers become aware of the drifting process early enough, sometimes they can stop it and possibly even reverse it. Although in drifting we can be likened to a stagnant river, the water below the surface is not necessarily stationary, and our lack of awareness of these underlying currents poses a major risk to the romantic relationship.

Drifting into Marriage

My boyfriend and I live together, which means we don't have sex—ever. Now that the milk is free, we've both become lactose intolerant.

MARGARET CHO

Premarital cohabitation has become the norm in many cultures, and more than 70 percent of US couples now cohabitate before marriage. Advocates of premarital cohabitation say that it enables partners to get to know each other better and to find out whether they get along well enough to marry. Counterintuitively, however, many studies have found that premarital cohabitation is associated with increased risk of divorce, a lower quality of marriage, poorer marital communication, and higher levels of domestic violence. Finally, there is research (although less) that refutes the negative correlation between premarital cohabitation and divorce. Why is it that this phenomenon, which has become so common and aims at increasing compatibility, has such disputable results?

Commitment theory describes three major factors underlying romantic commitment: the degree of love, the cost of separation, and the availability of an alternative. Commitment is strengthened by the amount of satisfaction and the extent of the cost, and it is weakened by possible alternatives to that relationship. Satisfaction level is significantly more predictive of commitment than is the quality of alternatives or the cost of separation. The quality of the relationship has the greatest impact upon its continuation, much more than external factors, such as the cost of switching or the available alternatives. However, when satisfaction is not high, the extent of the cost and the attractiveness of the alternatives can carry greater weight.[23]

In a study conducted by Scott Stanley and colleagues, it was found that the decision to get married while cohabiting was arrived at via a sliding (or drifting) process, involving hardly any deliberative decision-making. Thus, more than half of the couples living together had not discussed it and simply slid into cohabitation. In comparison to a simple affair or a relationship that has no committed framework, cohabitation involves a relatively greater cost of separation (e.g., financial obligations, a shared lease, sharing a pet, pregnancy, embarrassment), without necessarily including a significant increase in the intensity and profundity of love. Stanley and colleagues argue that the reduced weight given to love is likely to become problematic after marriage, when the couple will have to face various obstacles together. It is interesting

to note that the negative effects of cohabitation on marriage are greatly reduced when cohabitation begins after engagement; that is, when the decision to marry is made before the couple cohabits. In this case, the decision
to marry occurs when the weight of cost, relative to love, is less, and meeting
others is still natural.[24]

An additional factor limiting the ability to reach an optimal decision
about marriage is that cohabiting couples tend to minimize the differences
between cohabitation and marriage, particularly those differences concerning lasting commitment and challenges. Many cohabiting couples who decide to get married assume that the difference between the two lifestyles is
minor. This assumption is, after all, a major justification for cohabitation before marriage: it is a kind of test of the couple's suitability for marriage. As it
turns out, this assumption is wrong. While cohabitation seems like marriage,
it is a horse of a different color altogether. It lacks marital constraints (such
as exclusivity and less freedom) and challenges (such as raising children). It
appears that cohabitation is a kind of deluxe test, a test with less commitment
and fewer challenges. Indeed, research indicates that marriage is qualitatively
distinctive from cohabitation and that it involves a higher degree of commitment and stability than cohabitation.[25]

This does not apply, of course, to those couples who do not believe in the
institution of marriage, who never intended to marry, and who cohabit on
principle. Their partnership is not a trial marriage or a test to see if marriage
might be a future option; rather, it is a committed relationship between couples who feel they do not need legal or religious sanctions to confirm their
pledge to each other. This holds also for gay couples in places where gay marriage is not legal, and these couples cohabit without anticipating marriage in
the future.

When a couple enters a marital relationship after having cohabitated, their
passion is not at its peak. If people have reached their peak of passion during
cohabitation, they arrive at the challenging years of marriage without the drive
of passion that provides the energy to overcome the challenges in a marital
framework. It is also possible that after cohabitation, people take divorce more
lightly, because cohabitation made them experience and consider separation
as more natural.

Commitment theory rightly considers the presence of quality relationship
alternatives to decrease romantic commitment. Cohabitation indeed limits the
number of quality alternatives, and in this sense strengthens the relationship.
However, since cohabitation is a stage in the process of *choosing* a partner,
this limitation can hinder finding the optimal partner. This is an additional
reason why cohabitation can be valuable when the decision to marry has been

taken—and the main issue is to strengthen this relation—and can be harmful when you are still searching for the best romantic partner.

In contrast to the above considerations, there are scholars who emphasize the value of premarital cohabitation as a kind of "trial marriage," which enables the couple to become better acquainted before committing themselves to marriage. Advocates of this theory claim that those who cohabit prior to marriage tend to have a greater risk of marital dissolution, not because they cohabited, but for other intrinsic reasons, such as their personality and previous history, which led them to cohabit in the first place. Thus, it has been found that cohabitation, relative to marriage, is selected by less committed individuals.[26]

A study by Michael Rosenfeld and Katharina Roesler suggests that premarital cohabitation affects marital stability differently in the short and long terms. In the first year of a marriage, couples who have cohabited before have a lower breakup rate than couples who have never cohabited, which may be due to the initial experiential advantage of couples who have already lived together when they enter into marriage. This advantage, however, lasts only for the first year. The marital stability disadvantage of premarital cohabitation emerges most strongly after five years of marital duration, and has remained roughly constant over time.[27]

Without getting into the details of the empirical dispute, it seems that the nature of premarital cohabitation can have significant effect on marital duration in both the short and long term. This impact, however, is multifaceted and should take into account personal and contextual factors.

Inequality and Envy

The flower which is single need not envy the thorns that are numerous.
RABINDRANATH TAGORE

Equality in friendship is an old, well-discussed topic. Thus, for Aristotle and many others in ancient Greek society, friendship was ideally a relationship between equals. Aristotle also considers friendship between people of unequal status but maintains that in this kind of asymmetrical friendship, there must be some proportional exchange of benefits, which bestows a "distributive equality" upon the relationship.

A lack of equality often generates envy and decreases martial satisfaction. I have argued that envy is mainly concerned with *our undeserved inferiority*. Envy does not involve a general moral concern for justice, but rather a particular, personal concern for what we consider to be our undeserved inferiority.[28] The central place of inferiority and deservingness in generating envy demonstrates the role of inequality in envy; when such inequality is perceived to be undeserved, envy is likely to emerge. Inequality is often perceived to be negative, as equality is typically associated with a positive norm. Thus, we speak negatively about the growing inequality between the rich and the poor. Inequality is defined as "an unfair situation in which some people have more rights or better opportunities than other people." It is often expressed in socioeconomic terms as the gap between the "haves" and the "have-nots." Various egalitarian societies have tried to eliminate such gaps by allocating similar resources for fulfilling their members' basic needs, such as food, health, education, and living accommodations. The kibbutz movement in Israel is a prime example. Yet this has not reduced, and has even increased, the level of envy in the kibbutzim.[29]

The utter failure to eliminate or even to reduce envy in egalitarian societies has to do with our inability to reduce the inequality associated with natural differences, such as being handsome and wise, or with those arising from other impersonal causes, such as one's background. Since such inequalities do not entail anyone's unjust behavior or attitudes, we cannot blame anyone for this situation. Nevertheless, the situation can be considered undeserved or unfair: it represents some kind of injustice, since it places us in an undeserved situation. We often envy beautiful people or those born with natural gifts. In feeling envious toward these people, we do not accuse them of behaving immorally; rather, we consider ourselves to occupy an undeserved inferior position. The situations perceived as unfair by envious people are often not perceived as unfair by others. The urge to find some kind of unfairness in our inferior position could also be explained by referring to the saying "Injustice is relatively easy to bear; it is justice that hurts."

The most suitable partner will often not be the person with the best "objective" traits, but someone who is ready to invest in improving your joint flourishing. We can love a person who is "objectively" not the most handsome or the wisest person in the world, but with whom our connection is nevertheless profound and fulfilling.

The value of equality in intimate relationships is clear, but determining equality can be hard. In some cases, the gap is obvious, and both partners are aware of it. In other cases, where love is absent, each partner thinks that she (or he) is the superior person and therefore the one who is making the compromise. In many cases of profound love, each person adores the partner and considers the partner to be (almost) perfect. Self-deception might be common in all these situations.

One's comparative value is of less importance when the differences are insignificant and refer to different domains. They are disturbing only when they fill your mind and heart to the extent that you believe you are making a profound compromise. However, since there are various domains of comparison, such as kindness, attractiveness, wisdom, social status, and achievements, and since it is, to a certain extent, up to the lover to decide on the relative weight of each domain, not considering your partner to be inferior or superior to you depends somewhat on you.

The combination of being in an inferior situation and being in what is perceived to be undeserved circumstances is exemplified in a study indicating that being in an undeserved position in your marriage could encourage extramarital affairs.[30] Equity theory states that those involved in an inequitable romantic relationship consider themselves to be in an undeserving situation. This is the case for both the "superior" person, who feels that she could do better, and for the "inferior" one, who feels indignant at being unappreciated by the partner. Involvement in extramarital relationships is more likely for these "superior" and "inferior" people than for those who are considered by their partners to be equal. The superior person might perceive extramarital relationships as something she deserves because she is getting "less" than she merits. The inferior person tends to be involved in extramarital relationships to escape the unpleasant state of inequity and to prove to herself and to her partner that she is equal to the partner and is regarded as attractive and desirable by others.

Generally, inequities might give rise to great admiration in the short term; hence, they can increase the initial love and sexual desire. However, in the long term, significant inequalities become a problem for both sides, whereupon superficial short-term goals (such as being in a relationship with a famous person) become less important. For example, the "higher status" person might begin to show a lack of reciprocity, which will eventually damage the "lower status" person's love and spur envy, jealousy, and anger.

The situation is made more complicated by the fact that the extent of the gap and the overall comparative value of each partner also play a part. Feeling bad about an inequality in a certain domain, such as intelligence, can disappear if the overall comparative value is perceived to be similar. In these circumstances, the partner's inferiority in one domain is compensated for by superiority in another. Thus, when people are certain of their worth, they may prefer a partner who is a bit superior to them in one domain and hence will be more beneficial for them. In this case, admiration might be the relevant emotion. For example, in one study, 89 percent of high-achieving men report that

they would like to marry or have already married a woman who is as intelligent as they are, or who is more so. These men believe that in marrying such a
woman they have made the better deal. However, there is some limit to the desirable gap. Thus, one study found that both men and women pursue partners
who are on average about 25 percent more desirable than themselves. People
are aware of their own position in the hierarchy and adjust their seeking behavior accordingly, while competing modestly for more desirable mates.[31]

Interestingly, while constant inequality is unsustainable and emotionally
damaging, a shifting power dynamic in a relationship is often what keeps it
alive. Such shifting indicates the basic status of equality in the relationship.
The profound value here is not in the shifting itself, but in the equality enabling the shift. If this value is not solid, people may always fear that their current inferior status is here to stay. If the equality in status is robust, such fear is
unlikely to pan out—taking the current inferiority to be superficial and brief.

Romantic Reciprocity: When the One You Love Doesn't Love You (as Much)

If equal affection cannot be, / Let the more loving one be me.

W. H. AUDEN

Loving someone who doesn't love you back is like hugging a cactus. The tighter you
hold on, the more it hurts.

UNKNOWN

Unrequited love is one of the saddest of all loving experiences. Some people,
however, prefer a lack of reciprocity to a complete lack of love. Despite the
importance of reciprocity in love, someone can love her partner without having the partner fully reciprocate that love.

Each partner's romantic involvement will always be somewhat different
than that of the other, but some measure of profound reciprocity should exist
in order to prevent other types of inequality that would lead one partner, or
both, to consider the difference unfair. When this happens, we can expect to
see resentment and a decline in marital quality. Compromising on romantic
reciprocity is an example of the "principle of least interest." The least-interested
partner is less committed and has more control over the continuation of the
relationship. Accordingly, this partner is often the one who terminates the
relationship.[32]

Unequal romantic involvements are hard to gauge, given the differences
in people's personalities and in the manner and pace that they form loving
relationships. Accordingly, inequality in romantic involvement is common, at

least in the early years when the romantic relationship is being formed. The difference in romantic involvement can lead to the following two types of circumstances:

1. You are in love with your partner, but your partner does not love you (as much).
2. Your partner is in love with you, but you are not (as) in love with your partner.

Another true story. Albert is a handsome divorced man in his early fifties. He met Debra on a blind date, and they were together for about a year. He left her because although he liked her and enjoyed her company, he did not love her very much. After their separation, he dated a few other women. Then, on his birthday, almost a year later, Debra invited him to dinner at her house, after which he decided to get back together with her. Albert told his friend: "This is the woman I want to live with." The friend was clearly surprised and reminded Albert that nearly a year before he had said that he didn't love her enough to be with her. To this Albert replied, "Yes, but she loves me like no one else ever has before and this is what is most important at the end of the day." In fact, Albert had asked Debra the same question: "Why do you want to be with me, knowing that I do not love you as much as you love me?" Debra replied that she preferred being with a person she loves very much and who might not love her that much, rather than vice versa.

Given these choices, which shoes would you rather be in, Albert's or Debra's? My students and friends were divided in opinion. When speaking about unrequited love, people usually refer to painful experiences in which one partner feels no love whatsoever toward the other. However, most cases are not that extreme: both people love each other, but the nature and intensity of their love is different. As in our example, while Debra is madly in love with Albert, Albert just likes her. Albert's attitude is not without any traces of romantic love. It involves caring and companionship but a lesser degree of romantic intensity. There is a point of love's robustness (referring to both intensity and profundity) below which it is not worth being together, but Albert's feelings exceed this point.

Both Albert and Debra have decided on romantic compromise—but it is unclear which compromise is the more painful of the two. The major advantage in Albert's situation is the great love bestowed upon him; hence, he has greater control of the situation, and there is less probability that Debra will leave him. The disadvantage in Albert's situation concerns giving up a major human dream: to be madly in love with someone. Albert compromises his present in an effort to secure his future. Debra is more vulnerable, as she has less control over the situation. She gives up control of her future in an effort to enjoy profound love in the present. Personality traits also influence the choices in Albert and Debra's situations. More egoistic people might opt for Albert's choice, while more romantic people often prefer Debra's choice. Age can be another relevant factor: older people, whose romantic choices are decreasing or who might look for companionate love rather than passionate romantic love, will tend to choose Albert's situation.

Happy ending. A year after I heard this story, I was informed that Albert got back together with Debra, and they are now a loving couple—although each partner lives in his or her own house.

Concluding Remarks

Comparison is the death of joy.
MARK TWAIN

A major claim of the dialogical approach, which this book adopts, is that the interactions between two partners determine the robustness and quality of the relationship. This chapter, which examines the nature of the romantic connection, provides the foundations for this claim.

The need to belong, which is a vital human need, is expressed in the romantic connection, making this connection hugely important to us. However, romantic belonging does not imply one partner possessing another, as autonomy and equal status are essential in romantic relationships. Belonging is meant here in the sense of mutual acceptance as a natural part of the couple's joint interactions and development.

The connection between love and marriage has become more complex in contemporary society. Marriage, which is a social framework, was primarily designed to fulfill pragmatic goals related to improving living conditions, including reproduction. Once love, and then personal fulfillment, were introduced as ideals in marriage, the quality of marriages began to rise, but so did the prospects of failing to achieve such love and personal fulfillment. This has led to an increase in marriage breakdown.

I have examined the wish for establishing an enduring, perfect, romantic relationship with a perfect person by distinguishing between two senses of "perfect": flawless and most suitable. In the context of romantic love, I consider the second sense helpful and the first one less so. Moreover, we discussed the comparative and uniqueness approaches to assessing the nature of a partner. Both approaches are common and valuable in choosing a romantic partner, though the uniqueness approach is more significant in long-term romantic relationships.

The issue of the replaceability of the partner is central to romantic love, which involves a certain level of mutual commitment—in some cultures, till death do us part. However, people and circumstances change, and romantic separation is a common phenomenon. Nevertheless, love is not like a library book; you cannot replace your partner every week.

The decision-making mechanism of drifting is not as beneficial as the mechanisms of emotional intuition, intellectual deliberation, and intuitive reasoning. Indeed, in many cases, romantic drifting is problematic and is unable to provide romantic stability and depth. In some other circumstances, drifting is valuable and can enable a slow but steady process of cooking to deepen romantic profundity. Slowly comes, slowly (if at all) goes.

Profound love, whose bread and butter is joint activities and experiences, involves autonomy and equality. When a person perceives his or her partner to be unequal to him or her, envy enters the scene (and possibly extramarital affairs as well). The couple equality should not be a mechanical equality, in which the partners add up each person's contribution, but rather one that takes account of their different inputs and especially their status equality.

7

Romantic Compromises

And the only way to do great work is to love what you do. If you haven't found it yet,
keep looking. Don't settle. As with all matters of the heart, you'll know when you find it.
And, like any great relationship, it just gets better and better as the years roll on. So keep
looking until you find it. Don't settle.
STEVE JOBS

Sometimes the heart needs steering.
ALICIA FLORRICK, in the TV series *The Good Wife*

Jobs's rejection of settling, or compromise, is a commendable ideal. It gives
our emotions the leading and even exclusive role in making major decisions
about work and love. However, this ideal is not practical and, in many circumstances, not appropriate. Combining the heart and the head often works
better, because in this combination, emotional regulation is possible. In the
US television series *The Good Wife*, the protagonist, Alicia Florrick, is asked
how she makes love outlast passion. "I think it's not just about the heart," she
says. "Sometimes the heart needs steering." Florrick is right (even though in
later seasons, she has left her husband); sometimes and somehow, you must
compromise, as this can ultimately increase your personal flourishing.

In this chapter, we turn down the road of romantic compromises. The
major forms of such compromises are (a) giving up alluring alternatives and
(b) compromising on the choice of the partner. In this chapter, and throughout the book, I discuss the first type of compromise. (The second type is discussed in the next chapter, which examines the issue of choosing a romantic
partner.) Then I discuss the following issues: whether love involves sacrifice
or compromise, the distinction between good and bad compromises; the
value of being the first, second, or the last lover; being a good-enough partner; and the complexity of romantic compromises.[1]

The Nature of Romantic Compromises

You can't always get what you want, But if you try sometime you find, You get what
you need.
THE ROLLING STONES

In romantic compromises, we give up a romantic value, such as intense, passionate desire, in exchange for a nonromantic value, like living comfortably. Nevertheless, in our hearts, we keep yearning for the possible that we desire, for the romantic road not taken. We do not know when the yearning heart's cry is real or when the cry is momentary and can be compensated for as the relationship develops.

Romantic compromise is the most common and painful syndrome of our modern romantic life. It seems that half of all married couples are unable to accept the romantic compromises they have made, and this can result in divorce. Among the rest—those who do remain in their marriages—many feel that they have compromised themselves. The lucky group of couples who are most profoundly in love have hardly needed to steer their hearts; they have been free to follow their loving hearts, which have taken them to the type of relationship they want to sustain.

Being happy with someone does not mean that there is no other person in the world with whom you would be happier. However, finding that person is problematic for multiple reasons. One is the cost of separation, such as the risk of losing your good-enough relationship now; the cost of the search for this ideal partner, which involves investing time and effort in looking for her; and the risk of not finding the more suitable partner soon. If we assume that the interaction between the two partners is most important for establishing romantic profundity, then, to discover this ideal partner, one would need to be with many people before making a decision. This might lead to the discovery of a better-suited partner (although still not necessarily the best in the world). However, if this search endures for fifty years, so that happiness is only achieved, say, at age seventy-eight, the preceding half century could be quite miserable.

Romantic compromises imply a more favorable attitude toward the role of time in romantic love. Thus, some people who were not profoundly in love with their spouse when they got married say that they decided to marry because they hoped that time and greater mutual understanding would deepen their relationship. Sometimes, time does improve a relationship, and the initial compromise is found to be a good one. In other cases, time does not improve, and even worsens, the partner's view of the spouse, and separation becomes inevitable. Hence, the distinction between romantic intensity and profundity can explain many cases in which the spouse was perceived at the wedding as a romantic compromise intensity-wise, but years of spending time together and sharing intrinsically valuable activities considerably increase the couple's romantic profundity.

Types of Romantic Compromises

But a woman is checkmated at every turn. Flexible yet powerless to move . . . Whenever
a desire impels, there is always a convention that restrains.
GUSTAVE FLAUBERT, *Madame Bovary*

There are two major types of romantic compromise: (1) compromises on romantic freedom that are made when entering a marriage (or another committed relationship) and (2) compromises on the choice of a partner. In the first type, the major concern is that we might give up alluring possible alternatives while continuing to yearn for them. In the second type, another concern is added: accepting negative aspects of the partner.

When the negativity of the relationship is significant—involving domestic violence, for example—the concern regarding negativity becomes most dominant, and the decision to end the compromise should be taken immediately. However, if the negativity is not severe, then yearning for the possible will usually be the dominant concern. Often the two concerns are combined, and the feeling of romantic compromise is an outcome of both.

Consider the following candid comments made by a married woman: "I didn't feel that I was compromising too much when I married my husband. Initially, the positives outweighed the negatives by quite a lot. Over time, the negatives started to increase, but it was years of this that caused my feelings of love to start to weaken. I want to improve the negatives, but I also began to realize the value of the alternatives. I go back and forth between these two options!"

Both types of romantic compromise—giving up romantic freedom and accepting a partner with obvious weaknesses—reveal the necessity of compromise in committed romantic relationships. Many couples in less-than-perfect marriages would stay together if they understood that compromise is essential for committed relationships. These people often take an unnecessarily harsh view of their marriage and their partners because they fail to see the value of compromise in a less-than-perfect world. On the other hand, many people stay in appalling relationships because they do not understand the difference between good and bad compromises. The major issue here is whether the romantic compromise ultimately enhances (or damages) our flourishing in life and love.

Giving Up Alluring Alternatives

Two roads diverged in a yellow wood. And sorry I could not travel both. And be one
traveler, long I stood.
ROBERT FROST

What I wanted—I didn't get; and what I got—I didn't want.
HANOCH LEVIN, *The Labor of Life*

The tension between stable boundaries, which secure our comfort zones and within which events are familiar and predictable, and the wish to experience novelty, which is often produced by stepping beyond those boundaries, is basic to human life and the experience of love; this is also the tension between the ideals of freedom and commitment. This tension leads to the major romantic compromise in marriage: giving up romantic freedom, which leads people to feel they are in captivity.[2] The greater flexibility of marriages today and the greater feasibility of tempting romantic alternatives have enhanced the role of love in our life and the need for some revisions in the current form of marriage.

The proliferation of alluring romantic options today can tempt people in a good relationship to go in search of an even "better" (or, at least, different) one—and the very fact of such a search can lead them to neglect and ruin their current relationship. You might believe that your partner is good, or at least good enough for you; but the presence of many seemingly attractive and feasible options can make you restless. In the words of Nat King Cole, "In a restless world like this is, love is ended before it's begun." And since Nat King Cole first sang this beautiful song, the romantic world has become much more restless. These days, romantic excitement often endures only until the morning after. As an older divorced woman said, "Men's love for me lasts as long as my make-up does. Their intense romantic desire at night disappears in the morning when my make-up dissolves."

Coping with the presence of available tempting alternatives is difficult, in part because of "choice fatigue" and the cost of pursuing these alternatives. Moreover, fast change is the hallmark of our throwaway and restless society, which is based on overconsumption and excessive production of short-lived or disposable items. We are addicted to rapid novelty that takes place in constant flux.[3] For many people, remaining in one place is tantamount to treading water. There is no rest for lovers, and not because the road of love on which they are traveling is not good; it might be a bit boring, but it is still a valuable road—probably one of the best in the history of humanity. Yet the novel road not taken is seen to be more attractive, and there appear to be many roads from which to choose. Chasing after a short-term fantasy is often the problem, not the solution. Fantasies about what is or might be "out there" often prove to be a poor substitute for what we already have. We can become enslaved by our own fantasies about the possible; as the Eagles sing it in "Hotel California," "We are all just prisoners here, of our own device." A better understanding of the nature of romantic compromises might free us from this prison, or at least make life within the prison walls more enjoyable.

Romantic compromises are functional, and, in this sense, many of them are good; they mediate between romantic ideals and reality. Romantic ideals are important even if one cannot implement them, at least not fully; in such cases, they can still be a kind of beacon, guiding our way in an imperfect world. If this beacon is to be of any value, we must also be aware of actual reality, and this is precisely what romantic compromises enable us to do.

We base our commitment to a relationship more on our expected future satisfaction with the relationship than on our current satisfaction with that relationship.[4] This can be one reason why people make romantic compromises—for example, why unhappy couples stay together despite feeling that they are compromising. Including the temporal dimension in our romantic decision-making process helps us consider the difference between short- and long-term considerations and decide on the best road to follow. A romantic compromise gives up a romantic value for a nonromantic value, as when people marry not for love but for a comfortable life. However, marrying someone who is highly attractive to you while ignoring the person's equally high opinion of himself, say, might be considered a romantic decision in the short term but could prove to be a romantic compromise in the long run. Many romantic compromises involve a conflict between short- and long-term considerations.

Why Is It So Painful to Compromise in Love?

Don't compromise yourself. You are all you've got.
JANIS JOPLIN

Love is full of compromises, as much of what we want we cannot get. We compromise on our love because of reality. Romantic ideology denies such complexity and hence opposes the need for compromises. Indeed, the very term "romantic compromise" appears to be a contradiction in terms—you cannot tell your partner: "I love you, darling, even though you are a compromise for me." But we often feel this way.

Romantic compromises, like other types of compromises, have both positive and negative aspects. In making them, we give up some of our values, and we wind up feeling some degree of dissatisfaction. However, the idealistic and comprehensive nature of romantic love and the frequently reversible nature of romantic compromises mean that romantic compromises are particularly difficult to make.

Unlike financial compromises, which are made in response to a specific situation and have a finite impact, romantic compromises are *ongoing experiences*—you might live with this compromise all your life. Moreover, romantic compromises are usually *reversible*. This nagging notion that there are seemingly "better" options can prevent lovers from being satisfied with their own lot and can pose an ongoing threat to enduring love.

We live in a complex world that demands compromise. This calls for an order of priorities that can guide us when we must give up something of lower value for something of higher value. Hence, we need to compromise when applying our values to reality. In fact, the ability to seek compromise in a conflict and to understand the concern of the other is considered the height of reason. Relative to young and middle-aged people, older people make more use of higher-order reasoning schemes that emphasize the existence of multiple concerns, allow for compromise, and recognize our limitations.[5]

Romantic compromises involve a lack, or a lower degree, of at least one of the major basic evaluative aspects of the partner—namely, physical attractiveness or praiseworthiness of traits and achievements—in our attitude toward the partner. Some people compromise on physical attractiveness and base their choice more on praiseworthiness of traits and achievements, such as being a good provider or parent. Others may prioritize intense passion, while issues such as friendship, establishing a family, or supporting one's personal development are compromised. Compromising on romantic passion is expressed, for instance, by women who say, "This is the man I want to be the father of my children." These women do not necessarily consider this man as the most attractive but see him as a good friend and a trustworthy person with whom to raise a family. Conversely, a woman can consider a certain man to be a great sexual partner but not the finest friend and companion.

As both physical attractiveness and praiseworthiness of the partner's traits and achievements are essential to falling in love, and since neither tends to show up as an all-or-nothing proposition, romantic compromise is all about proper degree. When both of these aspects are weak, the feeling of romantic compromise can be strong. However, since it is impossible for both to be at maximum level, at least all of the time, each person needs to decide when these aspects drop to a level that feels like a romantic compromise. In our selection of a partner, we are initially less likely to compromise on the partner's attractiveness, which has greater weight at the beginning. Later, considerations of shared activities, caring, and reciprocity, which are more relevant in the long term, become more central. Economic developments in modern society have reduced the need to choose "a good provider," and this allows for greater freedom in our choice of a partner, which means that we can focus more on finding a partner with whom we are in love.

Does Love Involve Sacrifice or Compromise?

A thing is not necessarily true because a man dies for it.

OSCAR WILDE

When we sacrifice, we give up something meaningful to get something else. Romantic *sacrifices* involve giving up a significant *nonromantic* value for *romantic* reasons—for example, devoting less time to one's work so as to engage in joint romantic activities with the beloved. Sacrifice is a personal, voluntary decision in which one goes "beyond the call of duty." In compromises, one gets less than is normally expected.[6]

Close relationships are peppered with sacrifice and compromise, as people have many different desires and values. These conflicts can be minor, such as choosing which restaurant to eat at, or significant, such as having another child or choosing a new place to live. Two ways of dealing with such conflicts are sacrifices and compromises. Whereas many people consider sacrifice to express genuine love, romantic compromises are not perceived to be a part of genuine love.

In close relationships, a willingness to sacrifice is associated with greater relationship satisfaction and stability. People identify sacrifice with caring, trust, respect, and loyalty and hence with what they consider as love. Accordingly, sacrifice is a potent longitudinal feature of marital adjustment. The tendency to sacrifice expresses profound love and enhances a sense of security, which is central for marital success. Reciprocity is important in sacrifice, as it shows a basic balance, in the idea that one's partner would make sacrifices if necessary. Despite the fact that sacrifices are intended to promote the other's well-being and not that of the sacrificer's, the latter can also benefit from the sacrifice, as it increases their self-esteem, others' evaluations of them, and the likelihood that their partner will make sacrifices for them in return. Accordingly, they also could gain from their sacrifice. Generous giving is good for both our health and marital quality.[7]

Romantic compromises are closely related to romantic sacrifices. The two differ, though, in some important ways. Romantic compromises involve giving up a romantic value in favor of something that serves a person's immediate self-interest, whereas romantic sacrifices involve giving up one's immediate self-interest for romantic reasons: promoting the well-being of the partner or the relationship. Thus, we tend to hide our romantic compromises but are proud to broadcast our romantic sacrifices, as these seem closer to moral behavior than do romantic compromises.

Sacrifices are more voluntary than compromises; in the latter, external circumstances "force" (at least from one perspective) the partner to give something up. Sacrifices involve a personal, voluntary decision where one gives up more than is expected to promote the partner's flourishing. In romantic compromise, one gets less than one expects to prevent worse circumstances. Although making compromises and sacrifices can be passive, active, or, as is frequently the case, both, romantic sacrifices are usually more active than romantic compromises. Since romantic compromises involve unfinished business, their negative impact can last for a long time and is expressed in a continuing yearning for the possible. As sacrifices are more isolated and concrete, their impact is usually more limited and focuses on the positive aspect of promoting the partner. Romantic compromise is generally accompanied by feelings of frustration, sadness, and hope; romantic sacrifice, for its part, by feelings of sympathy, compassion, and gratitude. We can feel regret about missing a valuable opportunity in compromise, but usually not in sacrifice; however, sometimes we resent the sacrifice we have made and its cost, although we might not regret having made it.

When making sacrifices, people might not even consider their behavior as a sacrifice. In romantic compromises, one still believes in the greater value of the possible alternative and hence does not fully accept the existing situation. Reflecting the frequent fact of unfinished business, it takes longer to adapt to romantic compromises. People continue to doubt the value of the compromise and yearn for the alternative, until they accommodate themselves to the new situation and no longer experience it as a compromise. Hence, compromises typically involve more emotional repercussions than do sacrifices.

Sacrifices can be harmful when they are extensive and are not reciprocal, such as when one partner carries the full burden of sacrifice for the sake of the other's personal flourishing. In these circumstances, in which we generally find inequality between the partners, those who lack power in the relationship (often women) are more likely to engage in sacrifice. This is made even worse when those making the sacrifice "silence" their own opinions and desires in the relationship.

Good and Bad Compromises

If you can't be with the one you love, Love the one you're with.
CROSBY, STILLS & NASH

I wanna be your vacuum cleaner, Breathing in your dust.
JOHN COOPER CLARKE

In a world without constraints, we would not need compromises, as we would get whatever we want. In a more realistic world, there are many constraints, and compromises are necessary. Take, for example, the issue of marital conflicts. Conflicts are inevitable in romantic relationships. However, conflicts are not necessarily bad, and in any case, the number of conflicts (up to a point) is not the most relevant factor with regard to the risk of divorce; rather it is how conflicts are managed. Although conflicts may provoke perturbation or even separation, they can also provide an opportunity to improve communication, and strengthen interconnections. Conflict management follows three major patterns: downplaying, integrative, and conflictive. The downplaying pattern puts great effort into minimizing the value of the disagreement. The integrative pattern involves acknowledging and negotiating the disagreement, while arriving at a fair and good compromise. The conflictive pattern leads to a further escalation of the dispute. While downplaying is beneficial mainly in the short term, the integrative compromise is the most valuable pattern for reducing risk of separation in the long term. The conflictive pattern, which in a sense denies any compromise, is the most harmful for a relationship.[8]

In characterizing good romantic compromises as opposed to bad ones, I would like to emphasize some of their similarities to (good) settlements. All compromises seem to be a sort of settlement (though not all settlements are compromises). I will describe their similarities in light of Robert Goodin's analysis of "settling." According to Goodin, (a) settling is a matter of setting one's mind at rest; (b) settling is for a limited time, which can be long, but not momentary; (c) settling has value of its own, in addition to its value in preventing worse circumstances; (d) settling and striving, which seem to be opposed, are actually related to each other in the sense that the existence of the one presupposes that of the other.[9] These characteristics all have a strong temporal element.

Setting one's mind at rest. As in settling, in good romantic compromises one's mind is set at rest for a while. When lovers adapt or accommodate to the values and desires of their beloved, they are not necessarily compromising their own values or desires but are sharing the other person's values and desires and beginning to consider them as their own.[10] Not every change in one's values is a compromise. Only when someone continues to yearn for a better alternative can her situation be considered as such. In the romantic realm, good compromises provide the lover's heart with a home in which to settle.

Limited in time, but not momentary. Good romantic compromises are ongoing experiences over time—they are not momentary but might also not last for a very long time. The lack of a constant, active search for an alternative in good romantic compromises does not mean that such an alternative cannot be considered when circumstances are suitable. In romantic life, there are many rocky points in which the continuation of the relationship is under consideration. After almost every fierce fight, the question of the relationship's future is on the table. In a good romantic compromise, the temporal perspective of the couple is broader than that of the immediate difficult situation.

Intrinsic value. Good romantic compromises have their own intrinsic value. They are valuable not merely because they prevent futile, frustrating searches for the perfect prince or princess, but also because they promote the partners' flourishing—typically, in nonromantic realms. Good romantic compromises are also valuable in the romantic realm when they promote long-term romantic considerations rather than merely satisfying short-term sexual needs. A common example of this is when, in choosing a spouse, people give greater weight to the partner's capacity for caring than to that person's attractiveness. Good romantic compromises include settling for a good-enough relationship, while continuing to try to improve it.

Striving. Although good compromises end futile and frustrating striving, they do not stop all forms of striving. The striving, however, is focused on improving the romantic relationship, rather than relentlessly seeking to replace it.

In bad romantic compromises, the above characteristics are absent, as people feel that in making compromises, they are actually compromising themselves. In such compromises, there is no setting one's mind at rest, and the person is actively searching for a better alternative. The value of bad romantic compromises is merely in preventing a bad situation, but the compromising situation is often worse than the previous situation. One significant difference between good and bad compromises is that in good compromises, the feeling of compromise vanishes when the relationship develops further, while in bad compromises, the relationship gets worse, and divorce is almost inevitable. Good compromises are those in which an initial conflict of values turns, in time, into a convergence of values.[11]

The only compromise that is acceptable in romantic ideology is temporal—lovers may postpone their romantic gratification by, for example, waiting for months or even years until the beloved is available. Thus, we are told in the Bible, "Jacob served seven years for Rachel, and they seemed to him but a few days because of the love he had for her." According to this ideology, true love can wait and prevail, even when suitable circumstances are not present. Such waiting is not due to a need for maturation, but to the great value of the beloved and the refusal to compromise for less than the perfect partner. Expressions such as "I will patiently wait for you till the end of time" and "waited in the darkness patiently" are common among lovers and appear in many popular songs and other cultural works. In these circumstances, people compromise on the temporal aspect, which they consider to be less significant, so as to avoid compromising on the more significant aspect: the identity of the beloved. In romantic ideology, compromises function as a necessary means to an end; they have no value of their own.

Let's consider another true story, this time about two sisters, Mildred and Janet. At the start of Mildred's relationship with Bruce, the romantic intensity was lower than in her previous relationships, in which her more "athletic" partners were, in her words, "much more outwardly exciting or adventurous." Despite that fact that she has "always appreciated masculine beauty" and continued to take "pleasure in seeing a handsome man," she chose to marry a man who "was not the most romantic of my loves as a young woman." Consequently, in the first year of marriage she had two brief extramarital affairs. When she cried as she told Bruce about her affairs, he generously comforted her. His wise and caring reaction to her brief adventures clarified for her that even if she had to relinquish tempestuous opportunities, she had gained so much more in her profound, loving relationship with him. Her flings became a small amount of poison that immunized and enhanced their relationship.

Mildred's younger sister, Janet, has a different tale, one of passionate, wild love that quickly ended in disaster. She gave up higher education and married a man whom others considered inferior to her. When asked about the quality of her relationship with this man, she answered, "We love each other and that is what really matters." Janet was madly in love with her husband at the time of her marriage, but from the start their relationship revolved around dining out, heavy drinking, and violence. Eventually, Janet left her husband and entered Alcoholics Anonymous. Her husband died two years after the divorce, aged fifty-three.

The two sisters held different basic attitudes: while Mildred tended to look ahead, Janet was more short-term in her thinking. In their marriages, Mildred made a good romantic compromise, while Janet made a bad one. Mildred gave up brief romantic intensity for enduring romantic profundity; Janet gave up romantic profundity for brief romantic intensity. No wonder Mildred's relationship turned into a great love story, while Janet's relationship ended in an ugly divorce. Mildred was wise enough to see the difference between long-term valuable characteristics and short-term superficial ones (though it took her two affairs to fully internalize the difference). Janet had to learn the difference the hard way.[12] While good romantic compromises do not neglect short-term aspects, they focus on the essential aspects of long-term, profound love.

Being the First, Second, and Last Lover

You may not be her first, her last, or her only. She loved before she may love again. But if she loves you now, what else matters?

BOB MARLEY

The temporal order of being the first, the second, or the last is often of some romantic value. Many people want to be their beloved's very first lover, others prefer to be the second, and most lovers want to be the last.

Being the First and Only Lover

First love is dangerous only when it is also the last.

BRANISLAV NUŠIĆ

The attitude of many lovers (though less so these days) toward virginity (that is, women's virginity) is positive; violating virginity before marriage carries a negative connotation. Virginity does not merely refer to a temporal order but to the pure normative state of a woman, who gives her virginity only to the one who loves her enough to marry her.

Leaving aside the religious aspect and focusing on the psychological one, it would be natural to assume that those who marry their first love are likely to regret missing better, or at least different, romantic options. Along these lines, research indicates that when negotiators' first offers are immediately accepted, they are more likely to think that they could have done better, and therefore they are less likely to be satisfied with the agreement than are negotiators whose initial offers are not accepted immediately.[13] This accords with the powerful impact of the romantic road not taken.

Contrary to the above expectation, however, we have evidence that people who marry their first love are more likely to still be in love, to have never thought about breaking up, and to be certain that they will be with their partner forever.[14] Among various possible explanations of these somewhat surprising results, the one most relevant to this book is the destructive nature of constant romantic comparisons.

People who are married to their first lover are less concerned than others with comparing their beloved to other people. This is because their love is often profound, and they have invested serious time in developing their unique connection. Compatible with this assumption are findings suggesting that if a woman has a history of multiple sex partners, the likelihood of her having a secondary sex partner during a current relationship greatly increases.[15] It seems that personality tendencies and sexual habits are the main factors here rather than the presence or absence of a strong interest in novel sexual encounters.

A Secondhand Love

Men who think that a woman's past love affairs lessen her love for them are usually stupid and weak.

MARILYN MONROE

I never get jealous when I see my ex with someone else, because my mom always taught me to give my used toys to the less fortunate.

UNKNOWN

In its literary, temporal usage, a "secondhand" love is a relationship with someone who has been in a (committed) romantic relationship in the past. However, is there something wrong about not being the first? Given that these days, people begin their romantic relationships quite early in their lives, it is rare to find the one and only on your first romantic journey. In many cases, however, from a time-oriented point of view, being secondhand implies a sort of contamination. And here, not only do you not get a brand-new commodity, but, as is the case for many other used items, you assume that it is defective in some way.

Being a secondhand love does not necessarily carry this humiliating connotation. Thus, a single woman said, "I do not want to marry someone for whom our relationship is his first, as he may feel that he has missed out on something and might therefore have extramarital affairs." However, this single woman adds, "I don't want to marry a divorced man with kids, as he has already experienced with someone else the excitement of the birth of his children and he might also have to cope with difficulties raising his own kids. I would have to find him extremely charismatic and highly attractive to compensate for my compromise in marrying such a person."

A married person's lover might feel that her married lover feels a more profound love for the woman with whom he has a shared history, but she would still like to be unique for him. As a married woman said, "It's so important to be special and unique. Then I can at least be first in *some* area. Then I can deal with my friend being with his wife, who is really his first choice. I know he doesn't have any other relationships like ours, and I can't imagine he ever will either. That is how I cope."

The issue of being a second love is more acute in the case of widows or widowers or others whose deep loving relationship has ended for nonromantic reasons. Those people can keep a unique place in their hearts for their late husband or ex-lover while loving another person. As one widow writes, "Second love is different, but it's very good. I will always love and miss my late husband. It's really hard to understand sometimes how I can go from tears for my late husband into smiling and thinking about my new guy. There's an odd 'divide.' I love both of them, the one here and the one gone." It seems that we are blessed with a heart that is flexible and big enough to accommodate several people at the same time.

When "secondhand" refers only to a temporal aspect, it has a more positive sense than "second best," as a temporal second might be first in quality. However, when "secondhand" involves being defective somehow, it is more negative than "second best," as it can be much lower quality than being second.

The Value of Being the Last

You can dance every dance with the guy who gives you the eye. . . . But don't forget who's taking you home. . . . So darling save the last dance for me.
THE DRIFTERS

In this song, the man allows his partner to have her personal space by dancing "with the guy who gives you the eye," providing she remembers who will be taking her home and for whom she should save the last dance.

First love has its own intense excitement, which can be remembered for a long time. However, last love can achieve greater profundity. It is easy to be exciting when you are the first lover, but such excitement might stem from being first and novel and not from romantic profundity. Being the last can involve profound satisfaction. Although you and your partner can have the attitude of "been there, done that," which often expresses a measure of boredom or complacency, you are still in love. A married woman, who in her thirty years of marriage had two lovers, compares her attitude toward them: "The situation with my first lover was very exhilarating. We shared intensity that both of us did not feel with others. Although the second love affair may have been less exhilarating, it was not 'lesser' from an overall perspective, as in many aspects it was more. Above all, it was more profound, lacking the pain that my first lover gave me; the second lover gave me security and calmness that the first lover never did."

The negative view of second-best and secondhand love is associated with the all-or-nothing attitude of "I will be the very best and the very first, or there is no value whatsoever in this relationship." This attitude, which dismisses the value of human flourishing, implies that previous relationships contaminate the purity of one's heart. But things can work in just the opposite way: such relationships can educate our hearts, enabling us to discover the value of our current relationship as compared to previous ones.

In our dynamic and restless society, when many loving relationships are very brief, the order in which relationships take place is of lesser significance. As a married woman said about the fact that her married lover had had many lovers before her, "The issue of not being the first or the second is less important as long as he loves me greatly. He may have had greater loves in his life, but who knows: I may be the last. I see myself as his dessert—the hot fudge over cool, sweet ice cream." Thomas Fuller claimed, "A conservative believes nothing should be done for the first time." In the case of love, some people believe that nothing should be done for the second time. Both views are wrong.

There is nothing wrong with second-best love, secondhand love, or last love. Each of these loving relationships can be of great value. In our competitive, individualistic society, it is sometimes difficult to believe that there is enough love to go around for everyone. However, our hearts are flexible and big enough to enjoy love with various people, without ranking them in light of their temporal (or other) properties.

Being a Good-Enough Partner

You only live once, but if you do it right, once is enough.
MAE WEST

In romantic compromise, you have settled for less than your dreamed-about romantic partner. The question is, how much "less" can your partner be and still be a sufficiently good partner? This is a complex issue, as someone who initially seems barely good enough can turn out to be the most suitable partner.

"Enough" can be considered "as much as necessary." Ideal love, however, seems to be about getting much more than that. In ideal love, enough is not enough, and you can't get enough of your partner—the better she is, the more you want of her. Nevertheless, some people are not fortunate enough to have even a good-enough partner—they might merely have a "just-enough" partner or a "barely enough" partner. Consequently, many people settle for a romantic partner who is no good for them at all. As Carrie Bradshaw says in *Sex and the City*, "Some people are settling down, some people are settling, and some people refuse to settle for anything less than butterflies." However, it is possible that with age and experience it is somewhat easier to accommodate ourselves to what we have and to be satisfied with it. Indeed, Confucius said that it was only when he reached seventy that "I could follow the dictates of my own heart; for what I desired no longer overstepped the boundaries of right."

Herbert Simon combined the words "satisfy" and "suffice" and came up with "satisfice," a term used to express an adequate solution rather than one that maximizes utility.[16] A "satisficing" solution can be the best choice when we take into account the cost of looking for alternatives. In Simon's view, since the human capacity for knowledge is so limited, we would do well to take a realistic approach to seeking optimal solutions, which are not necessarily those that maximize their possible gains.

Simon's considerations are relevant to the romantic realm, in which there are further complications concerning our inability to predict the partner's attitude in the long term, as well as our response to that attitude. This makes finding a good-enough partner even more important.

Relevant to the romantic realm is Harry Frankfurt's rejection of the "doctrine of economic egalitarianism," which states that it is desirable for everyone to have the same amount of income and wealth. In his view, termed the "doctrine of sufficiency," what is morally important is that everyone should have enough. When following (economic) egalitarianism, people focus their attention on what others have, rather than on what is intrinsically valuable for them. For Frankfurt, being content is a matter of one's attitude toward what she has and not toward what others have. Thus, Frankfurt claims, "suppose that a man deeply and happily loves a woman who is altogether worthy. We do not ordinarily criticize the man in such a case just because we think he might have done even better." A nicer-looking, wiser, and wealthier woman might not be good for you if her attitudes don't jibe enough with yours. It is not mainly the external, objective, measurable qualities that count in what is good for you, but the interactions between you and the other person. In Frankfurt's view, having enough money should stop us from having an active interest in getting more. This notion frees us in the following ways: our attention and interests need not vividly engage in the benefits of having more, we do not need to consider having more as important, we do not need to resent our circumstances, there is no reason to be anxious or determined to improve them, we do not have to go out of our way or take any significant initiatives to make them better, and our contentment need not be dependent upon comparing ourselves to others.[17]

It would be wise to adopt a similar attitude with respect to a good-enough romantic partner. It implies that we are content with our partner inasmuch as the person suits us and not necessarily because this person is the most perfect partner in the world. Accordingly, we do not have an active interest in seeking someone else, and we do not see our situation as needing urgent improvement. We are content with our lot, and in the current circumstances we do not need anyone else. It seems that the more satisfied we are with our own situation and activities, the more we tend to be happy with a good-enough partner, as we would not expect Mr. Right to fulfill all our needs—some of them we have fulfilled by ourselves. Thus, one survey found that women with PhDs are twice as likely to settle for Mr. Good-Enough as women with a high school education.[18]

There are important differences between having what someone else has and having enough. In the former, one makes a superficial comparison to others who might be very different from you, and thus what they have is irrelevant. In the latter, it is one's own attitude that is important, and the satisfaction gained comes primarily from within. Although we cannot avoid making comparisons with others, what counts most in romantic love is the flourishing of our own, unique connection.

When we think of our partner as good enough, we realize what is most valuable for us. This does not mean that people should not aim at increasing the profundity of their romantic relationship, but that such improvement will mainly relate to developing the connection with our current, good-enough partner. As in the story of the pot of gold buried in the garden, sometimes the treasure can be found right at home.

Concluding Remarks

And in that moment, everything I knew to be true about myself up until then was gone. I was acting like another woman, yet I was more myself than ever before.
FRANCESCA, in Robert James Waller's *The Bridges of Madison County*

Romantic compromises are sometimes viewed as a pitfall of the romantic experience—distracting us from what should be an all-inclusive love that only gives and never takes. However, romantic compromises that involve giving up a romantic value for a deeper, nonromantic aspect of life are often good for love as well. Beyond that, it is sometimes the case that with time, these compromises end up being experienced not as negative, but as productive parts of the relationship, as they benefit the other partner and the connection. In compromises, people relinquish romantic tendencies to overvalue the partner's nonrelational properties and to consider alternative partners. Good compromises are intrinsically valuable: they set the mind at rest by solving most of the pressing problems that are disturbing the relationship, and they leave room for striving, which is an aspect of flourishing that involves the capacity to achieve more. A romantic sacrifice, on the other hand, involves giving up time spent doing something you value personally, like work or a hobby, to make room for activities that deepen the romantic connection. In the case of profound love, these sacrifices are often made willingly and happily, as they benefit both partners and the relationship.

In considering the order of priorities in romantic relationships, and how having had multiple partners might have an impact on a current relationship, it remains vital to prioritize the quality of the current partnership. Although staying with a first love often enables us to maintain a high-quality relationship, when we do so out of complacency, fear, or laziness, it can take the taste out of life. A relationship in which the partner pales in comparison to previous partners, so much so that one cannot concentrate on the current relationship, fails to work out not because of the ghost of those past relationships but because the current connection is not profound. Once we embrace the seemingly unfavorable circumstances of a relationship and show a willingness to devote ourselves to an imperfect but good-enough partner, then love can flourish. Profundity does not require any single set of circumstances; rather, it requires partners who are committed to each other and who, instead of constantly comparing their partner to past and potential lovers, try to be present for one another.

Choosing a Romantic Partner

I think men who have a pierced ear are better prepared for marriage. They've experienced pain and bought jewelry.
RITA RUDNER

In this chapter, we arrive at a major thoroughfare in our journey toward romantic love: choosing a romantic partner. The chapter begins by discussing the distinction between "nonrelational" and "relational" traits, at which point the suitability scale is introduced. This scale, which measures the degree of the partner's suitability to the other, is the most important measure for predicting long-term profound love. I then discuss the value of meritocracy (being chosen for accomplishments rather than circumstances) in seeking a romantic partner, and ways of choosing a long-term romantic partner, while taking account of the comparative and the uniqueness approaches.

The Suitability Scale in Love

I love you not only for what you are, but for what I am when I am with you.
ELIZABETH BARRETT BROWNING

When I love, I do it without counting. I give myself entirely. And each time, it is the grand love of my life.
BRIGITTE BARDOT

The dialogue model and the phenomena of synchrony, responsivity, and resonance have taught us that a couple's connection stands at the center of romantic relationships. Thus, the *suitability* issue looms large in establishing long-term profound love. A person's romantic value should be judged mostly on the basis of how suitable he or she is to the partner. There are two scales with which to assess romantic value: the nonrelational scale (which is a general measure of people) and the relational scale of suitability (which measures a unique connection).

The nonrelational scale measures the value of traits as they stand on their own (think sense of humor, wealth, etc.). This sort of measure has two advantages—it is easy to use, and most people would agree about the assessments. The suitability scale is much more complex, since it depends on personal and environmental factors about which we do not have full knowledge.

Let's think for a moment about assessing the relational suitability value in long-term relationships. Should you marry a smart person? Generally speaking, intelligence is considered good—but here is where things get more complicated. If there is a big gap between the IQ of the two partners, their suitability value will be low, as matching in nonrelational value is more significant here. This goes way beyond intelligence, though. The same goes for wealth. On the nonrelational scale, a lot of money is often good, but a wealthy person might score low on fidelity, as fat bank accounts open many romantic doors. Moreover, wealthy people tend to believe that they are more deserving, and hence their caring behavior might be lower. In the same vein, having a good sexual appetite is usually good, but a large discrepancy between the partners' sexual needs is not conducive to that crucial romantic connection. If, for instance, a man wants to have sex once or twice a week and a woman wishes to have sex multiple times a day, would they be suitable partners? If all the positives on someone's nonrelational scale are reduced by aspects on the relational scale, this is likely to bode ill for the individual's personal flourishing. Even if both partners score high on the nonrelational scale, but they are not able to bring out the best in each other, then their value on the relational scale will be low.

As it turns out, we can tell precious little about how someone will be as a partner by knowing how he or she rates as a person. It is far from obvious that the higher your partner is on the nonrelational scale, the better the connection between you will be. In this context, the following friendly interchange comes to mind. Woman: "Why is it that the people I fall in love with are never interested in me, whereas the ones who do fall in love with me are never the ones I care about?" Coworker: "You're an 8 constantly chasing after 10s, and constantly being chased by 6s."[1]

Romantic love takes all traits into full account. Since love includes the wish to be together with each other for a long time, we should try to transform the pleasant interest that is evoked by attraction into something more profound that can be maintained in the long term. The relational scale can be of service here. It measures suitability to an actual person, not to people in general. This scale analyzes the general overall romantic value in terms of a specific partner.

At the initial stage of romantic relationships, suitability is not such a big deal. After all, information about long-term profound suitability is not yet available. Such information comes from interactions between the two partners, as a loving attitude becomes more knowledge-based. As time goes by, the issue of suitability gains greater importance, and the gap between the two scales could grow. We update and refine the two scales over time.

With time, changes in each scale relate mainly to the *weight* given to each trait, and to a lesser extent to the *score* of that trait on each scale. A woman whose spouse is not particularly sensitive might say that, over time, his lack of sensitivity disturbs her less (she assigns it less weight), since she finds that his other traits compensate for it. However, she might also say that he seems to her a little bit more sensitive than she initially thought. Scholars call this "trait adaptation." In hedonic adaptation, something beautiful or ugly becomes less so with time. In trait adaptation, some of the partner's characteristics, which were initially seen as very positive or very negative, come to be evaluated more moderately. Romantic breakups are often traceable to traits that have a low score on the suitability scale that become more evident with time rather than to traits that have a low score on the nonrelational scale, which people may adapt to.

These two scales raise interesting issues about the nature of long-term romantic love. One of these is the possibility of predicting the success of love. As others can assess the nonrelational scale quite well, this assessment is possible even before the partners meet. The relational scale, however, is different. There, many traits cannot be assessed by others, and most of this evaluation must wait until the partners meet and interact. Because reciprocal interactions are so important, the main traits can only be reliably assessed after such interactions. Indeed, the renowned expert on marital stability, John Gottman, who is immensely successful in predicting the likelihood of divorce, bases his judgments on partners' interactions during conflicts in verbal communication.[2] The relational suitability scale assesses the suitability of the partner's nonrelational traits to the individual.

Both nonrelational and relational traits can enhance romantic love. Although there is no direct positive correlation between the two groups, they often correlate—a high value in one group often increases the value in the other. Thus, rich and intelligent people are often able to enhance the romantic connection, and a caring person is frequently considered of higher overall value. Moreover, as the possibility of lasting love draws heavily on the connection between the two lovers, relational traits are far more important in the long term. Nonrelational traits have greater impact at the beginning of the romantic relationship, when the relational traits are not yet apparent. As the two lovers become more familiar with each other, the impact of their relational traits increases.

A high positive evaluation of one's nonrelational qualities is significant—but it is no guarantee of profound romantic love. This is because it does not take into account the partners' connection, which is vital for maintaining this kind of enduring love. We admire the traits of many people with whom we are definitely not in love. And we would not criticize someone who loves her partner profoundly, just because we think she could have found a person with better qualities.[3] As mentioned below, this is not true only when the gap between the two partners prevents the development of a profound connection. Thus, someone can adore her partner's relational attitudes, such as sensitivity and kindness, and still not love him, because, say, he is not intelligent or wealthy enough or has a low social status. So, a lack of high nonrelational traits can be significant—especially when the absence of these traits can prevent the lover's and the couple's togetherness from flourishing.

Being a *person* who has good nonrelational qualities does not make you a good *partner*—and it is only with a good partner that we can nurture an intimate, flourishing connection. People often search for the ideal *partner* by focusing on the qualities that make a perfect, flawless *person*. The problem is that this quest fails to focus on the connection between the would-be couple. Romantic relationships benefit from nonrelational traits in a kind of backhanded way; they offer better circumstances in which to enhance relational traits—and, therefore, the connection. Being married to an optimistic person, for example, can upgrade the couple's relational activities because a sense of optimism can improve dialogue. At the end of the day, though, the value of the relational traits on the suitability scale is what counts most.

Along these lines, Paul Eastwick and Lucy Hunt show that when people are picking partners, they focus more on relational characteristics than consensual, nonrelational traits, especially over time. They found that although there was a lot of agreement on desirable (nonrelational) qualities at first, this agreement was weaker than participants' tendency to see one another as uniquely desirable or undesirable over time. Eastwick and Hunt conclude that despite the unbalanced distribution of desirable nonrelational traits among people, "mating pursuits take place on a more-or-less even playing field, in which most people have a strong chance of being satisfied with their romantic outcomes."[4]

All of this boils down to the idea that constant comparison of your partner to others is contrary to the spirit of profound romantic love. Long-term lovers are not in the business of accounting and comparing—they are more occupied with bettering their relationship than in having a better partner than someone else.

Is Meritocracy Useful in Searching for a Romantic Partner?

I don't wish to be everything to everyone, but I would like to be something to someone.
JAVAN

I want a man who's kind and understanding. Is that too much to ask of a millionaire?
ZSA ZSA GABOR

In a meritocracy, people are chosen because of their performance rather than their personalities and circumstances. So, for example, whether or not you were accepted to a particular college or got a particular job would depend upon your achievements alone. Meritocracy aims to abolish different biases, some of which dearly deserve to be eliminated. The problem with meritocracies, however, is that disregarding a person's background is likely to create bias against those from less privileged backgrounds. Indeed, a common criticism against running educational systems as meritocracies is that doing so has created an elite class that represents a narrow segment of the population. Hence, it ignores diversity.

Scott Page argues that teams made up of different kinds of thinkers outperform homogeneous groups on complex tasks. Page strongly questions the ability of a meritocracy to build successful teams. He argues that the principle of meritocracy—the idea that the "best person" should be hired—runs counter to the multidimensional or layered nature of complex problems. In his view, there is no best person. Page claims that even if people have extensive knowledge about the relevant domain, no test or criteria applied to individuals will produce the best team. The depth and breadth of a domain is such that no test can ever suffice. He argues that optimal hiring of teams to fulfill certain complex tasks depends on context; hence, optimal teams should be diverse. When creating a forest, you do not select the best trees; rather, you choose trees that are compatible with each other, and this requires diversity.[5]

Is it wise to apply the meritocratic system when choosing a romantic partner? The nonrelational traits of the beloved, which stand on their own, can be considered the "meritocracy." As we have seen, such characteristics alone are poor predictors of long-term profound love, at the heart of which are the interactions between the partners. Thus, on their way up, successful people can be quite inconsiderate of others. Our partners might be highly educated, attractive, rich, and famous, but they might suit us about as well as a tight pair of shoes. We might not find them sufficiently sensitive to us or genuinely interested in our flourishing; they might even be threatened by our success or autonomy. More-over, being with a person who is, in the spirit of meritocracy, very "superior" or "inferior" to you is quite problematic. Low-quality relationships and extramari-tal affairs are often the fallout.

Nonetheless, the nonrelational traits of the beloved can be harnessed in the service of romantic love. These traits provide the suitable circumstances for per-sonal flourishing and the flourishing of their bond. The principle of meritocracy can easily assess nonrelational traits, while romantic uniqueness, which is pro-duced by the partners' unique interactions, does not do well under the com-parative lens. So, we can apply meritocratic tools to find our romantic partner, but we should understand that their value is limited in this area. Meritocratic behavior helps partners to get along in a meaningful and profound manner. Such togetherness requires, for example, a certain similarity of background and values. Togetherness is built on values that both partners can achieve together. The partners' capacities should be complementary, and here the meritocracy is important.

But romantic partnerships are much more complex than basketball teams. Because of this, romantic matches are hard to predict without considering the partners' joint interactions. In any case, we ought to aim not for the best person in the world but rather the most suitable person for us.

Choosing a Long-Term Romantic Partner

There is no perfection, only beautiful versions of brokenness.
SHANNON L. ALDER

There may be "fifty ways to leave your lover," but there are many fewer good ways to choose the one who will stay with you for the long term. We've seen some signs on our trip toward profound love that point us in the right direction. At this next junction, we have a new signpost. Choosing a long-term romantic partner should take into account the following two major ranges: (1) positive-negative and (2) profundity-superficiality. The positive-negative range expresses the range of the partner's traits that can help or harm the relationship and the partner. The profundity-superficiality range situates this helping or harming in terms of time and depth. Thus, the impact of the partner's positive or negative trait lasts a short or a long time and can be either substantial or shallow.

If we combine the two dimensions, we discover four main ways of choos-ing a long-term romantic partner:

1. The checklist: rejection at first meeting (superficial and negative)
2. Love at first sight: attraction at first meeting (superficial and positive)

3. There is nothing wrong with him: detecting profound flaws (profound and negative)
4. Bringing out the best in each other: accentuating the positive qualities (profound and positive)

The first two ways mainly refer to nonrelational, superficial traits that others can see, and so, one can note with a superficial acquaintance. The profound ways primarily refer to deep traits on the suitability scale. Each way has its own advantages and disadvantages. So, none should be ignored when choosing a romantic partner. We might say that the methods appear in ascending order of importance: the first way is the least important, the second more important, and the third even more so; the fourth way is the most important way of choosing a romantic partner.

The Checklist: Rejection at First Meeting

We all know the drill. After compiling a checklist of the perfect partner's desirable and undesirable traits, you mark next to each trait whether this is a quality of the prospective partner. This kind of search, which is pretty much how online dating works, focuses on negative, superficial qualities and tries to quickly filter out unsuitable candidates. This is interesting, because of course you are dating to make a good catch, not merely to eliminate a bad one. But this is natural in an environment of abundant romantic options.

The checklist practice has two major flaws: (1) it typically lacks any intrinsic hierarchy that would grant each quality a different weight—hence, it ignores the issue of romantic profundity; (2) it focuses on the other person's qualities in isolation and gives scarcely any weight to the connection between the individuals—that is, it fails to consider the value of the other person as a suitable partner.

These checklists are long—easily a few dozen traits or more—and one merely checks the presence or absence of each quality. In this mechanistic method, we can hardly take the significance of each quality into consideration. Thus, one's height can be given the same significance as one's kindness—again, the presence or absence of any attributes that are checked receive the same weight. Moreover, height—and how much more so, kindness—come in greater and lesser degrees, and this fact is also not expressed when ticking off presence or absence. So, from the checklist point of view, we are superficial machines with no intrinsic hierarchy or weight given to the different qualities. But unattractive hair color hardly carries the same weight as being unkind. Putting all the qualities randomly in the same basket considerably

CHOOSING A ROMANTIC PARTNER

decreases the value of employing such a process in a romantic search. In accordance with the negative bias, the checklist search has many properties that are deal breakers, and very few, if any, deal makers (perhaps sometimes being very rich or famous is such a deal maker).

The second major flaw of the checklist method is that it focuses on the qualities of a perfect *person* rather than the qualities of a perfect *partner*, thereby failing to take into appropriate account the connection between the would-be couple. This is a big problem, since the suitability and interactions between the partners are of far greater significance in long-term profound love.

Benjamin Franklin was one of America's Founding Fathers and a genius. Back in 1758, Franklin wrote that "an investment in knowledge pays the best interest." Franklin counseled his nephew to use knowledge to find a wife: one should proceed like a bookkeeper, he advised—list all the pros and cons, weigh up everything for two or three days, and then make a decision. Gerd Gigerenzer shows that computer-based versions of Franklin's rational bookkeeping manner—a program that weighed eighteen different cues—proved less accurate than following the rule of thumb "Get one good reason and ignore the rest of the information."[6]

In Graeme Simsion's popular novel, *The Rosie Project*, Don Tillman, a university professor seeking a wife, prepares a detailed list of the characteristics he desires in a woman: intelligence, good cook, nonsmoker, teetotaler, physically fit. He rules out many women until he meets Rosie, a bartender who smokes, drinks, and otherwise lacks most of his criteria. Together, they search for Rosie's biological father, and in the process, Don falls in love with Rosie. It is not her individual characteristics that generate his love. It is the harmony he feels while spending more and more time with her, which makes all the difference.

Love at First Sight: Attraction at First Meeting

This is going to sound crazy, but . . . from the moment I first set eyes on you I haven't been able to stop thinking about you.
     LEIGH FALLON, *Carrier of the Mark*

It wasn't love at first sight. It took a full five minutes.
     LUCILLE BALL

Choosing a romantic partner on the basis of love at first sight is also a superficial way with which to determine the value of the other, as it does not necessarily identify the absence or presence of the prospective partner's more profound qualities.

Love at first sight is intense love. The physical attraction strikes you like a flash of lightning and you want to spend forever with the other person. Love at first sight can be the basis of profound, long-term love, if characteristics revealed in later acquaintance enhance—or at least do not contradict—those assumed initially. Love at first sight cannot be profound, as there has been no time for creating such profundity. However, this kind of love should not be described as shallow; it is just that the issue of profundity is not yet relevant. Shallowness might arise when the phenomenon does not last long, but it cannot be said to be present when the phenomenon just begins. In the same manner, after thirty seconds of a football game, we would not say that the team's performance is shallow because no goal has been scored yet, or no impressive action has yet occurred. The most we can say is that so far we cannot tell whether their performance is shallow, but based on the high level of the team's engagement, such a conclusion is probably unwarranted.

The survival chances of initial love increase when we do not speak about love at first sight, but about love at first meeting (or acquaintance). Such a meeting provides more time to get to know other characteristics of the person, like sense of humor and kindness, and to become involved in common first activities, such as conversation. Moreover, signs of a unique, instant, intimate connection between the two agents might clearly appear at the first meeting and might be expressed, for example, in admiring the person's wittiness and wisdom, mutual attraction, enjoying the conversation, the wish to be closer to each other, and "accidental" touching. Love at first sight expresses the aforementioned "attractiveness halo," in which a person who is perceived as beautiful is assumed to have other good characteristics as well. Love at first acquaintance relates to the "personality halo," in which a person who is perceived as having a certain positive personality trait is perceived to be valuable and assumed to have some other positive characteristics. It should be noted that although attractiveness has a powerful impact at first sight, the weight of this impact decreases as time passes and after we get to know the person's other characteristics. Likewise, wittiness has a powerful impact at first chat, but its impact can decrease once we know the person's other traits.

The connection between love at first sight and the quality of a subsequent relationship is mainly influenced by two opposing factors: (1) the initial positive impression has a positive impact upon the quality of the relationship, and (2) the brevity of time in which the partner is selected prevents a person from identifying profound compatibility, which is vital for long-term profound love.

Research has demonstrated that initial evaluations have significant influence on long-term relationships.[7] The positive evaluations present in love at first sight therefore have a positive impact upon the relationship. In this sense, if love at first sight develops into a long-term relationship, that relationship has a greater chance of achieving higher quality. The importance of first impressions is illustrated in the well-known saying "You never get a second chance to make a (good) first impression."

While positive first impressions increase the likelihood of long-term profound love, the superficial manner of choosing the partner in love at first sight can have a negative impact upon the subsequent relationship. The fact that the beloved was a complete stranger to you gives rise to the possibility that you do not have much in common. The love might be intense, but not profound. Indeed, studies have found that partners who fell in love at first sight, in comparison to partners who got involved more gradually, entered into intimate relationships more quickly after they met and had mates with less similar personalities, especially with regard to levels of extraversion, emotional stability, and autonomy. This, however, does not necessarily lead to a low relationship quality, as the positive impact of the first impression can compensate for the superficial manner of choosing the partner.[8]

The volatile nature of love at first sight is vividly expressed by a married man in the following description:

> The very first time that I laid eyes on her from across the room I knew that I wanted to spend the rest of my life with her. I was currently married to someone else at the time, and this was the first time that had ever happened to me. It had nothing to do with sexual attraction or lust, as she was pretty ordinary-looking. We did end up getting married a few years after my divorce and had a mostly positive marriage. No real issues until I was deployed for eighteen months and when I came home, she had fallen in love with someone else. We divorced shortly after. To this day, she is the only woman that I have ever truly loved. I love her as much now as I did then. I believe that she was my one true love. It just stinks that I wasn't hers.

Falling in love in cyberspace is akin to love at first sight: we do not have all the required information, but we fill in the gaps with idealized assumptions. As in love at first sight, the chat skips, in a sense, the usual process of information processing, and is directly "injected" into the brain evaluative centers. Thus, we can speak about "love at first chat." For example, one might detect in the first chat a sense of humor and wittiness, and instantly fall in love with the sender.[9] As in the case of attractiveness in offline relationships, humor also has a powerful impact at first chat, but this impact can decrease once the person's other characteristics begin to surface. If wittiness is perceived as superficial, and more profound characteristics such as kindness and wisdom are found to be wanting, the weight of the initial positive impact of wittiness is likely to diminish.

Although love at first chat can reveal more profound qualities than those involved in love at first sight, those qualities might still be superficial, as the agent has no way of knowing whether the prospective partner is presenting herself authentically. And even if love at first chat does reveal profound qualities, the spectrum is too short for having a comprehensive, complex communication. However, when the first chat turns into an online relationship, and then an offline one, the likelihood of finding profound love increases.

Interestingly, although sight, which is significant in generating physical attraction, plays a substantial role in falling in love, research indicates that voice-only communication increases empathic accuracy over communication across senses. Hearing is more accurate than sight when it comes to identifying someone's emotions; accordingly, it might sometimes be easier to perceive the other's emotions over the phone than when meeting face-to-face.[10] Online conversations are a kind of intellectual interaction; the fact that they have a powerful impact on falling in love is another indication that love can be ignited by many different ways of interacting. In successful cases, greater diversity increases profundity, since such diversity can reveal more aspects of the prospective partner.

There Is Nothing Wrong with Him: Detecting the Profound Negative

The art of being wise is the art of knowing what to overlook.
WILLIAM JAMES

Unlike the two previous methods of choosing a romantic partner, this way takes into account profound qualities, and when no such negative qualities are detected, the prospective partner can be accepted. Compared to the checklist manner, the manner of detecting profound flaws is more sophisticated and realistic. It assumes the presence of flaws and so focuses merely on profound flaws. Here, we find the assumption that whereas one can learn to live with superficial flaws, profound flaws pose a real danger to a long-term loving relationship.

Lori Gottlieb tells the story of Madathil, an Indian-born researcher in the United States, whose parents arranged her marriage. When she met her prospective husband, there was no spark. Although Madathil could have met as many men as she wanted until she found the right match, she nevertheless decided to marry him. Her reason was that "there was nothing wrong with him." Now, after ten years of marriage, they are profoundly in love with each other.

Madathil's process in evaluating her prospective partner was also focused on detecting negative qualities, but her hierarchy of values excluded a mechanical count of negative qualities. Here, the process aims to determine whether the person is "harmless," and this becomes a significant reason for giving the person a further chance. This method of seeking a partner doesn't totally devalue appearance, but it does not rank it as most valuable in an enduring relationship. Thus, Madathil said: "Physical appearances matter—I thought, yeah, he looks cute. But he didn't have to be gorgeous."[11]

In contrast to the almost universally positive effects of increased levels of attractiveness on new relationships, there is no significant association between levels of attractiveness and the subsequent quality of marriages, except for the fact that more attractive husbands were found to be less satisfied when their level of attractiveness was greater than that of their spouses.[12]

Focusing on profound flaws seems to be a smart decision, but it involves a more complex search and a greater investment of time. Thus, detecting profound qualities, such as insensitivity, is more difficult than detecting superficial qualities, such as not being tall. Detecting compatibility—in the spirit of "there is nothing wrong with him"—is valuable, but in many cases, it is insufficient. We should also detect profound positive qualities.

Bringing Out the Best in Each Other: Accentuating the Profound Positive

> You make me want to be a better man.
> MELVIN UDALL, in the movie *As Good as It Gets*

We have learned that detecting negative qualities is more important than detecting positive qualities. But this does not mean that detecting positive qualities is of no value at all. In establishing long-term love, profound positive qualities are very important. A positive quality that is particularly valuable for maintaining and enhancing the connection is the ability to bring out the best in each other. This is the aforementioned "Michelangelo Phenomenon" in which close romantic partners behave toward each other in a manner that is congruent with their own self-ideal, spurring them to move nearer to their own ideal self and thus feel good about themselves. Sometimes, as Finkel argues, we see the Michelangelo Phenomenon in reverse—cases in which relationship partners bring out the worst in each other, rather than the best. The two kinds of sculpting can be done by our parents, siblings, and children.[13]

Detecting profound positive qualities that are valuable for a long-term relationship is complex, in part because they are more clearly revealed through shared activities that take place over time. Since, at the beginning of a relationship, we do not have all the relevant information concerning these profound positive qualities, trying to predict the partner's future behavior by calculating the qualities in the checklist manner doesn't work well. Instead, we might have to imitate the experts: use rules of thumb that increase the probability of solving problems without deliberative thinking, which cannot be used when we lack relevant information.

Here, the decision is made by assuming a hierarchy of values and focusing on the significant positive or negative qualities. If you believe that your prospective partner is likely to bring out the best in you, you have a very good reason to choose this person as your life companion. This method, which seems helpful for finding profound love, can hardly be used in the fast and superficial world of dating sites. The profound positive qualities that bring out the best in each other require ongoing, shared experiences and joint activities.

The first two ways of choosing a partner—that is, the checklist and love at first sight—are shallow processes that, despite offering certain benefits particularly in eliminating unsuitable candidates, often have limited value in the long run. The other two ways—that is, detecting profound flaws and bringing out the best in each other—are more profound and combine intellectual and emotional processes crucial for the development of profound love. Although we tend to focus more on the partner's negative qualities at the choosing-a-partner stage, it seems that in the long run, positive qualities gain at least the same importance and might eventually outweigh negative qualities.

Online Dating Sites and Romantic Profundity

In the end when the sexual rush dissipates, the novelty of an online extramarital affair is gone and the lack of profoundness becomes clear. . . . Online relationships leave me feeling empty.
A MARRIED WOMAN

In recent years, online dating has exploded in popularity. Online matchmaking sites promise to facilitate two different types of romantic activities: (1) identifying romantic partners and (2) developing long-term profound love.

These sites excel at the first objective, and today the internet is the foremost place where singles met their last first date. Indeed, a greater percentage of romantic partnerships are created through the internet than offline. The value of an online search is especially evident in locating potential partners for individuals who face a thin dating market, such as gays, lesbians, and middle-aged heterosexuals; these are also the groups that are most likely to rely on the internet to find their partners. Whether or not these matchmaking sites fulfill the second objective remains unclear. The algorithms used by these sites can be highly predictive in avoiding pairings that are unlikely to succeed, which constitute most possible pairings, but they still leave a considerable minority from which to choose.[14]

I am not suggesting that the online origin of romantic partnering is, in itself, an obstacle to developing profound love. Rather, I am suggesting that dating sites, which provide many alluring romantic options, do not encourage nurturing a single person as long-term partner. Similarly, the breakup rate is scarcely influenced by whether the couple met online or offline. However, couples who have been together longer, especially couples who are married and coresidential, are much less likely to break up.[15] Spending time together increases the cost of separation and enables the partners to develop romantic profundity.

Because profound love is generated by many and various joint activities, the limited types of such activities available online reduce the likelihood of generating profound love. It is very hard to accurately identify the major profound flaws and advantages of your partner through online dating alone. One cannot bring out the best in the other when the relationship lacks diverse mutual interactions and hence a profound dialogue. Indeed, Finkel and colleagues argue that the matchmaking sites' claim that the essential qualities of a relationship can be predicted from characteristics of the potential partners that exist before they have met counters substantial scientific research indicating that preexisting personal qualities account for a small percentage of variance in relationship success.[16] This is even truer in cases where the matching, and sometimes even the wedding, are done without the two even meeting each other.

It is usually good to integrate the advantages of offline and online activities. Such integration occurs when online dating is used to locate possible suitable candidates with whom to start a romantic relationship, after which the partners meet and then establish a relationship offline, where the traits essential for profound love can be more reliably detected. This subsequent offline relationship should not eliminate online communication between the two—on the contrary, such communication can reveal additional significant information about each other.

Harmful integration between online and offline dating occurs when, together with the offline relationship, each person continues her activities on dating sites to further examine other possible candidates. Continuing such use of online dating services is a major cause of failing to achieve profound love, as it is very difficult to develop romantic profundity when alluring romantic options are further explored. These dating sites are excellent tools for locating possible romantic candidates, but they are less successful in establishing long-term profound love. The sites are best used like a kind of a virtual café, mainly to locate and get an initial impression of a prospective partner to date offline from then on.

"I Would Never Sleep with a Trump Supporter": The Impact of Political Views on Hooking Up

I would never sleep with a Trump supporter, though I slept with a few Bush supporters.

A LIBERAL SINGLE WOMAN

I would not be able to marry a man who is a leftist, even if I found him very attractive—although most of the men I have slept with are leftists.

A CONSERVATIVE DIVORCED WOMAN

I sleep with a Trump supporter every night, but I am happy to have a lover who is different, as I love to talk a lot with my lover.

A LIBERAL MARRIED WOMAN

Political views seem to be these days essential in choosing spouses, but their role in hooking up is less clear. We may not want to live with our political enemy, but what's wrong with having sex with him?

Relevant Factors

I can't stop hooking up with Trump supporters.

KOREY LANE

Factors that are relevant to this issue are (a) the depth of the relationship, (b) the negativity seen in the political view, (c) the person's support of this view, and (d) the person's traits that are unrelated to the political view.

The depth of our relationship with someone determines the types of traits that are relevant for us. The deeper the relationship, the more traits of this person become relevant. Thus, in choosing a spouse, many more profound traits of the person are relevant than is the case in choosing a sexual partner. Hence, spouses, and romantic partners in general, show strong similarity in political and religious attitudes. Our conservative divorced woman makes clear that she would never marry a leftist, but most of her lovers have been leftists.

Are we to understand that leftists make better lovers? As I am not aware of any research supporting this claim, I tend to account for her feelings by noting that in the short term, opposites attract, but in the long term, similarity is more significant.

Of course, casual sexual relationships come in different flavors: one-night stands, booty calls, fuck buddies, and friends with benefits. While in the case of friends with benefits, political issues are likely to be relevant, one can have a one-night stand without a lot of talking, and especially not about political issues.

The depth of the negativity seen in a given political view, and its connection to moral issues, is another factor in deciding whether or not to sleep with your (political) enemy. Political attitudes are associated with moral ones, but the connection can be of various degrees. The negativity can refer to major issues, which are related to significant immoral, criminal deeds, and minor issues, which are more a question of taste. Let's take the liberal single woman mentioned above: she does not consider her disagreement with Trump a matter of politics as much as a matter of good versus evil. Hence, although she would never sleep with a Trump supporter, she slept with a few Bush supporters; apparently, her opposition to Bush's conservative policy was indeed a matter of politics rather than profound moral lines. She even mentioned in a nostalgic tone that the conservative president Ronald Reagan was the president who, more than any other president, enlarged American national parks.

The depth of the person's support of the negative view is another relevant factor in deciding whether or not to hook up with someone supporting the "wrong" political view. There are, of course, various degrees of support. Thus, one can support the "wrong" view while criticizing some basic elements of this view but thinking that there is no better choice. Alternatively, one can show extreme and absolute support of the "wrong" view, and this will be evident even at the first meeting, and thus be a big sexual turnoff.

The person's traits that are unrelated to the political view are also very significant in determining whether to pursue the sexual encounter. If the person is kind, sensitive, and considerate, it will be easier to initiate the sexual encounter despite his "wrong" political view. The problem here is somewhat similar to the problem of loving a criminal. In a song written by Martin, Shellback, and Amber, Britney Spears says, "He is a hustler, he's no good at all, he is a loser, he's a bum, he lies, he bluffs, he's unreliable, he is a sucker with a gun," but, Mama, I'm in love with him. She further explains that this love "isn't rational, it's physical," but, she continues, he is okay for me. Loving a criminal may be sexually exciting in the short term, but for moral people, the immoral nature of the criminal will significantly hinder the establishment of a flourishing romantic relationship.

If the person is highly sexually satisfying, then even if your head says that he is the wrong person because of his appalling political views, it may be quite hard to stop hooking up with him. As Korey Lane nicely puts it concerning hooking up with a Trump supporter, this is probably not a sustainable relationship that she would want to have in the long run, but "for right now I can highly recommend hooking up with someone whose politics you hate. As long as you don't forget to vote."[17]

Polarized Political Views

When I was young, I certainly spent too much time with hustlers, bums, and suckers. However, these guys were not in favor of any radical political views, at least as far as I know. And if I do not know about their political views, it does not seem to have been important to me at that time.

A MARRIED WOMAN IN HER FIFTIES

If we begin to exclude Trump supporters and his ilk from our sexual interactions, soon we will have to abstain from sex altogether.

A MARRIED WOMAN

Our society seems more politically polarized than ever, and politics is a popular partner in the bedroom. Should we have the feeling of sleeping with the enemy while having sex with a person with different political views?

There is no golden rule for when to wed someone with opposing political views (though extreme opposition tends to be destructive) and when to keep the relation at the level of a hookup. There are many factors to consider, and each has various degrees. However, since we are dealing here with a combination of two emotions—namely, love and hate—I would guess that following the heart here would often be the way to go.

Concluding Remarks

I love going out to dinner with good-looking men, even though good-looking does not buy the meal; however, with an ugly man, I cannot eat at all.

A SINGLE WOMAN

The main reason for the complexity in choosing a long-term partner is the fact that a good match can hardly be determined by preexisting nonrelational traits; only ongoing interactions can reveal and establish a suitable match. The major issue here is not how good each partner is, but rather how suited they are to each other. In choosing a partner, the suitability scale is much more significant than the nonrelational scale. Accordingly, meritocracy, which is a system in which people are chosen for their nonrelational past achievements, is of limited value in choosing a romantic partner, whose main value is his suitability and not his performance.

When assessing methods of choosing a partner, it is important to consider which kinds of qualities are prioritized in each. While our minds tend to latch on to both positive and negative superficial qualities, these are less useful in ensuring profound love. Employing a checklist in an attempt to screen out a partner with superficial, negative qualities that one has deemed unacceptable is unreliable, as such qualities are of little value in predicting an enduring profound romantic relationship. Similarly, in the love-at-first-sight scenario, the passion and intense love that come from appreciating a partner's superficial positive qualities in no way secures the development of a relationship with deeper meaning. It is the profound qualities, particularly the positive ones that should be one's focus in choosing a partner. The ability to bring out the best in each other is one of the best predictors for the success of a romantic relationship. It is difficult, however, to identify this ability at the initial stage of a relationship.

Romantic Relationships

How deep is your love? I really need to learn, 'cause we are living in a world of fools breaking us down.

BEE GEES

Having traveled down the road of the nature of romantic love and romantic compromises, we now turn to consider how this view is expressed in actual romantic relationships, while focusing particularly on the issue of time in these relationships. Among the issues discussed in this chapter are unfinished romantic business; romantic curiosity; addiction to love; loving too much; the nature of the wish to be with the one you love; loving longer or loving more; and deciding on the best time to say, "I love you."

Unfinished Romantic Business

Where you used to be, there is a hole in the world, which I find myself constantly walking around in the daytime, and falling in at night. I miss you like hell.

EDNA ST. VINCENT MILLAY

Maria Elena used to say that only unfulfilled love can be romantic.

JUAN ANTONIO, in the movie *Vicky Cristina Barcelona*

Unlike enduring, profound romantic experiences, intense, brief romantic experiences tend to be incomplete, a kind of unfinished business. And we are usually excited by anything that is incomplete, unusual, unfinished, unfulfilled, unsettled, unexplained, or uncertain. Although such experiences are often associated with sadness and frustration, we continue to seek them out. People desire much more than they have or are ever likely to have. We have limited capacities and finite resources, but our desires are almost infinite. Consequently, many human desires are doomed to remain unfulfilled, even though we try our best to fulfill them.

An incomplete romantic experience is a kind of unfinished business; it is an experience in which love is present, but not entirely fulfilled. Incomplete romantic experiences are emotionally loaded. In such experiences, love has been partially attained, and there is yearning for its completion. The absent part is like a hole in the lover's heart that can be neither filled nor ignored; hence, the strong feeling of frustration. It seems that like dissatisfaction, a moderate measure of frustration can beneficial in some circumstances.

In characterizing the perfect seducer, Robert Greene writes of elements that maintain the incomplete nature of the romantic interaction. These include increasing ambiguity, sending mixed signals, mastering the art of insinuation, confusing desire and reality, mixing pleasure and pain, stirring desire and confusion, toning down the sexual element without getting rid of it outright, refusing to conform to any standard, being able to delay satisfaction, and not offering total satisfaction.[1]

Incomplete and intense romantic relationships are the stuff of endless books and movies. There, lovers spend most of their time without the beloved, and the inability to overcome this incompleteness is a significant compromise for them. Despite lacking the essential features of profound love that are present in normal circumstances, incomplete romantic experiences have their own advantages, in particular that of maintaining high romantic intensity for a long time.

Another kind of incomplete romantic relationship involves close emotional ties but no sexual intercourse. In this case, the intensity of the romantic relationship is due to, among other things, its incomplete nature—to the unfulfilled desire to include another aspect in the relationship. Unfinished business does not carry with it merely thrills, but suffering too, since the element of frustration at not achieving what we fully desire, and believe to deserve, is central here as well. Once such a relationship becomes complete, for instance, after the sexual component is added, the great romantic intensity tends to dissipate, and the relationship is terminated. This is the incomplete courtly love of twelfth-century troubadours. The troubadours sang about "a new kind of tender, extramarital flirtation which (ideally) was sexually unconsummated and which, therefore, made the chaste lovers more noble and virtuous."[2]

Online relationships usually have the characteristic of "unfinished business," since so long as they are not transformed into offline relationships, there is something missing from them. In this sense, they are similar to an extended period of courtship. Accordingly, emotional intensity remains high—in the words of one woman, "passion at an unbelievable peak"—even for a long period. A paradoxical aspect in this regard is that although online relationships are intense because of, among other factors, their incompleteness, such incompleteness involves the wish to transform the relationship into a more complete one—something that usually decreases the intensity and can lead to terminating the relationship.[3] Cyberspace lacks a closed and unitary structure. Being in cyberspace involves a perpetual state of searching, an endless chase that will rarely settle into a stable form of life. Online events often lack a stable narrative, with an expected beginning and end. Such never-ending events, which are analogous to unfinished business, increase uncertainty and frustration, and hence, emotional intensity.

Romantic Curiosity

I want to know what love is, I want you to show me, I want to feel what love is, I know you can show me.

FOREIGNER

One who is too curious in observing the labor of bees, will often be stung for his curiosity.

ALEXANDER POPE

There is a long philosophical tradition, from Plato and Aristotle to Spinoza and Kant that views knowledge as a necessary part of moral behavior and the key to a good moral life. Accordingly, profound happiness is seen as dependent upon having enough knowledge. There is also a long cultural tradition that considers knowledge to be a stumbling block to happiness: Adam and Eve were expelled from the Garden of Eden because they ate from the Tree of Knowledge. The myth of Pandora carries a similar warning: all of the world's sufferings were released because Pandora *had* to know what was inside the box that the gods gave her.

Knowledge in romantic love is also a mixed bag. Popular songs indicate the close connection between knowledge and romantic love—for example, "The more I know you, the more I love you." A different view emphasizes the advantages of lack of knowledge, the role of mystery in romantic love, and particularly in sexual desire. As Rabindranath Tagore said, "Love is an endless mystery, for it has nothing else to explain it." These opposing traditions express the complex nature of the relationship between knowledge and love. In my view, knowledge in love is usually good, but positive illusions, ignorance, and limited curiosity can also be beneficial.

Does Knowing Him Mean Loving Him?
Certainly Not Always

A bride at her second marriage does not wear a veil. She wants to see what she is getting.

HELEN ROWLAND

Some people think having large breasts makes a woman stupid. Actually, it's quite the
opposite: a woman having large breasts makes men stupid.

RITA RUDNER

A former student of mine told me (while walking together at a funeral) how
much she enjoyed my course on emotions, which she took quite a few years
ago. "I frequently recall," she said, "that in the class you played the song 'To
know him is to love him' and commented, 'This is a wonderful song, but
with a minor problem—its main claim is often wrong.' In the years that have
elapsed since the course, living with my spouse, I have realized how true your
claim is." I told her that nowadays I believe that the situation is more complex;
the claim is indeed often wrong, but there are many circumstances in which it
might turn out to be at least partially true.

Knowledge certainly does not solve all problems. Yet, it puts us in a better
position to address complex circumstances in the romantic realm. Knowledge can increase our ability to adapt and help us recognize our capacities
and limitations. Of course, knowledge can make us sad, but that doesn't mean
that overall ignorance is the way to go. Although in specific circumstances,
ignorance, illusions, and limited curiosity can have a local value, as a way of
life they tend to trip us up badly.

The more we know about our beloved and our own romantic attitudes, the
more able we are to bring out the best in both partners. This does not mean
that we should dwell, day and night, on our problems and our beloved's flaws.
Quite the contrary. While being aware of such difficulties and doing our best
to reduce their painful impact, we should focus on the positive aspects of our
lives together. Ruminating about things we cannot change merely increases
their centrality in our lives, and hence their impact. Romantic intelligence is
information-based wisdom that enables us to give greater weight to positive
qualities and lesser weight to negative ones.

Realizing that each quality of the partner can be weighted differently and
that the significance of a single quality might shift over time can even help
to rekindle the flames of romance and increase the depth of love. In Fisher's
survey of people in love, about 60 percent of respondents agreed with the
statement that they love everything about their beloved and that although the
beloved has some faults, those do not really bother them.[4] Attaching different weights to different qualities is different from the approach of "expecting
less from marriage." Lowering our level of expectation can reduce the risk of
disappointment and temper our excitement, yet it does not offer a solution to
long-term difficulties; it merely indicates one way of escaping from them. Giving greater weight to certain qualities and less to others is more constructive.

Granting different weights to various qualities is basically a subjective task, yet it is not entirely in our control, as it is influenced by various biological, sociological, and psychological factors. The subjective allocation can help increase the perceived value of our partner, but certain constraints cannot be ignored, even while we retain positive illusions.

Can One Have Too Much Romantic Curiosity?

My spouse said that if I (sexually) go elsewhere, he does not want to know about it.
A MARRIED WOMAN

Never wanna hear about it [your new girlfriend], Keep her stains away.
KAREN MARIE ØRSTED

There is no doubt that knowing each other can contribute to a loving relationship. Sometimes, however, too much knowledge, or curiosity, can be hurtful. In the romantic realm, people often seek to know as much as possible about their beloved, since this gives them a fuller picture of him or her, which can further enhance their intimacy. However, we do not need to know everything. For example, information about the beloved's past lovers can help us understand the beloved's personality, but it can also cause pain. For many people, a detailed description of the beloved's previous sexual interactions could cast an unpleasant cloud over their sexual interactions with their partner. Ignorance can also be preferable in some cases of unfaithfulness, as the above citation from the married woman indicates. Others might want to be told about their partner's affairs but not about sexual specifics. Yet others would prefer not to discuss such things at all.

Romantic curiosity is tightly tied to a practical attitude; we want to understand what love and sex are about, but we also want to experience them. Relatedly, people tend to not want to leave any possible romantic door unopened. And, with our powerful imaginations, we wish to see and experience what is beyond our present circumstances. Opening every romantic door along our way, however, can have costly consequences. Those open doors can block the path to your own home. In order to leave all romantic options open, we would have to disregard reality, since reality has its own limitations, including limiting our resources. Keeping all our romantic options open can spread our investment too thin. But closing romantic doors doesn't sit so well with our natural curiosity, nor does it jibe with the change and improvement that are such a big part of our lives. Rarely, people say that after meeting their spouse, they felt no passion toward other people. More commonly, romantic curiosity remains, but it is not translated into actual deeds.

The question "What is love?" reflects a valuable profound curiosity; however, being haunted by never-ending curiosity about other romantic options is a kind of unproductive curiosity. Closing some open doors limits our curiosity and may lead to the feeling of being romantically compromised. This is an unpleasant experience, but a necessary one in a world of limitless options, limited resources, and conflicting values.

Romantic Window-Shopping

You're window shopping . . . You're not buying, you're just trying.
HANK WILLIAMS

When I was not married, I did not realized my genuine market value. Now, when I am married and have wrinkles, it is too late.
A MARRIED WOMAN

Window-shopping—browsing through goods with no intent to purchase—is a popular pastime that is fueled by human curiosity. Romantic window-shopping involves browsing through people with no intent to initiate a profound romantic relationship. Window-shopping and romantic window-shopping are superficial, intrinsic activities. They are enjoyable in the short term but normally do not have a direct profound impact or a long-term outcome. However, given that they improve our sense of well-being, both types of window-shopping can also have accumulative value. In both of them, people are only looking around "to find the best deal in town."

Shopping is an extrinsic activity whose success is measured in its efficiency: paying as little as possible for superior merchandise. Window-shopping is an intrinsic activity; it is an enjoyable, free, and relaxing experience. Like other intrinsic activities, it is not a stressful, hurried activity. When people enjoy the activity itself, there is no reason for them to want to terminate it quickly.

Romantic dating is like shopping: both are originally extrinsic, goal-directed activities, intended to obtain something or someone we desire. A main activity of dating, like that of shopping, is searching for a suitable "item" (person, merchandise). To succeed in the task, the search should be efficient: getting the optimal product while investing the least resources (such as money and time). Unsurprisingly, economists and other scholars often use the market metaphor when discussing mate selection.[5] Like window-shopping, some kinds of dating are intrinsic, having their own value with no intent to "purchase" anyone or to make any commitments.

Window-shopping, which is a superficial intrinsic activity, can improve your current mood, but it does not profoundly develop your essential capacities. The same is true of romantic window-shopping, such as flirting. Flirting is enjoyable, harmless playing and teasing; it involves the pleasant, magical charm associated with romance, but it lacks profundity. As is often the case, little things can contribute a lot to our sense of well-being. As I indicated above, superficial activities are not necessarily bad or worthless. We should not aim to be constantly immersed in profound activities; sometimes we need to enjoy the superficial ones. Superficial activities have short-term value when pursued in a moderate manner. It is mainly when we engage in them excessively that they become harmful.

Studies indicate that women are more active shoppers than men and enjoy browsing more; accordingly, they are more involved in window-shopping. Most men claim to dislike shopping and browsing. Many women view most types of shopping as a leisure experience, just like dining, drinking in cafés and bars, sightseeing, and simply walking around a city. Although men have increased their participation in the traditional task of shopping, they are more likely to be efficient; they tend to "grab and go," rather than enjoy the social or therapeutic aspects of shopping.[6]

It seems, however, that men are more prone to romantic window-shopping. Men's greater involvement in romantic window-shopping is evident in both passive romantic window-shopping, such as looking at erotic pictures, and in active romantic window-shopping, such as flirting. Men's intrinsic activity of romantic window-shopping is more tainted with utilitarian motives than women's romantic window-shopping. When men flirt, they are more likely to move the conversation toward sexual aspects, thereby making it easier to turn the romantic window-shopping into actual "hard-core" shopping.

To sum up, window-shopping and romantic window-shopping are enjoyable in the short term, but they rarely have a direct profound impact or a long-term outcome. It may be enjoyable or even advisable to engage in romantic window-shopping, but it is also prudent not to sell or buy cheap.

Can Love Become an Addiction?

Love is like a drug and we don't care about the long-term side effects; we just care about how high we can get.
UNKNOWN

When love is not madness it is not love.
PEDRO CALDERÓN DE LA BARCA

Romantic love as addiction or sickness is an old idea. A less extreme version of this view is that certain people simply love "too much." There is no doubt that love can involve a persistent preoccupation with the beloved; such preoccupation is often part of addiction and excessive behavior in general. However, is the persistent preoccupation that characterizes some loving relationships always bad? Should this love be regarded as a type of addiction?

The identification of love with addiction can be found in literature, philosophy, psychology, psychiatry, and brain studies and it remains common today. However, "love addiction" and "sex addiction" are disputed terms that do not appear in some classifications of diseases; a common alternative terminology is "excessive sexual drive." This dispute exposes the extreme complexity of the issue. In my view, profound romantic love is not an addiction, although some features of addiction, such as preoccupation, can also be found in profound love. However, intense sexual desire or lust can become addictive. Moreover, not all types of preoccupations are harmful; when the preoccupation moves someone toward a flourishing life, it is good for the person and is not an addiction.

An obsession, which is considered the primary symptom of any addiction, is defined as "a persistent disturbing preoccupation with an often unreasonable idea or feeling."[7] The terms "disturbing" and "unreasonable" are crucial here. Persistent preoccupation with an idea or a person is not harmful in itself, as long as it does not harm one's flourishing. To clarify this issue in the romantic realm, I turn to discuss the notions of "repetition" and "loving too much."

Repetition is an action or event that recurs regularly or intermittently. In human behavior, repetition is often treated in a negative manner, especially when nothing is gained in saying or doing the same thing again and again. Indeed, repetition generates boredom and damps down human capacities. Why should we waste mental resources on something repetitive? This is compatible with the fact that emotions are generated by the perception of a significant change in our situation rather than by a repetition of the same event.

Can we speak about valuable repetition? As mentioned above, many human capacities, such as dancing and swimming, are enhanced by repeatedly utilizing them. In these cases, the repeated activity is valuable, since without it, the capacity will deteriorate or fail to develop. A repeated activity can be harmful when it is excessive, or when it damages other major flourishing activities. As profound love involves a positive preoccupation that enhances one's personal flourishing, it is not obsession, which by definition is a negative experience. Profound love involves a process of intrinsic development that does not generate boredom or damp down human capacities; on the contrary, such intrinsic development promotes one's capacities and flourishing.

Neither romantic profundity nor the unfinished nature of romantic intensity should be identified with obsession. The unfinished nature of intense romantic love refers to the never-ending desire to be sexually (and otherwise) with the beloved. It is not a meaningless, mechanistic repetition but rather a persistent urge to be with a meaningful person.

When a repeated activity does not contribute to the agent's development and flourishing, it is likely to either lose its value or become addictive. One such example is sex. Sexual activities are often rather repetitive. Because of this, excessive sex is likely to lose its value and even become addictive. One study found that although more frequent sex is associated with greater happiness for people in a relationship, this link was no longer significant at a frequency of more than once a week; hence, "the association between sexual frequency and well-being is best described by a curvilinear (as opposed to a linear) association."[8] Other repetitive activities, such as watching television, gossiping, or playing computer games, can also become addictive.

Loving Too Much

We have too much of everything and still we do not seem to have enough.
PETER KURZECK

Too many bitches, not enough queens.
MARILYN MONROE

Most people desire many more things than they have: more money, houses, types of chocolate, "likes" on Facebook, sexual interactions, and exciting romantic experiences. This wish, which appears to be natural, is problematic, since there is a price to pay for having too many options. One of these costs is that, faced with an abundance of options, we are likely to feel less satisfied with the option we have. I begin the discussion on this issue by considering the circumstances in which many options can be "too much" or "not enough," and then discuss the issue of whether love can ever be "too much."

When Many Are Too Much and Too Many
Are Not Enough

Only those who know when enough is enough, will ever have enough.
LAO TZU, Tao Te Ching

In continuation of our discussion of a good-enough partner, I turn to Barry Schwartz's distinction between people who tend to maximize and those whose tendency is to "satisfice." Schwartz argues that maximizers are hell-bent on making only the best choices; "satisficers," for their part, seek to make satisfying choices. Accordingly, maximizers engage in more product comparisons than satisficers, and it takes them longer to decide on a purchase: "Maximizers spend more time than satisficers comparing their purchasing decisions to the decisions of others. Maximizers are more likely to experience regret after a purchase. . . . Maximizers generally feel less positive about their purchasing decisions."[9]

Our rich romantic society is the perfect setting for applying Schwartz's ideas. If we replace Schwartz's word "purchase" with "romantic partner" in the passage quoted above, we have a good description of the different inclinations of people seeking a romantic partner.

The two senses of perfect (the "flawless" partner versus the most suitable one) come to mind here. Romantic maximizers are determined to find the "best" romantic partner; romantic satisficers focus on finding the most suitable, or a good-enough, partner. Accordingly, romantic maximizers spend more time making comparisons than satisficers do: they compare their current romantic decisions with partners they have had in the past, with other existing romantic options, and with the romantic partners of others. Romantic maximizers are more likely to experience regret after a romantic "purchase" and to spend time deliberating about hypothetical romantic alternatives. Like nonromantic maximizers, they tend to feel less positive about their romantic decisions than romantic satisficers do.

Schwartz has constructed a scale that measures the tendency to maximize or to satisfice. People with high maximization scores, he reports, experience less satisfaction with life, are less happy, less optimistic, and more depressed than people with low maximization scores. This is equally true of romantic maximizers, whose futile search for the "best" partner makes them restless, dissatisfied with life and with their current romantic relationship, and less happy and optimistic than satisficers. So, while romantic maximizers may manage to get themselves a romantic bargain, they wind up paying a high price in terms of personal well-being.

Moreover, says Schwartz, while maximizers might do better objectively than satisficers, they often do worse subjectively. The maximizer can have a partner who has better nonrelational properties, such as appearance, education, and social status. However, as maximizers walk around with the nagging sense that they have relinquished something in making their romantic decision, they tend to feel worse in the relationship, thereby reducing the relationship's overall quality. Romantic satisfaction has to do with being happy with your romantic lot, which is very difficult when you are plagued by the idea that there may be someone "better" yet to be discovered.[10]

Richard Thaler and Cass Sunstein also discuss the drive for incessant options. In their view, there is a big problem with the notion—popular in economics and ordinary life—that you can never be made worse off by having more choices because you can always turn some of them down. This principle, they argue, fails to take into account self-control, temptation, and the conflict between short-term desires and long-term welfare. Schwartz points out that maximizers' unending desire for more leads to general dissatisfaction and reduces their sense of well-being. Thaler and Sunstein criticize the wish to have more mainly because it tends to privilege many superficial, short-term desires and ignore our fewer, profound long-terms needs. Both are powerful criticisms.[11]

Oftentimes, it is, in fact, not good to have more or to be searching for more. And so, we hear: "More is less," "Less is more," "Too much of a good thing," and "Too many are not enough." Although all these expressions denote an opposition to having too much, they often focus on slightly different aspects of the negative effects of overabundance.

The idea that "More is less," which is similar to the idea "Many are too much," often refers, as in Schwartz's view, to a decision-making process. In the romantic realm, it refers to the current abundance of romantic options, which put people in an ongoing process of choosing, thereby hindering their ability to establish profound long-term love. Such circumstances often lead to frustration, sadness, and feelings of loneliness. The idea "Less is more" has a similar meaning. In focusing on fewer romantic partners, you can achieve greater profundity and meaningfulness. In this sense, less romantic quantity—that is, fewer romantic partners—is often associated with greater quality and romantic profundity. The expression "Too many are not enough" also refers to an imbalance preventing us from settling on what we have.

More and less, and too much and too little, are domain- and context-dependent. Aristotle believed that the most important aspect of an activity is not its quantity, but whether it is appropriate—that is, how suitable it is in the given circumstances. Finding the appropriate balance here is the key to romantic flourishing.

Can We Love Too Much?

In this world of extremes, we can only love too little.
RICH CANNARELLA

I love you much too much . . . but yet my love is such, I can't control my heart.
DEAN MARTIN

Too much of a good thing is wonderful.
MAE WEST

Profound love is morally desirable, as it entails caring and personal flourishing. It is difficult to see how such a phenomenon can be criticized. Nevertheless, people do criticize lovers and especially those whose love appears to
be excessive. Can one tell her beloved that she loves him too much? I begin
examining this issue by discussing the related issue of whether people can be
too happy.

Happiness is of great value to our well-being; indeed, research indicates
that in the central domains of health, work, and love, happy people did better
on average than did unhappy people.[12] Nevertheless, there are still cases in
which too much happiness can be harmful. Shigehiro Oishi and colleagues
argue that the optimal level of happiness depends on various personal and
contextual factors. Thus, people who experience the highest levels of happiness are the most successful in terms of close relationships, but those who
experience slightly lower levels of happiness are the most successful in terms
of income and education. They further claim that whereas wanting more may
be an important motivation for income and education, in the domain of intimate relationships, wanting more might be detrimental because it prompts
individuals to search for alternative partners.[13]

Love seems to be similar—it is typically beneficial for our well-being, but
there are types of love and circumstances in which love can be too much
of a good thing. As I have suggested, profound love involves a process of
intrinsic development that does not generate boredom or deactivate human
capacities; on the contrary, such intrinsic developing promotes one's capacities and flourishing. Since profound love is an engine of human flourishing,
its benefits run deep. Just as we would not fault an author for writing a book
that is too profound, we would be unlikely to criticize a lover for loving too
profoundly. If this profundity leads us to neglect other valuable activities,
both profound and superficial, then we can say that it is "overly" profound.
Like other flourishing experiences, profound love is valuable because it resonates with the lover's character and unique circumstances. Hence, the issue of
harmful addiction does not arise.

Of course, we wish to be with our beloved! We enjoy intrinsic, meaningful
romantic activities for their own sake, and there is no reason why we should
not want to be involved in such activities repeatedly, while making them more
meaningful and enjoyable. This is also the case with profound intrinsic activities
such as writing or painting. There is no "appropriate" frequency for engaging
in profound intrinsic activities, providing, of course, that these activities do not
prevent the person from engaging in other flourishing and necessary activities.

Romantic intensity, unlike romantic profundity, can be excessive. Thus, the
lover's intense passion might prevent her from noticing, or at least admitting,

that her partner's attitude toward her is humiliating or that their relationship has little chance of surviving in the long term. In contrast, since profound love is constitutive of personal flourishing, we cannot speak about an excess of flourishing. However, translating one's profound love into concrete deeds can be detrimental if one does not recognize what is good for the beloved or for oneself.

Profound romantic behavior and "love addiction"/"sex addiction" are completely different animals. To understand this difference, let's think of the difference between profound and superficial activities. In this respect, Stanton Peele and Archie Brodsky, in their classic book, *Love and Addiction*, argue that the distinguishing feature of the addictive attitude is not the intensity of passion, but its shallowness.[14] Being profoundly in love involves pursuing a wide range of flourishing activities with the beloved; being a sex addict confines your world to a narrow band of repetitive activities. The repetitive and superficial attitude that marks a sex addict's interactions makes personal development and flourishing extraordinarily difficult. In profound love, the wish to be with the lover is worlds away from the obsessive need that drives addiction.

We can conclude that something good can cross over the line into excessive when such an attitude or behavior does not contribute to one's overall flourishing, and might even damage it, mainly by preventing the pursuit of less enjoyable, but more meaningful, activities that would advance flourishing. Thus, "the more the merrier" holds true up to a point, after which "one can have too much of a good thing." Sex is typically a wonderful experience, but sex addiction is negative and needs to be treated, like any addiction. Imelda Marcos, the former first lady of the Philippines, had a collection of 3,000 shoes. The country singer Dolly Parton revealed that she never wore the same clothes twice, so one can only imagine how many outfits she had. A documentary on Fidel Castro puts the number of his sexual partners at 35,000—two a day (one at lunch, one at dinner) for the entirety of his four-decade rule.

We don't need to own thousands of pairs of shoes or have a different sexual partner at every meal to have too much of a good thing. That is particularly true when those things are superficial experiences or commodities and when preoccupation with them robs us of the resources to pursue more profound activities and thereby flourish. In this vein, if a couple's time together interferes with each partner's personal flourishing, this can be considered "too much" couple's time.

When people speak about loving too much, they are referring to the intensity that overwhelms lovers and makes them blind to their partner's faults or their own obsessive behavior. How appropriate, then, that Cupid, the Roman god of love, is depicted as a blindfolded boy—showing graphically that lovers, especially young ones, can be blind to the faults or the unsuitability of the one they love. A remark such as "I couldn't help it; I was madly in love with her" indicates excessive love, which lacks the restraint and control that enable autonomy and personal growth to develop, and, in extreme cases, can lead to possessiveness and domination.

Loving Longer, Loving More, and Loving Most of the Time

If you can't live longer, live deeper.
ITALIAN PROVERB

At this point in our road trip toward long-term profound love, we'll consider two related questions concerning the duration of this type of love: (1) Does loving longer mean loving more? (2) Can we be profoundly in love most of the time? As not everyone likes surprises, here's a hint: the dispositional nature of profound love makes the answer to both these questions no. But let's find out why.

Does Loving Longer Mean Loving More?

Susan Lowenstein: Just admit it. You love her [your wife] more.
Tom Wingo: No. Not more, Lowenstein. Only longer.
PAT CONROY, *The Prince of Tides*

Susan Lowenstein is Tom Wingo's twin sister's psychiatrist. Tom's wife cheats on him, and the two nearly divorce. Tom and Lowenstein fall in love with each other (while both are married). Tom then receives a call from his wife, who has finally decided she wants him back. He loves both Lowenstein and his wife. He returns home, not being the sort of man to abandon his wife and three daughters. Tom continues to love Lowenstein and considers her a blessing for him.

Does loving longer (time-wise) necessarily mean loving more (romance-wise)? Loving more is a combination of loving more intensely and more profoundly. As we have seen, time typically does not increase romantic intensity, but it can sometimes enhance romantic profundity—if a process of meaningful development exists. However, loving longer is usually part of living, or, at least, of knowing and interacting with someone for a longer period. Such joint living involves creating more nonromantic commitments, such as having a family, having friends in common, and sharing a joint, meaningful history of coping together in the face of various challenges. These commitments do not necessarily increase love, but they do reduce the likelihood of separation.

This is, indeed, Tom Wingo's case. He would probably have chosen Lowenstein if he had met her and his wife and at the same time. In his present situation, he chooses to make a romantic compromise and give greater weight to his life circumstances and family commitment. This is a dilemma between the value of love and the moral value of commitment to one's family and shared history. There is no rulebook in the world that can tell one what to do when one loves two people, albeit not with the same profundity. Despite the length of time that Tom has loved his wife, their love has not developed into profound love. Hence, in his case, loving longer has, indeed, not meant loving more.

Will we suffer Wingo's fate? As far as we can tell, many will—but many won't.

Being in Love Most of the Time

I have loved Berta for sixty years.
YA'AKOV HAZAN

I am in love with him most of the time.
BLAKE LIVELY, describing her love for her husband, Ryan Reynolds

When, at age ninety-two, the Israeli politician and social activist Ya'akov Hazan said that he had loved his wife, Berta, for sixty years, he did not mean that he thought about her or sexually desired her every minute of every hour of this long period. Romantic love is a complex emotion, and it is present even when thoughts about or sexual desire for the beloved are not.

Romantic love can endure even when the two lovers are not together. In fact, not being with each other all the time can enhance the endurance of such love, as it provides greater personal space. Romantic love includes the desire to be close to the beloved, but increasing numbers of romantic couples live at a geographical distance from each other. As indicated below, compared to close-proximity relationships, such long-distance relationships are characterized by higher levels of relationship quality.

Blake Lively's claim that she loves Ryan Reynolds "most of the time" might appear to run counter to the nature of profound love. However, she probably desires him sexually most of the time, but loves him all of the time. Lively said, "The secret to our marriage is our unwavering friendship. . . . We were friends for two years before we were ever dating. And I treat him like my girlfriend." She considers friendship to be the foundation of her loving relationship with Ryan. Friendship is, indeed, the basis of enduring profound love. As in the case of profound love, you cannot be a friend just "most of the time." Possibly, too, Lively did not announce an unwavering love because love seems to disappear during a disagreement or period of frustration with one's romantic partner. I would say that the love is there, under the surface. If Blake Lively is profoundly in love with Ryan Reynolds, her love is continuous and exists even when they fight with each other. She probably means that such love is at the center of her awareness most of the time, but she does not mean that it disappears when they are not making love or not thinking about each other.

Profound romantic love is a complicated emotional attitude that includes occasional eruptions of intense positive emotions, such as sexual desire, happiness, and admiration, and of negative emotions, like resentment, anger, and jealousy. Those acute intense emotions can be frequent, but they cannot be continuous; they can recur often or only infrequently. Profound romantic love just doesn't go away. It seems that Blake does love Ryan all the time, although she might sexually desire him "only" most of the time.

When Should You Say, "I Love You"?

The regret of my life is that I have not said "I love you" often enough.
YOKO ONO

I conclude this chapter on the issue of time in romantic relationships by discussing a practical lover's dilemma about timing—the question of when to utter the expression "I love you." Hearing a partner say "I love you" for the first time is often one of the highlights of a romantic relationship. However, people tend to be uncertain as to when to declare their love and whether to be the first to do so or to wait until the other has given an indication of feeling the same way. Is there an optimal time to reveal your feelings? Does timing make no difference, or all the difference?

When Should You Say It?

Love isn't saying, "I love you" but calling to say, "did you eat?"
MARLON JAMES

Romantic love expresses our genuine attitudes. There is nothing that boosts communication and personal flourishing more than exposing our loving heart to a partner. However, such self-disclosure makes us more vulnerable and can put our partner in an uncomfortable situation, especially if his or her feelings are different from ours. Consider, for example, these common (and conflicting) pieces of advice about when to say "I love you" to your partner:

- Go on at least five dates.
- Say it only after two months.
- Don't wait too long.
- Wait until you're absolutely bursting.
- Do not do it before, after, or during sex.
- Don't say it when you're very emotional and cannot think rationally.
- Don't say it when you want to reward your partner for something.
- Never say it first, and don't echo it back until you've spent some extended time together.

All of the above suggestions have to do with *timing*. However, is timing more important than honesty and self-disclosure?

As discussed above, when it comes to long-term love, it is time, not timing, that knocks the ball out of the park. Some wrong turns along the road, stemming from bad timing or political incorrectness, will not blot out an entire romantic picture. They might even enhance trust and honesty between lovers. Since profound love needs time to develop, it isn't reasonable to say, "I love you profoundly" after being together for just a short time. Such a statement could show that you are not serious about what is, in fact, a serious matter. However, since love at first sight can occur, you can say "I love you" after a short time together if you are just expressing what you feel at that moment. You might add that you see great potential for the relationship to grow. We can see potential, but we cannot see its end.

In profound love, *actions* speak louder than words. There can be many reasons for not saying "I love you" that are not necessarily related to the lack of love. When Tevye, in *Fiddler on the Roof*, asks Golde, his wife of twenty-five years, whether she loves him, she is surprised by the question and wonders whether he is upset or tired. "Go inside, go lie down! Maybe it's indigestion," she says. When Tevye insists on being answered, Golde says: "For twenty-five years, I've washed your clothes, cooked your meals, cleaned your house, given you children, milked the cow. After twenty-five years, why talk about love right now?" And when he insists upon receiving an answer, she finally says: "I suppose I love you."

Different Paces

Never seek to tell thy love / Love that never told can be; / For the gentle wind does move / Silently, invisibly.

WILLIAM BLAKE

When one is sincere, confessing one's love is usually not problematic. There could be a problem, though, in expecting a like-minded *answer* to the declaration. This difficulty derives from two major points—the different paces at which love develops, and the different personal tendencies in revealing one's heart.

It might matter, too, whether you happen to be a man or a woman. Men tend to confess love earlier than women do, and are happier than women are when receiving confessions of love from a partner. According to one survey, men take an average of 88 days to say "I love you" to a partner, compared to women's 134 days. Moreover, 39 percent of men say "I love you" within the first month of dating, compared to just 23 percent of women.[15]

Personality differences also cause people to fall in love at different paces. However, differences in pace do not indicate differences in romantic *commitment*—the one who falls in love more quickly might also be the one who will fall *out* of love more quickly. There are also differences in pace of *expressing* love: shy people tend to express love later than outspoken people do, even when their emotional intensity is similar. One shy woman told her lover, who had confessed his love to her: "Don't weigh my words now; weigh my deeds." She is right: in love, deeds are more real than words.

Lovers, then, are often counseled to reveal their love only when the *other* feels the same and is ready to express it. Romantic etiquette does not dictate that when a lover has confessed his love, you are to do the same. It is, in fact, probably best *not* to respond by saying "I love you too," but rather to say that although right now you do not know whether you love them, you do know that you like them a lot, that you want to get to know them better, and that you want to give the relationship a chance to develop further. Love at first sight is not required. Less preferably, one might postpone discussing the issue of love and simply enjoy the (presumed) bliss of ignorance.

Love does not grow at the same pace for all of us. While it is true that profound romantic flourishing involves mutual loving attitudes, this does not mean that you should hide your love just because your beloved is not (yet) as in love with you as you are with her or him. We should be open about our attitudes and give our partners the time they need for their feelings to develop. This development might be gradual. It might reveal itself in "softer," more indirect expressions of love, such as calling someone "My love," or saying, "I send you my love" or "I love what I see in you," until, finally, the direct declaration "I love you" might be heard.

Moving slowly is different from being at a standstill, nor does it mean that one is less committed to the journey. Often, the opposite is true. We should respect different personalities and not expect our partner to feel and express the same things that we do at the same time. Profound love is a long-term commitment, and so it is possible that sometime in the future, both lovers will feel profound love and be able to reveal it. Rushing to achieve an unripe romantic profundity is often harmful—patience and calmness are the name of the game.

The same is true of other expressions of romantic robustness, such as "You are the love of my life" or "You are my greatest lover." Such expressions create a ranking between past and present partners, making the declaration even more complex, as it involves not merely the two lovers, but also others from the past. If, for example, you tell your partner, "You are the love of my life," you should not be insulted if she does not reciprocate by saying the same about you. Comparing loving relationships is often impossible and even distracting. One loving relationship might be very passionate, another more profound, and a third more companionate. Even if comparisons *can* be made, the fact that your beloved's first love, many years ago, was and remains his or her *greatest* love does not diminish their love for *you*—the circumstances of the relationships are different, and you might have many good qualities that were absent in the former partner. In any case, your relationship is *unique*, and a comparison, even if it were possible, is of little value.

Concluding Remarks

You can take my husband but do not dare touch my lover.
A MARRIED WOMAN TO HER FRIEND

As with most things in life, virtues in love, such as romantic knowledge and curiosity, are useful in moderation but dangerous in excess. We should aim to know and understand our partner and our love, as this is of practical use. However, when curiosity pushes the boundaries toward adultery, and even in less extreme cases, such as romantic window-shopping, the superficial benefits are sometimes outweighed by the profound costs. Superficial intrinsically valuable activities are enjoyable and are an important aspect of the good life; however, they can be harmful when they become addictive. Whereas we would hardly ever speak about excessive romantic profundity, we do speak about excessive romantic intensity. Profound love is the ideal to aim for because it offers deep and meaningful reciprocity, which is intrinsically valuable. While such profundity does not mean experiencing intense love at every moment, it does entail constant appreciation and respect for one's partner, who is viewed as a valuable, essential part of one's life.

Sexual Relationships

I am happier in my marriage when I am dating other married men. Sad but true.
A MARRIED WOMAN

This chapter focuses on some major types of sexual relationships, discussing in particular casual sex, friendship with benefits, one-sided sex, sexual generosity, makeup and breakup sex, and sex and eating.

Casual Sex

I want to have sex all night long. Just not with my husband!
A WOMAN IN HER EARLY SIXTIES

My marriage is pretty great. But I think about other guys all the time.
A MARRIED WOMAN

Casual sexual relationships, which consist of sexual encounters outside of committed relationships, are attempts to overcome what seems to be the greatest compromise in a marriage (or other committed relationships): the loss of sexual freedom.[1]

Types of Casual Sex

I implied to my lover that I'd rather be a fuck buddy, rather than more. Trying to keep the emotional attachment at arm's length.
A MARRIED WOMAN

My wife wants sex in the back of the car and she wants me to drive.
RODNEY DANGERFIELD

Jocelyn Wentland and Elke Reissing divide casual sexual relationships into four major types: "one-night stands," "booty calls," "fuck buddies," and "friends with benefits." Each type is distinguished from the others by both its degree of romantic superficiality and its temporal aspects. One-night stands, which are the most superficial encounter, involve the least emotionally intimate experience and often take place between strangers or after brief acquaintance. One-night stands occur only once, and the relationship usually ends when the individuals part company. Booty calls refer to a communication initiated with the urgent intent of having a sexual encounter. Unlike one-night stands, the purpose of booty calls is to engage in repeated sexual activity with an acquaintance. Despite the acquaintance, individuals participating in booty calls do not consider each other friends, they typically do not stay overnight, and they share minimal affection. Booty calls are not planned in advance. Their unpredictability and spontaneity are one of their characteristics. When booty calls become too regular or frequent, the participants are considered to be fuck buddies. Fuck buddies are already friends, but their friendship is largely limited to sexual interactions. Friendship with benefits involves the most profound activity among casual sexual relationships. In this type, the partners are first of all friends, and then they add the bonus of the sexual benefit.[2]

Friendship with Benefits

> Between men and women there is no friendship possible. There is passion, enmity, worship, love, but no friendship.
> OSCAR WILDE, *Lady Windermere's Fan*

Among the above types of casual sex, I briefly discuss friendship with benefits, which is the closest to romantic love, as it involves the two major components of such love: friendship plus sex as a benefit. As in love, this friendship involves a concern for your friend for her own sake and not for your own; the other has her own intrinsic value. However, it does not constitute romantic love, since the relationship lacks the profound commitment of a long-term partner whom the lover deeply cares about and consistently engages in various sorts of activities with. Having both friendship and the sex together, while dropping commitment and most of the sharing, is different from profound romantic love; nevertheless, it is usually a pleasurable and exciting relationship.

In economic terms, friendship with benefits is a relationship that cuts the costs and reduces the revenue. It cuts the costs in that there is hardly any price to pay for being together or switching; one can replace the partner and the type of relationship in a relatively cost-free manner. The revenue is reduced because the greatest prize of all, profound romantic love, is excluded.

Friendship with benefits is a kind of disorganized relationship; the time between the meetings is not fixed, and the length of the relationship in its present form is not determined. People are aware of its relatively brief duration, but this does not bother them much, as this relationship enables them to exercise their romantic freedom. Friendship with benefits is relatively brief, since at some point in their lives most people will want to settle down and find a long-term partner for their primary relationship. However, such friendship is often not a matter of weeks or months, but of a good few years. Given the restless nature of our world, such duration is also of value. Moreover, unlike marriage, friendship with benefits does not prevent its participants from looking around and finding another, more fulfilling relationship.

Friendship with benefits is not suitable for all people or for all periods of our lives. It is particularly difficult when the friends are married (to other people), or when they wish to build a family and raise children. A major difficulty for such a relationship is the common case in which one partner wants more than just sexual intimacy. This dissonance complicates the relationship and can become humiliating for the friend who wants more. The optimal circumstances for friendship with benefits are those of young people before marriage and older people who have older children.

How Quickly Should Couples Fall in Love (or into Bed)?

> You can't hurry love; no, you just have to wait: You got to trust, give it time, no matter how long it takes.
>
> THE SUPREMES

> I love when you surprise me with a quickie.
>
> MANY PEOPLE

The paradox of quickness in love can be formulated as follows: there are persuasive arguments for not rushing love and good reasons for the value of quickies. Can we both not rush love and still enjoy having quickies?

Quickness, Rushing, and Hurry

> Fastness is not one of my top priorities. I'd rather be "sensitive" and "wise," which takes time—it takes the time it takes. I ask my lover to give me some time.
>
> A MARRIED WOMAN

When we wish to talk about moving fast, we have lots of terms to choose from: "quickness," "haste," "rushing," and "hurry" all fit the bill. Each of these words, however, has a slightly different sense—haste involves moving hurriedly and in a careless manner; rushing implies doing something too quickly without thinking carefully enough; and hurry refers to acting unusually quickly. Notice the common denominator? Negativity. Quickness seems to stand out as the one neutral choice in the list.

Quickness, then, is not negative by nature. But quickness can take on a negative feel when it prevents profound activities that take time. There seems to be a kind of quickness paradox: we can do a great deal of good while moving quickly, but we can get stuck in the quicksand of superficiality.

Time is indeed essential for profound love. Yet, that does not mean that quick—and yes, even superficial—activities are of no value in specific circumstances. As we will see, it's all about balance.

Why Are Quickies Often Good?

Seize the moment. And go for a quickie.
SLOGAN

A sexual quickie is a brief or spontaneous episode of sexual activity. Sometimes, this is 100 percent appropriate. In the heat of passion, it would be completely inappropriate to observe the niceties of polite society. Leave folding one's clothing for another time. Passionate quickies are often the right thing to do—as the old saying goes, just what the doctor ordered.

Yet, for many, slow sex remains a perennial preference. Partners can derive pleasure and meaning from enjoying their time together, growing closer and strengthening their connection. Both types of sex—wild and brief, and long and tender—are of great value. It is only when quickies are the only ice cream flavor available that things tend to sour. When it's a quickie or nothing, the development of more profound activities may be blocked.

Modern society has a problem: it loves "fast," but many things require "slow." Make no mistake: fast food and fast sex have their place. But the ideal of efficiency can go haywire. Orgasm—or any other satisfaction—can be achieved quickly. But romantic profundity takes time.

Why Is Rushing Love Bad?

Most men pursue pleasure with such breathless haste that they hurry past it.
SØREN KIERKEGAARD

Don't rush into love, because even in fairytales, the happy ending takes place on the last page.
UNKNOWN

When we speak of rushing love, we are talking about trying to establish a profound relationship without giving love its due course for development. At the risk of cliché, love, like a garden, must be cultivated, becoming more and more lush over time.

When they follow the in-due-course policy, the romantic partners take the time necessary for their own attitudes to develop. This policy supports a kind of prolonged courtship, which is quite beneficial for the development of the relationship.

Bibi Deitz has penned a helpful "Don't Rush" list:

1. Don't rush deciding if you're with "The One."
2. Don't rush spending lots of time together right away.
3. Don't rush your quality time.
4. Don't rush saying "I love you."
5. Don't rush moving in together.
6. Don't rush trust.
7. Don't rush important talks.
8. Don't rush commitment.
9. Don't rush marriage.[3]

Deitz's list includes features of a full-fledged, committed romantic relationship. Trying to have all of these features immediately is rushing, for it includes doing things hastily, which we may regret. Our own list should be taken slowly, adding features gradually. Instant gratification can feel great—but sometimes, it feels great only for that instant. For example, it can be useful to endure the pain of postponing desirable, often sexual interactions, or to refrain from having intimate conversations before the time is right. Of course, every couple moves at its own pace. But a perspective that aims to achieve these aspects all at once is harmful because it interferes with the natural progression of establishing romantic profundity.

"You can't hurry love" is true with respect to profound love. And Deitz's "Don't Rush" list is a healthy reminder. Let's return to our balance, for a moment, however. Some people go to the opposite extreme and refuse to even enter the waters of romance. They often have good reasons, typically related to fear of vulnerability. But drifting with the romantic current is important. Without it, we get marooned on the island of solitude.

To sum up, from the point of view of the good life, quickness can go either way. In our accelerated romantic environment, it is easy for quickness to turn into rushing, preventing the development of romantic profundity. But let's not throw the baby out with the bathwater and avoid quickies entirely (in the bathtub or elsewhere). Aristotle, we might mention, considered harmful not only emotional excess, but also emotional lack. It's all about balance.

You should not rush love in order to reach the sexual goal as fast as possible. The pace of gaining sexual satisfaction can vary, and quickies are not the only, and typically not the main, game in town.

One-Sided Sex

I have sex with my husband to maintain industrial peace in the home, but all my emotional resources are focused on my lover. After I check sex off my "to-do list," I feel bad
about trading sex for this peace. I never talk about this with my husband.

A MARRIED WOMAN

Reciprocity is central to romantic love and to sex. The lack of reciprocity—the
knowledge that you are not loved or desired by your partner—usually leads
to a decrease in the degree of love and ultimately to humiliation and breakup.
However, one-sided (unrequited) love and sex can also be found in long-term
relationships. Even more common is the presence of unequal romantic or
sexual involvement between partners—for example, when you love or desire your partner, but your partner does not love and desire you as much. In
some relationships, one partner might not be sexually attracted to the other
or might have a lower degree of sexual desire. One common option in these
circumstances is to allow the partner to find sexual satisfaction outside of the
relationship. Another option is to participate in one-sided sex.

Sex is typically a pleasurable experience, but there are some circumstances
in which sex is not pleasurable for one partner. Some of these kinds of one-
sided sex occur in long-term relationships; others are occasional. Sexual interactions based on the motivations of those who are not sexually attracted to
their partners include pity sex, charity sex, and peace-inducing sex.

Pity (or mercy) sex. In pity sex, a person is not particularly attracted to
someone who is in love with them and who wishes to have sex with them,
but sleeps with that person because they feel sorry for her or wish to provide
her with some momentary happiness. Consider the following description by
a woman of her pity sex experience: "I've been friends with this guy for five
years. He is the sweetest guy and I know he would treat me like gold, but I'm
just not physically attracted to him. He's not attractive *at all.* . . . After confessing his love to me . . . I had sex with him . . . pity sex. I just wanted him
to be happy and I do really care about him . . . *I wish I never slept with him.*"
A similar description of a pity sex experience is provided by another woman:
"I would say my sex drive is about zero right now. Last night we had sex. I
couldn't wait for it to be over. Even kissing made me nauseous."

Charity sex. Common in ongoing long-term relationships, charity sex
occurs in an effort to avoid deterioration of the relationship. It is a sort of
investment in the relationship. Like other investments, we might not see the
benefits at the beginning, but we increase the prospects of reaping these benefits later on. In charity sex, you love your partner, so you have sex despite the
fact that you do not feel like having sex at that moment (or at all). Charity sex,

which is a kind of consolation prize, might not be enjoyable, but it typically does not involve suffering, as pity sex does. In both pity sex and charity sex, someone engages in sex in order to meet the needs of another person, but in charity sex, it takes place in a more profound and enduring relationship.

Peace-inducing sex. "Industrial peace" refers to an agreement by an employer and employees to abstain from industrial actions, such as strikes and lockouts. In the same vein, we can discuss industrial peace in marriage, or in other long-term committed relationships, as a state in which both partners abstain from sexual sanctions, such as sexual deprivation or frequent "headaches," engaging instead in peace-inducing sex. The purpose of this type of "peace" is to ensure an ongoing, smooth relationship in which the two parties decide to stay together even in the absence of profound love or intense passion.

The value of industrial peace in organizations is clear: the employer and employee often have common interests and goals and can fulfill them without necessarily liking each other. Is marital industrial peace also valuable? In marriage, the partners also have common interests and goals. They can try to fulfill these without being profoundly in love or feeling intensely passionate toward each other. If they decide that the show must go on, they need to find a way to peacefully coexist in which they both benefit—even if there is a lack of passion. However, such peace can have emotional costs.

It is very common for romantic partners to experience situations in which they have conflicting sexual desires. When lack of sexual desire and situations of one-sided sex become permanent, they can involve considerable mental cost. Less extreme cases of one-sided sex, in which the lack of sexual desire is not permanent, but limited to specific circumstances, can be valuable. Thus, research reveals that the motivation to meet a partner's sexual needs, termed "sexual communal strength," enhances relationship and sexual satisfaction. However, whereas pursuing sex for promoting goals, such as to enhance intimacy, fuels satisfaction, pursuing sex for preventing goals, such as to avoid disappointing a partner, detracts from satisfaction. The former clearly involves sexual generosity.[4]

Sexual Generosity

For it is in giving that we receive.
FRANCIS OF ASSISI

Generosity is the virtue of giving to another without expecting anything in return. It is characterized by a willingness to give the other person good things freely and abundantly and by giving more than expected—beyond the call of duty. Many religions and moral traditions praise generosity. This praise is not unjustified: studies show that generosity is good for us, physically and mentally. Generosity can decrease blood pressure, reduce stress, help you live longer, boost your mood, promote social connections, and improve the quality of your marriage.[5]

Generosity is positively associated with marital satisfaction, and the lack of it is associated with marital conflict and perceived likelihood of divorce.[6] Whether or not generosity within marriage stems from merely altruistic motives or from a wish to be treated generously in return is an open question. It is probably associated with both—kindness and reciprocity are high on the list of desired qualities in a romantic partner. Conversely, when people are asked to name three negative qualities that would make them shun a prospective partner, stinginess appears on most lists. Generosity is an essential positive framework for prosperous marital relationships: it is natural to be generous toward the one you love.

These considerations indicate the obvious: it is easier to be generous toward the unfortunate, or to admire, rather than envy, those who are well above us or far away from us. These people are less likely to demean and threaten our self-esteem.

Two Types of Sexual Generosity

The charity (and sometimes, pity) sex with my long-term spouse is not a big deal—a few hugs, some kisses, a very brief act of penetration, and it is all over. Such a small sacrifice for so much gain (making my spouse happy). And then after a few such experiences, it becomes easier and (surprisingly) even somewhat enjoyable.

A MARRIED WOMAN

Generosity is very valuable for our well-being and health. Is this also true of sexual generosity? And should we aim to be more sexually generous?

Sexual generosity has come to refer primarily to caring about the pleasure of one's sexual partner. The generous lover is often perceived as someone who takes pleasure in giving pleasure—a phrase that is often used with regard to oral sex. In fact, saying "He's a generous lover" has become code for "He gives great oral sex." Two major types of sexual generosity within a committed relationship are, then, taking part in undesired sexual interactions with one's partner, and passively allowing one's partner to get sexual satisfaction with someone else.

The first type of sexual generosity concerns the willingness to engage in sexual interactions with one's partner even when lacking a real desire to do so and with little prospects of enjoying it. Above, I have discussed a few major kinds of such one-sided sex: pity sex, charity sex, and peace-inducing sex. In the second type of sexual generosity, one is more passive, allowing the partner to be active in seeking sexual satisfaction somewhere else. This can occur, for example, in polyamory, open marriages, or when one spouse is unable or unwilling to have sexual interactions. The first type—in which the generous person tries to fulfill the unfortunate spouse's desire for sex—is more common than the second—in which the fortunate spouse is allowed to be even more fortunate. Somehow, being kind to an unfortunate spouse is easier and feels better than being kind to a fortunate spouse, perhaps because the first is less threatening.

The moral evaluation of these two types of generosity is complex. The positive and negative consequences of active sexual generosity are more limited. It might temporarily alleviate the situation, as an aspirin does, but it does not substantially improve the overall state of affairs. The negative impact is also minor, as the quote above from a married woman who is involved in active sexual generosity indicates.

The positive and negative consequences of passive generosity, in which one's partner is sexually more active, are more complex. In this regard, Berit Brogaard argues that since sexual and emotional satisfaction is a good (possibly intrinsically valuable), "denying one's partner this value outside of the narrow context of a monogamous relationship is inconsistent with the core feature of romantic love, which is a genuine concern for one's partner's agency, autonomy and well-being."[7] Such generosity is common in polyamorous relationships.

The greater prospects of this generosity relate to bigger risks: opening the romantic field can result in the partner abandoning or reducing attention to the primary relationship. This generous attitude could in many cases, though not in all of them, undermine an essential aspect of love—the unique connection between the two partners. Passive sexual generosity is associated with moral and emotional complications due to the traditional sacred status of marriage and the (probable) increased risk it poses to a long-term romantic relationship.

Generosity is two-pronged: giving to the other good things abundantly and doing so in a manner that is beyond the call of duty. Being sexually generous is not the same as having sexual affairs. Generosity is giving good things to others, not to oneself. In having sexual affairs, the main concern is one's own pleasure, not the well-being of others. Generosity involves recognizing the other person's uniqueness and enhancing it while protecting them from becoming a mere object of one's own will. Therefore, the issues of sacrificing and caring for the other are central to generosity.

The major benefit of generosity in romantic relationships is not getting something from your partner but having the two of you establish a positive atmosphere that can nurture a profound, loving relationship.

Sexual Generosity in Elderly Couples and Those
Coping with Alzheimer's Disease

> That's what I consider true generosity. You give your all, and yet you always feel as if it
> costs you nothing.
>
> SIMONE DE BEAUVOIR

The issue of sexual generosity is more complex in the context of aging and Alzheimer's disease. Such circumstances can perhaps indicate future ways of coping with sexual generosity in less stressful circumstances as well.

John Portmann claims that both aging and Alzheimer's can transform a romance in the direction of increasing sexual generosity. The unaffected spouse is often required to exhibit both active and passive sexual generosity.[8] Having sexual interactions with a spouse suffering from Alzheimer's can be considered active sexual generosity. Portmann cites research indicating that many ill spouses make incessant sexual demands. However, healthy spouses are often disturbed by the idea of having sex with someone who cannot recognize them. They can feel guilty about withholding sex from their spouse but feel conflicted about granting it. This is a variation of pity sex. Healthy spouses may choose to exhibit the passive sexual generosity of letting sick spouses have sexual interactions with other patients—a common phenomenon, as sick spouses might no longer recognize their partners. This sexual leeway is more acceptable in the case of Alzheimer's sufferers, because they are no longer their previous selves and are not responsible for what they are doing. Portmann rightly indicates that the notion of sexual generosity does not impose obligation: it refers to favors freely granted, as opposed to earned. Earned favors, he writes, indicate a commodification of sex—the sort of transactions associated with prostitution. Generosity, which is a kind of toleration, should be voluntary.

The notion of "sexual self-generosity," which is associated with the popular notion of "self-compassion," is relevant to Alzheimer's circumstances. Self-compassion implies self-kindness—being kind to and understanding oneself in times of failures and strife, when harsh self-criticism might arise naturally. Just as you treat another person who has troubles with compassion, so should you be kind to yourself in difficult times. In the case of an Alzheimer's patient's spouse, sexual self-generosity means allowing oneself to find romantic and sexual fulfillment outside the marriage rather than waiting for the death of the sick spouse. Portmann argues that this type of sexual self-generosity is far superior to two other major options available to the healthy spouse—namely, deserting (or divorcing) a sick spouse or denying oneself romantic satisfaction. Portmann contends that the sexual generosity required in circumstances of aging and Alzheimer's should be praised and should lead the way to a redefinition of "fidelity" in regular relationships. Such circumstances could encourage all types of generosity.[9]

To sum up, emotional generosity, like other positive attitudes, is often valuable for a good life and for enhancing the quality of a committed relationship. Is sexual generosity valuable as well? All types of sexual generosity, active and passive, are valuable in certain circumstances. In others, their value depends on the dosage: too much sexual generosity can make a relationship toxic, but a moderate dosage can be an antidote.

Why Do Makeup Sex and Breakup Sex Feel So Good?

> The make-up sex was 10 times more intense than I'd ever experienced.
> TINA NASH

Makeup sex is wild and extremely gratifying sex that people report experiencing after having had an intense fight. Why, in the wake of having had a bitter fight, is everything forgotten while the couple engages in what many say is amazingly wild and enjoyable sex? And why is breakup sex similarly so exciting?

Arousal Transfer

> I feel more love during makeup sex because I know that no matter what happened, our love has survived it.
> A MARRIED WOMAN

Makeup sex is considered by many to be the best kind of sex, and in many cases, worth the fight. Its excitement seems to stem from a transfer of arousal from one situation to another. When we are excited by one stimulus, we are likely to be easily excited by another one.

We see the arousal (excitation) transfer in Donald Dutton and Arthur Aron's classic bridge experiment.[10] In this study, male passersby were contacted on either a fear-arousing suspension bridge or a non-fear-arousing bridge by an attractive woman, who asked them to fill out questionnaires. Sexual arousal toward the woman was greater in subjects on the fear-arousing bridge. Their fear arousal was transferred to sexual arousal, generated by the presence of an attractive woman. But even without scary bridges, we can see this in action. When we watch certain movies, our anger toward the villain can easily turn into the arousal underlying happiness upon seeing the villain punished.

Makeup sex excitement can be explained along similar lines. The high arousal state associated with the fight is transferred to a high arousal state during the makeup sex. The great sex that ensues is to some extent due to the change in mood and the relief at reconciliation with the partner, but it is also the result of arousal transfer from the fight to the sexual encounter. Makeup sex takes place after an unpleasant, heated fight with a partner that has created a gulf between the two and threatened the very existence of the relationship; makeup sex then reestablishes their bond in a very tangible manner. As one woman said, "Our relationship is that much more secure after makeup sex, on top of the added relief of being reconnected to my closest companion. It's a reminder that though we can hurt each other, we're still there for one another."

A similar manner of increasing sexual arousal by transferring arousal from a different state is when one partner acts wildly, and even sadistically, toward the other. Here, the arousal underlying anger and even revenge is transferred into sexual arousal. A subtler manner of increasing sexual arousal is teasing, which involves a gentle and humorous argument (simulating a "fight") that increases sexual arousal.

The arousal transfer can arise not merely from negative emotions, such as the anger that prevails during fights, but also from positive emotions, such as enjoying a good dinner together or engaging in other pleasurable experiences. It can also be activated by sexual arousal that is triggered by another person, such as a good-looking neighbor or the protagonist in a movie, and that is then transferred to one's own partner. As Rodney Dangerfield quipped, "Last time I tried to make love to my wife nothing was happening, so I said to her, 'What's the matter, you can't think of anybody either?'"

Emotions are dynamic and contagious phenomena: they spread easily from one person to another. Thus, when we see a sad person crying, many of us become sad as well. When someone loves us, we are more likely to love that person in return. And when we are aware of a sexually aroused person near us, we can also become sexually stimulated.

Breakup Sex

Breakup sex is amazing! It's really hard to explain till you experience it! Way better than makeup sex!

AN ANONYMOUS MAN

Breakup sex is the bittersweet, passionate sex you have with your partner shortly after, while, or shortly before breaking up with them. The exciting nature of "goodbye" sex, the "one for the road," is due to its unique circumstances: this is the last chance to enjoy sex with each other. As Ted Spiker said, "It's like the day before a diet. Tomorrow I'll start, but today I'm going to enjoy one last order of chicken wings." The sex is especially great when the relationship was basically good, but nonromantic reasons, such as different life plans, force the couple to separate. Breakup sex is flavored by the caring that remains, despite the separation. As Aradia describes her breakup sex, "We'd have one last hurrah and it was a damn great one! What a way to end the relationship! It actually really helped, and it'll be a nice memory down the line."

Because of its terminal nature, people often feel no inhibitions or constraints during breakup sex and behave however they wish, without worrying about the aftereffect or the future. In this moving, but sad experience, people usually do not speak of the bad times and what ruined the relationship; they are immersed in the exciting present, knowing that no future awaits. Nothing is meaningful except the present sexual togetherness. In breakup sex, the excitement stems from experiencing a togetherness that is unconstrained by past and future circumstances. In makeup sex, the excitement stems from overcoming past difficulties and looking positively toward the future. The total lack of constraints is what makes breakup sex (usually) the more exciting of the two.

The Risks of Makeup and Breakup Sex

I am an expert in makeup sex and have done it so many times.
A MARRIED WOMAN

I've never had makeup sex in my life, despite a lot of fighting.
A DIVORCED WOMAN

Makeup sex poses its own risks to long-term relationships, one of which is that it could lead to reinforcing fights, or at least not taking fights as seriously as they should be taken. This is particularly true when the fights are violent, as in the case of men who beat their partners. Sometimes, immediately after domestic violence, men force their partners to have makeup sex; it goes without saying how appalling such behavior is. In addition, makeup sex can make it easier for these women to return to their violent spouses as if nothing had happened.

Consider the true story of Tina Nash, a severely battered woman who stayed with her boyfriend despite his violent behavior. After a particularly violent episode, she returned the next day to pick up her car from outside his apartment, and although he smashed her car up, she took him back. She writes: "We made passionate love that night. The make-up sex with him was 10 times more intense than I'd ever experienced before. He was slow and loving and looked at me like he wanted to own my soul." A few months later, she lost her sight after he beat her severely.

Makeup sex is a superficial remedy for fights. The remedy works when the relationship is positive, and the fights are local and limited. In these circumstances, this sex can act like small amounts of poison that boost the immune system. When more profound problems underlie the relationship, or when the amount of poison is significant, such sex can be deadly.

It is not necessary to provoke serious fights to have great sex, as there is a price to be paid for fighting. Moreover, if a fight is deliberately provoked, the subsequent sex can lose its value as a reaffirmation of love. In addition, as there is no shortage of disagreements, misunderstandings, and fights in enduring healthy relationships, there is no need to artificially provoke them—there is only the need to overcome them in a positive manner.

Breakup sex can be of value in two main situations: (1) you still like each other and want to remain friends; (2) the decision to separate was mutual. In some cases, the breakup sex can be quite sad and painful. As Scott writes, "My girlfriend took me out on a romantic weekend with the idea of having sex as many times as possible and then dumping me before checking out. It made me very angry and bitter." For other people, especially those who are no longer in love with their partner, the "goodbye bed" can make them feel sad at being used and for giving in and having a kind of pity sex. As one woman wrote, "It made me feel dirty . . . and I will never do the 'goodbye bed' again." Breakup pregnancy or breakup STD (sexually transmitted disease) can have even worse effects.

Sex and Eating

I've been eating a sandwich with no mayonnaise, lettuce, tomatoes, or cheese with my spouse. Now I can eat the whole sandwich. My lover is the condiments and veggies, . . . my spouse the meat or stable foundation I've had for over twenty-five years! With both in my life, I am satiated but not overly full!

A MARRIED WOMAN

Catherine Hakim believes that sex is no more a moral issue than eating a good meal. Accordingly, meeting a secret lover for a casual encounter should be as routine as dining out at a restaurant instead of eating at home. In this sense, Hakim is in agreement with those who do not consider sexual desire to be an emotion, but a biological drive like hunger and thirst. In her view, eating most meals at home with our spouses does not preclude eating out in restaurants to sample different cuisines with other people.[11]

Scruton rejects the comparison between sexual desire and the appetite for food. He argues that only sexual desire is an interpersonal response involving the perception of another as a person that we do not see as an instance of his kind, replaceable by another substitute. This person is not a means to an end, but an end in his own right. Scruton concludes that what distinguishes sexual desire from hunger is not "the structure of the impulse itself, but an independent feature of those entities to which it is directed."[12] I believe that Scruton is right, and it is mainly the richer nature of the object that makes the essential difference between eating and having sex.

The richer nature of the object in sexual desire implies some differences in the nature of the subject as well. When considering the basic characteristics of typical emotions, sexual desire emerges as a typical emotion, quite different from hunger and thirst. Like typical emotions, sexual desire is mainly about a human being. Hunger and thirst are feelings, expressing states of deprivation; they are not directed at emotional objects. The role of belief and imagination in generating hunger and thirst is significantly smaller than in sexual desire and other emotions. You can imagine a good meal, but such imagination is no substitute for actually eating it. In this regard, it is said that the ancient Greek Diogenes the Cynic was found masturbating in the public square. When reproached for his behavior, he explained: "I wish I could rub my stomach to satisfy its hunger." Since a sexual activity involves higher and more complicated psychological activities (such as imagination) than eating does, it can be satisfied by an imaginative substitute.

It is true that like eating, sex can also be done in various places and with different people. However, the replaceable nature of sex (and romantic love) does not mean that democracy should be applied to it and that it is like linen—the more often changed, the sweeter. On the contrary, people who rapidly replace their romantic and sexual partners may have trouble forming profound loving relationships. Many of them are addicted to destructive sexual relationships and cannot achieve the stability and warmth of healthy, loving bonds. Eating is different; constantly dining out at different restaurants has no moral problems attached to it. Hence, we cannot be as unromantic about sex as we are about eating, although this is not to deny that there are cases in which sexual desire has nothing to do with romantic love. After all, many people think that love and sex can be separated but would prefer to have them combined. Moreover, most people would consider sexual involvement between their partner and a rival a threat to their romantic relationship.

Junk Sex and Healthy Romantic Relationships

> Junk sex is like junk food—not bad enough to avoid, but definitely not good enough to make a steady diet of.
>
> THE URBAN DICTIONARY

The very use of the term "junk" implies that both junk food and junk sex are inferior to the "real thing" and are therefore unhealthy. However, are they unhealthy in the same sense? The word "junk" refers to something of poor quality. What is poor quality in junk sex? Should we avoid junk sex, just as we are advised to avoid junk food?

Consider the following common claims about both junk food and junk sex:

a. Junk food and junk sex both have little long-term value for nutrition or for romantic love—they provide instant satisfaction, while time becomes a kind of obstacle that they need to overcome.

b. Junk food is high in fat, sugar, salt, and calories; junk sex is high in superficial, egoistic desires.

c. Many foods and sex activities are considered as either healthy or junk depending on their "ingredients" and on the way in which they are prepared.

d. Consuming or engaging in a limited amount of junk food or junk sex does not usually pose an immediate danger and is generally safe when integrated into a well-balanced diet or relationship.

e. Junk food and junk sex can easily become addictive.

In comparing junk food to junk sex, intimacy can be considered the "nutritional value" of sex, while one's overall flourishing is analogous to one's overall health. Intimacy involves a feeling of closeness and belonging, both of which are vital in healthy sex. We see the importance of intimacy in the following confession made by a married woman: "Last night I had sex with my husband, but he did not actually touch me—just penetrated me. I was so sad, I could cry." Intimate sex does not merely involve penetration; it also entails positive, close feelings between the partners. Without intimacy, junk sex has no romantic value, since it does not promote, and even reduces, the quality of the relationship. In good intimate sex, as with a good meal at a restaurant, the atmosphere is important; in junk food and junk sex, there is hardly any time or need for atmosphere.

Junk sex is all about one's own satisfaction; healthy sex is also, and often mainly, about the other. The positive experience of junk sex is over the moment that the agent is sexually satisfied. The experience of healthy intimate sex is not over when both people climax, but continues with embracing, talking, and just being together. Some people (more so women) claim that this is the most enjoyable part of intimate sex. As one married woman said after her first extramarital affair, "What I enjoyed the most that evening was the kissing, cuddling, and his emotional presence."

In contrast to junk food, we speak about healthy food—namely, food that is beneficial to health beyond the value of the normal diet required for human sustenance. Healthy food is an important element in healthy living. Similarly, in contrast to junk sex, we can speak about healthy sex, which fosters the flourishing of romantic relationships.

Living healthily is more than just eating healthily. It is a huge canvas on which many factors make their mark—some even before one's birth. Our genes and mother's actions during pregnancy start the list, and upbringing plays its part:

happy people are more likely to live longer.[13] Also important are outdoor activities, stress levels, social activity, and balanced meals. Some of these factors are within our control, others are not, and yet others fall somewhere in between.

It's hard to pin down exactly what makes up a healthy life. But longevity and flourishing seem like likely candidates. While longevity is easy to measure, it is more complicated to characterize flourishing. There is no one way to live a healthy life and no blueprint for achieving it. Of course, there are some essential elements without which we suffer or compensate for.

Junk sex is a superficial experience that typically does not contribute to our flourishing but rather reduces it. Furthermore, since junk sex is likely to become addictive, as is the case with junk food, it can have a significantly negative impact on one's life. Junk sex is usually very brief and can damage one's ability to engage in more profound romantic relationships, thereby having a negative impact on one's quality of life and longevity. Profound romantic activities have a lingering positive impact on our life and are basic to our flourishing. Positive sexual functioning plays a unique and fundamental role in human well-being throughout the life course.[14]

Love is important in forming a valuable marital framework. However, there are various types of loving relationships, and exclusive sexual intensity is not essential for all forms of marital frameworks.

What Makes You Feel Best about Sex?

Charm is a glow within a woman that casts a most becoming light on others.
JOHN MASON BROWN

Sexuality is significant in promoting happiness and satisfaction in enduring romantic relationships. But how can relatively brief and infrequent sexual experiences be so important for enduring romantic relationships? The answer seems to be less connected to the "hard-core" sexual activities, and in particular, orgasms, than to the "soft," affectionate experiences, like kissing and cuddling, that are associated with them.

Afterglow, After-Sex Affectionate Activities, and Orgasms

My married lover was cut off emotionally the moment he ejaculated. The speed by which he left me emotionally and physically was incredible. He actually left the bed to drink something and did not return to the bed.
A DIVORCED WOMAN

No woman gets an orgasm from shining the kitchen floor.
BETTY FRIEDAN

Sexual afterglow is the good feeling that lingers after pleasurable sexual experiences—a kind of intense shining that is both attractive and infectious. Research suggests that it is sexual afterglow more than orgasm that determines how people feel about their sexual partner. Although sexual afterglow is less intense than orgasm, it plays a greater role in enduring romantic satisfaction. Spouses who have experienced stronger afterglow report higher levels of marital satisfaction both at baseline and over time compared to spouses who have not. It appears, then, that sexual afterglow is a mechanism through which sex promotes pair bonding.[15]

Studies indicate that romantic partners view the time after intercourse as important for bonding and intimacy. Indeed, frequent physical affection, such as kissing, cuddling, and hugging, have been found to increase the duration and the quality of the relationship. The value of these behaviors is particularly high after sex, since they confirm that the relationship bond is deeper than the superficial, brief physical act. After-sex affectionate activities prolong the duration of sexuality, thereby enabling it to have a greater impact on the relationship. It seems that after-sex affectionate activities are crucial to sexual afterglow, and that they play a more important role in sexual and relationship satisfaction than foreplay or the duration of intercourse. Along these lines, it has been found that, within cohabiting marriages and romantic relationships, increased kissing significantly decreases total cholesterol and perceived stress, and significantly increases relationship satisfaction.[16]

Applying the intensity-profundity distinction to the sexual realm, we may say that orgasm is the most obvious example of sexual intensity; it is a momentary peak of sexual desire. Sexual afterglow and after-sex affectionate activities help to deepen the romantic bond. Indeed, in a study of newlywed couples, sexual afterglow remains for about forty-eight hours after sex, and those with stronger afterglow had higher overall marital satisfaction. No wonder that it is the afterglow, rather than the number of orgasms, that best correlates to the length and quality of the relationship.[17]

The French famously refer to orgasm as "la petite mort," or "the little death." Once orgasm is reached, it is, in a sense, the end of the experience preceding it, and hence, it is a little death. Along these lines, it has been claimed that "all animals are sad after sex." These ideas reflect the momentary nature of orgasm. However, once after-sex affectionate activities are added, and then supplemented by promoting romantic activities, the momentary peak can initiate a process that enhances enduring love.

When It Rains, It Pours

While having an affair I was sexually aroused and began to notice other men noticing me.
I paid more attention to my appearance, wore more attractive clothing, and began enjoying this attention. Even my husband was more attracted to me. When it rains, it pours.

A MARRIED WOMAN

We have seen that sexual afterglow promotes enduring, high-quality romantic relationships. However, afterglow also attracts other people to the individual's radiant sexual arousal. Thus, one study found that the merest interaction
with a member of the opposite sex can bring a glow to a woman's face. Even
nonsexual social interactions with men caused a noticeable rise in the tem-
perature of a woman's face, without them even noticing it.[18]

The pleasant sexual afterglow involves the wish to have more sex; this
attitude in turn attracts other people to this person. Sexual glow is a kind of
spell emitted by the individual that hits other people, who are attracted to the
individual much as insects and butterflies are attracted to light.

Sexual glowing experiences seem to make sexually rich people even richer.
Those who enjoy sex are more likely to enjoy it more, thereby enhancing their
current romantic relationship. However, since sexual glowing attracts people
beside one's partner, it might well ruin low-quality relationships.

Eleanor Roosevelt once quipped that "a woman is like a tea bag—you can't
tell how strong she is until you put her in hot water." The phenomenon of
sexual glow indicates that Eleanor was not entirely correct. You can feel the
love of women (or men for that matter) not merely when they are in intense,
hot romantic experiences, but also—and perhaps more so—before and after
being in such hot experiences.

Sexual interactions are important in enduring romantic love because they
involve more than the momentary peak of an orgasm. Even more important
for such love are the affectionate activities associated with orgasm that last
longer and express more genuinely the partner's loving heart. To paraphrase
Winston Churchill, we can say that orgasm is not the end of love. It is not
even the beginning of the end. But it is, perhaps, the end of the beginning
of love.

Sexuality and Friendship in Cyberspace

My excitement when physically touching my lover is higher than that of online excitement, though I have an orgasm quite often while having cybersex.

A DIVORCED WOMAN

Cyberspace is a kind of huge, dynamic, electronic bedroom loaded with imaginative interactions. This novel environment has a significant impact on offline romantic activities, as it offers increased opportunities, greater self-disclosure, decreased vulnerability, lesser commitment, an increase in boundary violations, and reduced exclusivity. Cyberspace provides technical tools that facilitate the opportunity to conduct several romantic (and sexual) relationships at the same time. Although cyberlove and cybersex are likely to become more popular, they cannot replace offline relationships. Nonetheless, they can complement them.

Like the physical romantic environment, cyberspace is multifaceted. Here, I will focus on online romantic and sexual relationships—cyberlove and cybersex.

The Interactive Nature

I like restraint, if it doesn't go too far.
MAE WEST

Cyberlove is a romantic relationship consisting mainly of computer-mediated communication. Despite the fact that the partner is physically remote and might be anonymous, love can be experienced as fully and as intensely as in an offline relationship. In a broad sense, cybersex (or in slang, "cybering") refers to all types of sexually related activities offered in cyberspace, including mobile applications. When people are involved in cybersex, they cannot actually kiss each other, but the kiss they might send is emotionally vivid, and its emotional impact can resemble that of an actual kiss.

The active personal role in cyberspace makes this environment more exciting and seductive than that of sexual fantasies, erotic novels, or X-rated movies; hence the massive temptation to engage in such sexual activities. The imaginary personal interaction is very seductive. Since the line separating passive observation from full interaction is crossed in cybersex, it becomes easier to blur the line separating imagination from reality. The presence of interactive characteristics in the imaginary realm of an online relationship is a revolution in personal relationships, as it enables people to reap many of the benefits associated with offline relationships without investing significant resources.[19]

The interactive revolution in online romantic and sexual relationships has promoted both greater social interaction and more solitary activities. In comparison to standard fantasies, online relationships involve greater social interaction with other people. However, in comparison to offline relationships, many romantic activities are performed while someone is sitting alone in front of a computer or a smartphone. Take, for example, cybersex. Compared with offline masturbation, cybersex (like phone sex) is a much more social interaction, as it is done while communicating with another person. While in offline masturbation, orgasm comes courtesy of the person's own hands and mind, in cybersex orgasm comes courtesy of another person's mind (and one's own hands). Cybersex narrows the gap between masturbation and offline sex, as it involves the active contribution of another person. However, compared with offline sexual relationships, cybersex is less social and can reduce the need for actual social interactions. Moreover, the virtual nature of cyberspace often fails to satisfy real needs. As a married woman wrote to her online lover, "I want a lover who actually touches me."

Greater Flexibility and Reduced Exclusivity

The paradox in my situation is that I'm cheating on my spouse with an online lover, whom I am cheating on with a real-time lover, who both have to compete emotionally with another online lover!

A MARRIED WOMAN

Human communities need boundaries: living with others necessitates limiting our desires. However, globalization, in which cyberspace is a central arena of action, is essentially an act of crossing, fracturing, and breaking boundaries. Once people get used to violating boundaries in virtual space, normative boundaries in real space are likely to be treated with greater flexibility too, which in turn can weaken the safeguards against further violation. The flexible nature of boundaries in cyberspace is not necessarily immoral. On the contrary, adhering to strict boundaries in our romantic life can be immoral, as it does not take into account the unique, specific, personal, and circumstantial aspects of the lover. In this regard, Stephen Toulmin argues that "we do need to recognize that a morality based entirely on general rules and principles is tyrannical and disproportionate, and that only those who make equitable allowances for subtle individual differences have a proper feeling for the deeper demands of ethics."[20]

Of course, greater flexibility has its own costs. Take, for example, cybersex, where romantic and sexual boundaries are much more flexible than in offline circumstances. This flexibility has not reduced the number of offline violations of boundaries but rather increased it. With the expanded use of the internet and particularly mobile applications, romantic and sexual cheating has increased. Moreover, even if the sexual cheating is limited to the online arena, partners can feel betrayed and traumatized.[21]

Romantic, and especially sexual, exclusivity has long been regarded as the hallmark of stable relationships. The current social trend leans toward reducing exclusivity in relationships, and this trend is being reinforced by behavior in cyberspace, where romantic boundaries are highly flexible. Reducing romantic exclusivity conflicts with partiality, which is one of the basic emotional characteristics and enables us to focus our resources. This reduction also goes against the heart of ideal love—namely, the perception that the beloved is the one and only person suitable for the lover's profound love. Such a reduction in exclusivity, however, enhances the need for change and novelty, both of which generate emotions.

The technology associated with online relationships, and in particular the various mobile applications, make it easier, more convenient, and safer to increase flexibility and reduce exclusivity. The romantic environment in cyberspace suits perfectly our accelerated society while making this society even more sexually efficient. Because of the hectic schedule of many people these days, they are too busy even to make superficial sexual contacts on a face-to-face basis. They let their mobile applications do the work.

Modern technology continues to improve the methods available for both initiating and maintaining sexual and romantic relations. In addition to the many websites offering potential partners, there are various mobile applications making the initiation of a relationship easier. The popular application Tinder makes the selection process extremely simple (selection is based mainly on external appearance) and very easy (one sweeps the smartphone screen to the right to say "like" or to the left to say "pass"). Motivations for using this application vary; users are looking not merely for casual sex, but also for love, communication, validation of their self-worth, thrills or excitement, and to be trendy. Hence, "Tinder should not be seen as merely a fun, hookup app without any strings attached," but also as a new way "to initiate committed romantic relationships."[22]

Modern technology also helps to maintain remote relationships. It doesn't only offer options for meeting willing people; it provides a more comfortable and efficient way to pursue several romantic relationships at the same time. The practice of whetting your appetite online while eating at home is a significant element in the process of violating marriage's monopoly on sex for married people. As cybersex is seen as a lesser sin—since it can be considered merely a process of talking that involves no actual physical encounter—some offline partners will tolerate or even support it. Letting your partner know about, and even watch, your sexual activity with another person is significant in the sense that the committed couple knowingly accepts that sexual exclusivity is not an absolute category that should never be violated. Sexual exclusivity is thus seen as a continuum, and, in some circumstances, certain points along that continuum can permissibly be violated.

In order to reduce the risk of ruining their primary offline relationship, some married people might accept their partner having an intense online sexual affair, but not agree to a profound online romantic affair. Others might further limit the sexual affair to a one-night cyberstand. All such limitations intend to minimize the harm done to the primary relationship. It seems, however, that a more substantial change in our emotional makeup is required for coping with these sexual opportunities while still maintaining some stability in the primary relationship.

The internet and mobile applications present a serious threat to monogamous relationships in general and marriage in particular, since they facilitate not merely pleasurable sexual activities, but deep romantic relationships as well. A one-night cyberstand is more available and easier to keep a secret. On the other hand, the conditions for nourishing a deep, loving relationship have also been improved. Both the internet and mobile applications provide an enjoyable and efficient means by which various people get to know each other intimately without the distractions of external factors, such as appearance, age, geographical distance, race, nationality, religion, or marital status. This is bound to increase the number of international, intercultural, and inter-religious marriages, ultimately modifying global social norms—in the main, making them more flexible and often more superficial.

The Alternative Romantic Environment

I fell in love with the way you touched me without using your hands.
UNKNOWN

Cyberspace provides an alternative environment to one's actual setting. It enables participants to explore exciting romantic alternatives without necessarily violating significant personal commitments. It offers an outlet for developing alternative emotional ties without completely ruining the primary offline relationship. When people confuse cyberspace with the actual world, the issue of commitment becomes problematic and emotional, and moral difficulties emerge.

The seductiveness of cyberspace and the effortlessness of becoming involved in online affairs also entail risks: people are easily carried away, and the risk of addiction is high. Like other types of addiction, cyberspace does not merely satisfy needs but creates new needs that often cannot be met. This can lower the probability of being satisfied with one's romantic lot.

The smart money is on offline and online romantic relationships both sticking around. The increased lure of the internet and mobile applications lower the likelihood that those with access to it will restrict themselves solely to offline relationships. However, since online relationships lack some basic romantic activities, such as touching and actual sex, satisfying offline relationships will continue to be considered an upgraded and more fulfilling relationship. Learning to integrate cyberspace with actual space in the romantic domain is a major task for our society. Indeed, many marriages now begin online. In comparison to marriages that began through traditional offline venues, those that began online were found to be slightly less likely to result in a marital breakup and were associated with slightly higher marital satisfaction among those respondents who remained married. This suggests that the internet may be altering the dynamics and outcomes of marriage itself.[23]

Today, dreams are no longer the major tool for imagining a better situation. Cyberspace has taken up that role and run with it. In cyberspace, two lovers feel as if they are directly connected—as if their bodies do not interfere, allowing their hearts to be in direct communication. People often describe their online relationship as "dreaming while awake" and delight in these dreams. However, a life of mere dreams is dangerous because of the disconnect from reality. Online romantic relationships are valuable when they complement, rather than replace, offline relationships. Dreams, like cyberspace, are valuable when they are interspersed with reality.

Future changes will probably modify present social forms such as marriage and cohabitation, as well as current romantic practices relating to courtship, casual sex, committed romantic relationships, and romantic exclusivity. Hakim argues that as the pill made premarital sex among young people a lot easier, the internet facilitates playfairs among older married people. Recent history teaches us that we can expect a further relaxation of social and moral norms.[24]

Friendship in Our Cyber Society

Social networks such as Facebook have become a central space for initiating and maintaining new romantic, including sexual, relationships. The new technological means of communication are shaping romantic relationships. The possibility of having so many friends further undermines the value and possibility of romantic exclusivity and often decreases romantic profundity.

In his article "Faux Friendship," William Deresiewicz discusses the current broad notion of friendship as it is viewed on Facebook, where we can have thousands of "friends," arguing that once we become friends with everyone, we forget how to be friends with anyone. As he sees it, friendships have traditionally been rare, precious, and hard-won; a "true friend" stood against the self-interested "flatterer" or "false friend." With the disintegration of the modern family, friends might become *the family we choose*. Yet the current concept of friendship has changed from a (profound) relationship into an (intense) feeling—from something people share to something each of us hugs privately to ourselves in the loneliness of our electronic enclaves. In these enclaves, we have stopped thinking of others as *individuals*; we have turned them into an *indiscriminate mass*—a kind of audience or faceless public. Deresiewicz argues that we are too busy to spare our friends more time than it takes to send a text message. Hence, the more people we know, the lonelier we get.[25]

Deresiewicz further deplores how many of us have become willing, even eager, to conduct our private lives in public. The value of friendship lies precisely in the *uniqueness* of the relationship—and social networks such as Facebook lack this exclusivity. While Deresiewicz admits that Facebook serves to connect people, particularly long-lost friends, he believes that it does so at the cost of reducing identity to information about mundane details. Friendship is built by investing time in joint activities and listening to our friends' stories, hopes, beliefs, pleasures, and worries. How can you do that when you have 500 or 5,000 friends? Intimate friendship takes patience, devotion, sensitivity, subtlety, and skill. As Deresiewicz puts it starkly, we have given our hearts to machines, and it now seems that *we are turning into machines*.

What does science say about these claims? Does the internet indeed increase loneliness? It seems that the internet can help many people build and maintain their social lives. This is particularly true for older people, people with different physical limitations, and people who belong to groups that suffer from a negative social stigma. The long-term effects of Facebook on friendship and loneliness remain unclear, although most of the communication on Facebook appears shallow, as friends are accumulated in much the same way as stamps.[26] We need to use the internet as a supplement for offline experiences, not as a replacement for offline lives.

Concluding Remarks

> Young men do not know what they do, but they do it for the whole night.
> MADONNA

The casual sexual relationship of friends with benefits maintains the major aspects of a romantic relationship—friendship and sexual desire—despite the absence of profound love. Nevertheless, this kind of relationship, the popularity of which is increasing, can lead to long-term romantic relationships in which friendship is essential. Sex is also of considerable importance in intimate relationships, and hence sometimes takes place even when one partner does not really want it. One option in these circumstances is to allow the partner to find sexual satisfaction outside of the relationship; another option is to participate in one-sided sex, such as pity sex or peace-inducing sex.

Sexual generosity, in the sense of allowing your partner to have another sexual partner, can be problematic if it damages the primary relationship. Instances of makeup and breakup sex are highly emotionally driven and often experienced as very positive. Considering the contexts in which these encounters occur, it is understandable that they would inspire renewed passion and excitement between lovers. However, this is an artificially positive experience, which should not be considered a replacement for achieving pleasurable sexual encounters in more typical romantic circumstances, with the underlying support of profound love.

Sex seems essentially different from eating because of the intrinsic value of human beings. Junk food and junk sex, however, have a lot in common. The benefits of junk sex, as an experience of intense love, are largely superficial and do not contribute to long-term profundity. Additionally, while enjoyable, it can easily become addictive. As it has a tendency to reduce flourishing, junk sex can be a misleading temptation that is often better resisted when a more profound experience is available. Sexuality is significant in promoting enduring romantic relationships. How can brief and infrequent experiences such as orgasms be crucial for enduring flourishing romantic relations? The answer relates to sexual experiences, such as after-sex affectionate activities and sexual afterglow, which last longer than orgasms, and genuinely express the partner's loving heart. They connect the momentary peak of the orgasm with a longer process that enhances enduring love.

The ease of establishing online relationships and the reduced investment that they require may make some of them superficial, alongside the superficial nature of our society that emphasizes the value of immediate satisfaction. However, online relationships can also be used to establish romantic profundity.

Cybersex provides more flexible boundaries than real-life sex. As a forum for communication, there is demand for greater social interaction, and the lines of intimacy are blurrier from behind the screen. This can be useful for maintaining long-distance relationships but poses a serious threat to general exclusivity in that there are virtually unlimited partners available on the web. It is easier and simpler to navigate the romantic realm of cyberspace than the physical romantic domain. We can expect that as technology develops, the norms of our romantic relationships will also morph to include cyberspace as a realm in which viable romantic love can be achieved. Online social networks have increased the number of people we are in touch with, but cannot sustain the profundity of a traditional friendship. Hence, it is unclear whether they reduce loneliness.

11

Love in Later Life

One is never too old to yearn.
ITALIAN PROVERB

Mature calmness is exciting. I am so thrilled by the calmness and acceptance of my older lovers who focus on the moment without calculating future prospect.
A MAN IN HIS THIRTIES WHO LOVES DATING WOMEN
IN THEIR FIFTIES

At this bend in the road toward profound love, the issue of time takes center stage as we examine mature love in old age and in times of illness. The belief has been that, along with a decay in physical and mental capacities, happiness and romantic love decline with age. We now know better. Older people, it turns out, are often happier and more satisfied with their lives and their marriages than younger people are. Perhaps when we realize that our years are numbered, we change our perspective and focus on positive present experiences, which are more likely to consist of peacefulness and serenity rather than excitement and joy. Sonja Lyubomirsky summarizes these findings, reporting that for most people the best years are in the second half of life.[1] Needless to say, there is a great deal of diversity here as well, and some older people become depressed and afraid of death. This chapter also discusses other phenomena characteristic of love in old age, specifically love after the death of a spouse and love when one spouse suffers from dementia.

Maturity and Love

It strikes me that we are "behaving" (actually we are *not* behaving) like teenagers. Can't we at least try to behave *as if* we were mature adults?
A MARRIED MAN TO HIS MARRIED LOVER

Maturity seems to run counter to novelty and excitement. No wonder young people are considered more emotional than older people. This of course does not mean that exciting positive as well as negative experiences do not occur at all ages. Intense emotions are typically elicited in the midst of unfinished business and hence are mainly concerned with the future; maturity is focused on the present and requires satisfaction with your current lot. Intense emotions are generated by change, while maturity involves growing accustomed to changes and perceiving them as less significant. Although at all ages we enjoy both familiarity and novelty, the relative weight of familiarity increases in maturity. As we've discussed, the happiness associated with intense love is excitement; the happiness associated with profound mature love is peacefulness (calmness) and serenity. Similar findings indicate that the transition from youth to older age includes a shift in close social relations, involving a change of emphasis from quantity to quality. It has been suggested that the main developmental task for younger couples is managing conflicts, while for older couples it is maintaining mutual support.[2]

People who behave in an immature manner are exceedingly attractive: they are very lively, joyful, and youthful, living in the moment as if there is no tomorrow. However, like children, they are often inconsistent and unstable, making you wonder whether they will love you tomorrow after meeting another exciting person enabling them to fully embrace romantic life from another perspective.

Romantic compromises express a kind of maturity. As in maturity, compromises reflect an acceptance of our limitations and current situation. However, unlike maturity, the acceptance in compromises is mainly a behavioral acceptance rather than an attitudinal one. So long as the situation is still regarded as a compromise, deep down the individual does not actually accept it. The moment people wholeheartedly accept a compromise, it stops being a compromise. Like habituation, maturity and compromise often reduce desire and thus can be deadly to romantic relationships. Maturity lessens both positive and negative emotional experiences, while compromises can reduce positive experiences and increase negative ones. In maturity and compromises, expectations are reduced, though not eliminated, and the desired object is often replaced by the possible and the reasonable. Mature love is often not what passionate romantic love is all about. Hence, many people say that they never want to become mature, because settling for what is possible while ignoring the desirable can be a sign of a decline in enthusiasm and spontaneity. However, this is precisely what people do when they compromise.

We want children to mature and learn to value long-term considerations, while we want older adults to worry less about long-term threats and to give greater expression to their emotions. We do not want to lose our positive child-like aspects. We want to be optimistic and sincere and to love passionately. We want to adore each other despite our obvious flaws. We want to understand each other well, but at the same time we would like our views of each other to be somewhat rosy so that we can harbor some positive illusions.

We want to maintain the buoyancy, naturalness, and ardor that we associate with children, while being mature adults who stand by each other through the pain that inevitably arises during long-term romantic relationships. We want to overcome problems, not so much by changing each other but by adapting to each other.

Love in Old Age

This is the first time that I am getting old. I have no experience in being old.

NAOMI POLANI

Love is the word used to label the sexual excitement of the young, the habituation of the middle-aged, and the mutual dependence of the old.

JOHN CIARDI

A common view considers old people to be incapable of experiencing strong love, as their sexual desire and physical abilities are expected to have declined with age. This is a simplistic and distorted idea. It is often the case that love in old age is deeper than love at a young age.

Carstensen informs us that although chronological age is an excellent (albeit imperfect) predictor of cognitive abilities and behavior, it is a poorer predictor in later age. An additional temporal aspect that becomes more important than the time since our birth is the subjective sense of our remaining time until death. The temporal extent of our horizons plays a key role in motivation. Carstensen argues that as people age and increasingly experience time as finite and their horizons as being gradually narrowed, they change their priorities. For example, they attach less importance to goals that expand their horizons and greater importance to goals from which they derive present emotional meaning. When time is seen as short, we tend to focus on short-term goals. Older people have smaller social networks, are less drawn to novelty than younger people, and reduce their spheres of interest. Nevertheless, they appear as happy as (if not happier than) younger people. This makes sense, as in a situation of decreasing horizons, people prioritize deepening existing relationships and developing expertise in already satisfying areas of life.[3]

Carstensen notes a preference for emotionally positive information over emotionally negative information in older adults' memories. This, she contends, is particularly intriguing because it has long been known that younger people find negative information more attention-grabbing and memorable than positive information. In contrast, older people process negative information less deeply than they do positive information, and at the very early stages of processing, older adults also engage in less encoding of negative material. Carstensen concludes that when people, young or old, see time as finite, they attach greater importance to emotional meaning and satisfaction from life and invest fewer resources in gathering information and expanding horizons. Thus, although their social networks grow smaller, older adults grow more satisfied.[4]

Elderly couples indeed more readily take the attitude of being happy with their lot. Consider the following confession of a single mother in her fifties: "I am looking for perfection and I have been mistaken in my choices. I turn down opportunities to be with men because I judge these men as far from perfect. As I get older, I seem to be softening, but I also seem to be getting clearer on what I like and want. I don't want superficiality—but for the first time in my life, I am considering having sex with someone I don't see as partner material!" An apparent exception to shrinking horizons in older ages is the benefit and joy derived from grandchildren that in part come from the expanding new horizons that grandchildren both provide and represent. Many grandparents talk about experiencing a "new lease on life" with their grandkids, and even observe, as the old saying goes, that "if I had known grandchildren were this much fun, I would have had them first!"

We have supporting evidence for these anecdotal comments. Older individuals often experience their spouses as affectionate both when disagreeing and when performing joint tasks, and they report high marital satisfaction. Older married couples have fewer marital conflicts than their younger counterparts do, although they report that erotic bonds are less central in their lives. Companionate love, which is based on friendship, appears to be the cardinal feature of their interactions. Intimate relationships in old age are largely harmonious and satisfying.[5]

Romantic compromises become less of an issue as we age. Over time, people become used to their spouse's negative traits. They learn to live with them, while minimizing their negative impact. When we realize that our time is running out and that our alternatives are decreasing, we are more likely to accept our limitations and not feel compromised by not pursuing an attractive option. Moreover, as older people are more dependent on each other, the marital chains tend to turn into helping hands. Despite feeling as much negativity as younger people, older individuals may be more resilient in the face of tensions in their closest relationships. Older adults are less likely to argue and often let issues go. They are better able to place conflict in perspective and to think that it is not worth fighting over issues.[6]

It seems that in old age, when cognitive and physical capacities tend to decline, the ability to be satisfied with one's own lot increases; this reduces marital conflicts as well as the experience of romantic compromise. Older people are more likely to adopt the constructive attitude of making the most of what they already (or still) have. Their concern is not with having more, but with losing less.

Love after Death

Broken crayons still color.
SHELLEY HITZ

While most of us have had romantic predicaments, those of widows and widowers seem particularly poignant. Should they actively search for another lover? And if they find another lover while still loving their late spouse, how can these two loves coexist in their hearts? Is loving again worth the effort of having to adjust to another person? And what is the proper time to fall in love again? (In what follows, when I refer to widows, I mean it to include widowers' experiences too.)

The End of Love and Death

For many people, romantic love forms an essential aspect of their lives; without love, life may seem worthless. Romantic love is a central expression of a meaningful and flourishing life. Without it, people can feel that an important part of them is dead. The lover is perceived as the sunshine in their life, and for many, without such sunshine, decay and death are all around. Even during one of the darkest periods of history, the Holocaust, people fell in love despite the risks they had to take to express it. People did not relinquish love, and love even enabled some of them to survive the horrors of the death camps.

Love and death are unlikely partners. Romantic breakups, for example, are often described as a kind of death. In the words of Dusty Springfield, after such a breakup, "Love seems dead and so unreal, all that's left is loneliness, there's nothing left to feel." Personal relationships without love are also often associated with death. We speak about "dead marriages," "cold husbands," and "frigid wives." People within a dull relationship often consider their situation to be a kind of death, and having an affair is described as living again. Thus, a married woman, having her first affair after twenty years, describes her relationship with her husband as being that of roommate. While having the affair, she said, "I felt like I had awoken from a coma. I felt connected to life and the people in it. I felt youthful, confident, and brave."

Since love is perceived to be vital to life, the end of love can cause some people to wish to end their lives as well or to kill others for love. In the name of love, there are men who kill their partners and commit suicide when the latter intend to leave them.[7]

Despite the crucial role of love in human flourishing, there are people who give up the search for it, believing that they will never find what they seek. These individuals say that they would not reject profound love if it found its way to them, but that they will not actively pursue it. This attitude is understandable—after all, love is not all you need in life—though people are often much happier with love.

A Widow's New Romantic Situation

Is the human heart large enough to hold more than one romantic love? This is entirely possible—both loving one person after another and having two lovers at the same time. Let's think for a moment of the complicated case of widows' love. Their love for two people is particularly complex, given the continuing impact of bereavement, even years after the death occurs. Their bond to the deceased can remain a personal defining force. They face the double challenge of loving two people at the same time and a huge practical change: a relationship with a current companion who provides active support and love and with the memory of someone who is no longer alive and cannot be active in their life.

According to romantic ideology, profound love should last forever. The end of love is a sign that it was superficial in the first place. In fact, however, love *can* end for reasons connected to different circumstances, and such changes do not necessarily indicate that the love was superficial. Profound love is less likely to perish, but it can nevertheless. Hence, there is no reason to assume that one's heart is not big enough to include several genuine loves during a single lifetime.

The death of a spouse and the end of love dovetail in different ways. But widowhood is unique. Whether a relationship is average, as most relationships are, or very good or very bad, the ending of any personal relationship changes one's circumstances. In most cases of widowhood, any positive attitude toward the spouse is enhanced. This is due both to the tendency to idealize the past and to our sense of propriety in not speaking ill of the dead. Although the late spouse is physically absent, the widow's love for him can remain—and even grow.

The newly widowed confront different situations when contemplating love. Here I will discuss two situations: (1) adapting to a new love while still loving the late spouse, and (2) falling in love with another person almost immediately.

Adapting to a New Lover

A widow's refusal of a lover is seldom so explicit as to exclude hope.
SAMUEL RICHARDSON

Falling in love again after losing a spouse is not the same as having a new love affair after a previous one has ended. This is especially so if, at the time of the spouse's death, both partners shared a profound love. In this case, the survivor's love does not die. Although a new love might develop, from a psychological viewpoint, the widow will now love two people at the same time. Her experience eloquently expresses the nonexclusive nature of love.

Importantly, love is a shape-changer. Seeking the same love with another partner can be devastating, as no two people are identical. In a sense, the new lover can bring a bereaved partner back to life. One widow told the friend who ignited in her the desire to make love again: "Thank you for bringing me back to life."

The widow faces the challenge of entering a new and meaningful romantic relationship without forgetting or negating the old one. Ofri Bar-Nadav and Simon Rubin compare the issues facing bereaved and nonbereaved women when they enter new relationships after a long-term one has ended. The bereaved experienced themselves as having changed more, but the nonbereaved reported the changes they experienced as more positive. The growth experienced by the nonbereaved at this stage of life is likely to be less conflicted, and while the bereaved experience such growth, it lags behind that of their counterparts. Bar-Nadav and Rubin argue that in the wake of loss and its aftermath, widows feel greater hesitancy than their peers do about engaging in intimacy with new partners. These concerns about intimacy arise from fears of further loss, of opening themselves up to new relationships, and of lack of fidelity to the deceased spouse.[8]

Our minds work wonders in these situations. While the deceased spouse ceases to disappoint and irritate us, the new (and very much alive) partner continues to do so, reminding us of the richness and challenge of ongoing living relationships. Although love for the deceased spouse might increase as time goes by, it may be less of a preoccupation, easing adaptation to the new relationship. A new loving relationship requires both letting go of and holding on to the previous relationship, creating a new equilibrium.[9]

Finding the right partner and learning to live with them can take a lot of time and effort. Some people reach an age at which they doubt whether it is worth the effort, especially when the memory of their late spouse remains ever present as the new relationship develops.

How Soon Should Widows Fall in Love Again?

Even if all the above obstacles to being with a new lover are resolved, the widow still faces a whole set of dilemmas. These include the proper period for grieving, whether and when to take off their wedding ring, when to begin dating, when to give away the late partner's belongings, how to dress for various occasions, how often to talk about the past, and what loving gestures toward the new lover can be shown in public. As widows tend to be judged critically, sensitivity, careful pacing, and moderation are in order. A widow dating a married man will be subject to greater criticism than a divorced or single woman—after all, she should know better what it is to lose a spouse. It seems that, like Julius Caesar's wife, widows are expected to be "above suspicion."

Consider the following true story. A widow who was dating a widower observed that her beau continued to wear his wedding ring—he had not taken it off when his wife died. In due time, the two became engaged and started to plan their wedding. The wedding ring remained on the widower's finger. Finally, just as the bride-to-be was choosing her new wedding band, her intended turned to her and said: "Would it be okay with you if I wore two wedding rings?" This poignant question (answered, incidentally, in the negative) exposes a deep dilemma—profound love cannot be exclusive in all its aspects. There are things that we cannot, and should not, erase from our partner's heart.

And now we come to a particularly contested point: the waiting period before dating. Different cultures have different norms: in some traditions, people wait at least a year; in others, it can be longer or shorter. Michelle Heidstra's experience is telling. Only four weeks after the death of her husband, Jon, she embarked on a new love affair with his best friend, Adrian, a pallbearer at the funeral. Lost in her grief, she found herself drawn to the man who could comfort her. Adrian was very supportive of both her and her infant. At the end of a day spent with a group of her husband's friends, including Adrian, Michelle found herself in his house. "We were both in turmoil and we needed each other. We made love," says Michelle. "We couldn't help ourselves. It seemed so right." It is, she says, exactly what Jon would have wanted. She was not even embarrassed to tell her friends about it. Michelle understands those who criticized her, but says, "How can you make rules about people's emotions? We all love and grieve differently. I have never stopped grieving for Jon. But that doesn't rule out a new love." After a year of seeing each other, they felt that the relationship was getting too serious too quickly, and they took a break. A year later, they started dating again. This time the pace was slower, and they moved in together only six months later. They are now engaged to be married.

Michelle says, "Blame me if you like, but grief hits people in different ways and I have no regrets."[10]

Such stories are far from rare; many people fall in love with their late partner's best friend within a short time after the partner's death. This can be a reasonable response to intense loss, when a supportive friend is the most natural person in the world to be with. The terrible grief can be shared.

To sum up, widows must manage a unique form of romantic breakup, which involves a final physical separation but not a psychological one. The breakup caused by the spouse's death is unwelcome and irreversible, and the surviving partner might still be in love with her late spouse. Different people do different things under such circumstances. Although it is often better to find a new lover than to give up and never search for a new love, this option is not always available. It is possible to fall in love again, but new loving relationships are always well populated: the deceased partner is always in the background.

Love and Dementia

Love is an act of endless forgiveness, a tender look which becomes a habit.
PETER USTINOV

What is the meaning of love in relationships between couples in which one partner has dementia? This is a question for which the role of time in love is highly relevant, since one of the partners has virtually lost a sense of the past. In such situations, the healthy spouse's sense of the past is a major factor in maintaining love.

In old age, the reduced ability to share various activities presents a challenge to the dialogue model, which is based on spouses' engagement in joint activities and thus creating a meaningful *we*. Dementia, which severely damages the ability to socialize, and especially the capacity to converse and share interests with others, magnifies this problem.

Orit Shavit and colleagues present a nuanced picture of the romantic attitudes of individuals whose spouses are living with Alzheimer's disease. They identify five major types of relationship development following the emergence of the disease: love died, love became weaker, love did not change, love was enhanced, and the healthy spouse fell in love again. These types are also common among the loving relationships of other couples in old age. Participants described their love in a compassionate manner and in the context of their daily routines of caring. Most spouses stated that their intimacy gained a new meaning; they reported greater intimacy with their spouses living with the disease. It seems that the increased romantic intimacy experienced by some is related to an enhanced component of care.[11]

On the face of it, the dialogue approach would seem to have trouble explaining love in relation to dementia, in which the partners' interactions decline in quantity and quality. It is the care model, instead, that leaps to mind as most appropriate. Although in old age and with dementia the shared time and activities are more limited and less diverse, they can still be part of love and intimacy. Thus, even if sick people cannot contribute to the loving relation as much as they did before, their loving relation is the continuation of what was before. This is compatible with the dialogue model.

Concluding Remarks

Romantic horizons indeed shrink at an older age; certainly, there are fewer possibilities numerically and emotionally. This makes many people too willing to stay in their comfort zone and not engage in a relationship or expect a relationship to just happen to them without doing anything.

HARA ESTROFF MARANO

Extramarital affairs express the determined refusal to grow older gracefully.

CATHERINE HAKIM

Later life is a patchwork for profound love—it presents some of the best circumstances for it as well as some of its greatest obstacles. Since time nurtures profundity, the deepest point of connection for romantic partners in healthy relationships is sometimes after they have accumulated decades of experiences that they can build upon together in later life. After the loss of a partner in old age, the severing of this bond can be extremely difficult to deal with. It can be tempting to give up on love completely after the death of one's lover. But, as love is so vital to flourishing and well-being, it is important to find a suitable new relationship, though the type and timing of such a relationship differs from person to person.

When one partner passes away and the other is left single, often for the first time in nearly a lifetime, there are unique challenges in achieving new love. Not only do widows tend to idealize their deceased partner, but their profound love might very well be everlasting, so dealing with mixed emotions when establishing new love becomes even more complex. Questions of whether to try to forget or to replace the previous partner further complicate the beginning of a new relationship.

Adding to the hurdles for love in old age, dementia presents a unique set of issues and questions, as the disease often unpredictably influences a crucial aspect of the romantic connection—profound meaningful interactions and experiences, including communication, sex, caring, friendship, reciprocity, and love. While individual experiences differ widely, dementia does consistently mark a change in the way that partners relate to each other and interact. This is not a barrier to profound, though limited, love, but it requires significant adjustments to the new type of relationship.

Emotional experiences in later life are likely to be marked by calmness rather than excitement. As both calmness and excitement are important in a romantic relationship, the issue is not one of either/or, but of choice of focus.

Obstacles to love are scattered throughout the life course. Old age can rebalance partners' ability to engage constructively in the relationship. When dementia figures into the equation, the maintenance of love calls for great sacrifice. Serious consideration must be given to the impact of such sacrifice on the relationship and one's personal flourishing. This is how we honor the wholeness necessary to sustain profound, romantic relationships.

12

Greater Diversity and Flexibility

The measure of intelligence is the ability to change.
ALBERT EINSTEIN

I love my husband and do not intend to leave him for my lover. However, my husband is not easy to live with—he is grumpy and tries to control me. My wonderful time with my lover helps me cope with the situation I have made at home. It gives me back my self-confidence. Without my lover, I would divorce my husband immediately.
A MARRIED WOMAN

Overcoming difficulties on the road to enduring profound love is one aspect of the complex task that lovers face today; another is making romantic norms, and in particular monogamous ones, more flexible. I begin by examining the attitudes of singles, which genuinely express what people want, while not having to take account of the chains of their present situation. Most of them keep the traditional value of an enduring, profound loving relationship, while still yearning for brief and diverse sexual interactions. Then the nature and feasibility of polyamory are discussed, and the issue of whether you can be happy with your partner's romantic affair is examined.

What Do Singles Really Want?

Marriage is like a cage; one sees the birds outside desperate to get in, and those inside equally desperate to get out.
MICHEL DE MONTAIGNE

Many married people envy singles for their greater romantic freedom in conducting casual relationships. Do singles envy married people for their enduring serious relationships? Match Eighth Annual Study on U.S. Single Population (2018), supervised by Helen Fisher, indicates surprising trends.

Seeking Serious Relationships

I have a rule, and that is to never look at somebody's face while we're having sex; because, number one, what if I know the guy?
LAURA KIGHTLINGER

Conducting a serious romantic relationship that includes the intention to stay together for a long time implies giving up much of your romantic freedom for the sake of your significant profound relationship. Strikingly, however, the Match survey indicates that 69 percent of today's singles are looking for something serious.

According to the survey, American singles use three major paths for fulfilling this wish for seriousness: hanging out, friends with benefits, and an official first date. All three paths require an investment of time and are governed by rules that send messages about their differing degrees of seriousness.

In *hanging out*, people do not engage in sex and have not gone out on an official first date. Although this type of relationship has the lowest degree of seriousness, it still has some rules of behavior that indicate some level of seriousness. Thus, many singles believe that a wider array of behaviors are appropriate when hanging out than when on an official first date, including asking out on the day of the meeting, splitting the bill, and moving slowly toward physical intimacy.

Friendship with benefits is more serious, and indeed, almost half of the people in such relationships have turned it into a committed relationship. Moreover, most participants in the survey who engaged in this kind of relationship think that the friendship part is more significant than the sexual benefits.

The experience of a *formal first date* has become increasingly popular (almost half of the singles surveyed had gone on such a date) and significant. The greater significance is expressed in asking someone out two to three days in advance, having the first date at a nice restaurant (rather than in a fast food place), and having a perfect ending, such as a peck on the cheek or kissing.

Seeking Diverse, Brief Sexual Interactions

I thought I was promiscuous, but it turns out I was just thorough.
RUSSELL BRAND

Alongside their search for serious romantic relationships, singles are experiencing diverse, brief types of superficial, sexual relationships. Thus, many singles have dated multiple people simultaneously—more women than men. Moreover, most heterosexual singles would be open to a threesome, and one in four singles would have sex with a robot, yet nearly half of singles would consider it cheating if their partner had sex with a robot.

In a fascinating finding, both single women and men reported having their best sex in their midsixties. This suggests that good sex is not mainly based on superficial novelty, as is often the case at a young age, but requires some profound familiarity. This is not to imply, however, that the best sex in a committed relationship with the same partner is best at an older age. On the contrary, the aforementioned "honeymoon-as-ceiling effect" indicates that marital quality rarely increases beyond its initial point of marriage, or prior to it.[1]

According to the Match survey, among those involved in a friendship-with-benefits relationship, most singles believe that one must disclose all other current sexual partners. The greater openness about romantic flexibility stems from the greater acceptance in society of such flexibility, as well as from the fact that such flexibility is expressed in many frequent and various types of experiences that can no longer be hidden.

What Do Singles Really Want?

I am too intelligent, too demanding, and too resourceful for anyone to be able to take charge of me entirely. No one knows me or loves me completely. I have only myself.
SIMONE DE BEAUVOIR

The huge number of alluring options in the current romantic environment presents challenges for everyone—but particularly for singles. To an outside observer, this environment is paradise, the wet dream of all lovers: having whatever you want, whenever you want it. A closer look, however, reveals that something is rotten in the state of romance. Flexibility without constraints and change without stability are the makings of many difficulties.

Singles really want to combine profundity with sexual diversity. They want to have it both ways—a serious, meaningful relationship, as well as diverse sexual encounters. Is this possible? In our current society, it is not easy to achieve. It contradicts the accepted norms that separate profoundness from sexual diversity—most people feel the two are incompatible and should not be sought at the same time. You first have the sexual diversity. You eat as much as you can from the sexual meal, then stop it, and turn to the phase of a serious relationship. This route is rather problematic, as most people want both of these phases to continue. They want to be married, but not dead; they do not want merely to breathe, but to be alive.

Current singles (and others) realize the intricacy of their conflicting desires. On the one hand, most of them retain the old dream of having a serious, profound relationship that will last for a long time. To achieve it, they develop different tactics to get to know others better through various interactions over time. On the other hand, singles also like brief and diverse sexual interactions, such as dating more than one person at a time, having a threesome, and for some even having sex with a robot.

Relaxing Monogamous Values

I see my extramarital affairs as a different nutrition. Just as I need extra minerals because I'm a mature woman, I need the affair because I am still beautiful and horny.
Calcium for my bones and chrome and zinc . . . all of these are not provided in my
regular diet, and so I need to take some additives with my food. My extramarital affairs
are additives for my health, regardless of my activities with my husband.

A   M A R R I E D   W O M A N

The Love Bird is 100% faithful to his mate, as long as they are locked together in the
same cage.

W I L L   C U P P Y

Monogamy—that is, the practice of being married to one person at a time, and
having a sexual relationship only with this person—is often regarded as the best
road for enduring romantic love. A central assumption of traditional monogamy
is that your partner should fulfill your entire romantic and, in particular, sexual
needs. Nonmonogamous relationships can be consensual and nonconsensual.
Nonconsensual nonmonogamy involves the prevailing practices of sexual infidelity. Two major types of consensual nonmonogamy are open sexual relationships (where a primary couple pursues outside, mainly sexual, relationships), and
polyamory (in which people maintain multiple loving or committed relationships). The first type also includes swinging (in which a couple may have other
sexual partners). The differences between these types are not always clear, and in
any case, we speak here about a continuum of breaching monogamous values.

The prevalence of flexible sexual practices indicates that the way of coping with the issue of romantic or sexual exclusivity is not to stage an all-or-
nothing holy war against them, but to look for ways to make romantic exclusivity more flexible, but still limited. A major feature of such flexibility is
abandoning the expectation that marriage will fulfill all your needs.

Couples can relax strict exclusivity by agreeing to various relationship
rules that allow a more flexible notion of fidelity, albeit within certain boundaries. Such an agreement can include rules such as the "doesn't count" rule,
which allows for oral sex, one-off sex, out-of-town sex, phone sex, and even
mental infidelity. Other similar rules are the "must-confess-all" rule; the
"don't know, don't care" rule; as well as "anything goes—except love," "sex and
nothing more," "no couple-like behavior outside the bedroom," and "anything
above the waist isn't cheating."[2] Within such agreements, "coloring outside
the lines" is not always a grave violation of normative behavior.

More and more, society is adapting its norms to cope with the greater
diversity and flexibility of actual romantic behavior. Many couples now allow each other greater freedom in their personal romantic relationships with

others. Certainly, many societies continue to disapprove of extramarital sex. Yet there is an increasing tendency to mildly criticize, rather than condemn or ostracize, the transgressor for such activity. Indeed, extramarital affairs are often described in terms that are more neutral; instead of highly negative terms such as "adultery" and "betrayal," some people use the term "parallel relationship."

A different tack toward more flexible types of romantic exclusivity would be to promote the value of uniqueness over that of exclusivity. Exclusiveness is characterized in negative terms that establish rigid boundaries, whereas uniqueness is characterized in positive terms that celebrate an ideal. The shift in emphasis from exclusivity to uniqueness is often a shift from a superficial "preventing" decree to a profound "promoting" value. It reflects the shift from basing love on the negative requirement of controlling the beloved's behavior to the positive feature of seeing the unique value of the beloved. It seems that the longevity of a romantic relationship can profit more from the latter attitude. While romantic love involves both features, uniqueness is much more important.[3]

Until rather recently, the sexual realm was limited (mainly for women) to marriage. Today, sex is considered an acceptable part of casual relationships before and after marriage. The only stronghold that the sexual revolution has failed to destroy is the prohibition against married people having sex with people other than their spouses. Married people seem to be allowed to do almost anything with other people—except engage in sexual activity. Will married people be allowed to join the party sometime in the future, and satisfy their sexual needs outside of their committed framework? Do the boundaries of marriage reflect profound moral or psychological boundaries, or are they rather, as George Bernard Shaw colorfully put it, "the Trade Unionism of the married"? Not unlike other trade unions, that of the married couple attempts to stay in business by erecting rigid boundaries. At the end of the day, do such boundaries make people happy? In Shaw's ironic formulation, "If the prisoner is happy, why lock him in? If he is not, why pretend that he is?"[4]

Taking a perhaps provocative tack, Hakim argues that an enduring marriage and extramarital affairs are the best formula for happiness. Attributing the high divorce rates in England to the "unforgiving, Puritan Anglo-Saxon" attitude to adultery, she advocates the French (and to a lesser extent, the Italian and Japanese) tradition, which considers an extramarital affair as a parallel relationship that, when conducted discreetly, has its own value. Hakim believes that a successful affair can make both parties happier, without hurting anyone. While the Anglo-Saxon tradition leads to serial monogamy and multiple divorces, in the French tradition affairs are simply ignored, and marriages last longer. Hakim praises the French tradition, in which marriage is a more flexible relationship and both spouses find friends and lovers outside marriage. This tradition rejects the common assumption that spouses must fulfill all of each other's needs, all of the time, exclusively. However, in order to avoid embarrassment, the affairs should be "conducted with great discretion."[5]

I do not think that the prohibition of affairs is just an external and socially dependent issue, as it closely relates to the partial and personal nature of emotions. However, the strength of this prohibition is being increasingly diminished in a more flexible social environment.

Loving Two People at the Same Time: Polyamory

One woman is too much for me—and two are far too few.

WOLF BIERMANN

I feel a polyamorous relationship fits the biopsychosocial needs of many! In my situation, my spouse can hardly sexually satisfy me, but my lover satisfies me immensely. If I could have both it would be ideal. I deeply care about my lover as a person, and I love my husband.

A MARRIED WOMAN

Monogamous romantic relationships involve a trade-off between the romantic intensity prompted by variety, on one hand, and the romantic profundity of a connection with one person, on the other. This trade-off rests on the premise that increasing the one inevitably decreases the other. Is this premise correct? Can nonmonogamous relationships offer *both* romantic intensity and romantic profundity?[6]

Consensual Nonmonogamy

The chain of wedlock is so heavy that it takes two to carry it—and sometimes three.

HERACLITUS

It takes a loose rein to keep a marriage tight.

JOHN STEVENSON

Consensual nonmonogamy comes in different flavors. Open sexual marriages and polyamory are two major such types, and each has many variations on its main theme. Both relationships, and their various variations, are open, though in different ways. Open sexual relation focuses on sex; polyamory is more comprehensive and involves romantic needs as well. In open sexual marriages, one or both partners seek sexual experiences outside the relationship, while in polyamory one or both partners desire an additional intimate, loving relation, which also includes sexual interactions. Consensual nonmonogamy involves adultery—namely, sex between a married person and someone who is not their husband or wife—but infidelity, which is the action of being unfaithful to a spouse or another sexual partner, is typically not part of it.

In open sexual relationships, it is easy to see that there is a primary and a secondary relation. In polyamory, such a relational hierarchy often exists, though it is less clear. The major concern in open sexual relationships is having sexual relations with those who are not the primary partner; in polyamory, it is bringing within the primary relationship an additional loving relation. The degree of involvement in the life of each partner is different. Thus, a prevailing form of open sexual marriage is swinging, in which the couple has other sexual partners, and their interactions often happen at social events designed for this purpose. In some forms of polyamory, the secondary relationship of each partner is separated, and in other forms, there are shared activities of all those involved.

In open sexual marriages, the basic attitude is that marriages are essentially fine—the most acute problem is declining sexual desire. This is taken care of by adding new sexual partners. The basic attitude in polyamory is more radical. While it is agreed that declining sexual desire is a problem, it is assumed to be part of a larger problem associated with the assumption that one person can fulfill our entire romantic (and other significant) needs. Hence, we cannot be satisfied with "merely" adding one or a few sexual partners; we need to add (at least) another romantic partner, who can also satisfy the sexual needs. This is a more drastic change of monogamous marriages.

The boundaries between open marriages and polyamory are blurred. In some polyamorous arrangements, one partner (or both) has more than one lover, and lovers are frequently replaced. There are also open sexual marriages in which the relation with the sexual partner lasts for months or even years. In light of the greater depth in polyamory, polyamorous people, and particularly polyamorous women, can feel rather insulted when they are seen as someone who is ready to sleep with every man who comes their way. As they see it, they only sleep with men they fall in love with—although it seems that they fall in love faster as they allow themselves to fall in love in circumstances that others would not. Moreover, since secondary relations require fewer deeds and commitments than primary ones, more people are suitable as secondary partners. Furthermore, polyamorous women usually have a more positive attitude toward sex.

Polyamory and Complexity

My lover has provided me with a profound love and unique sexual satisfaction that I have never experienced before. I hope, however, that my loving relations with my husband, with whom I raise our two children, will continue to flourish for many years.

A POLYAMOROUS MARRIED WOMAN

I don't want to own her, but I can't let her have it both ways. Three is one too many of us, she leaves with me or stays with him.

RUPERT HOLMES

I have emphasized the importance of complexity for the endurance and profundity of romantic relationships. Polyamory is more complex than monogamy in the senses we have discussed: diversity, ambivalence, and behavioral complexity. Thus, having multiple romantic relationships with different people yields more emotions (emodiversity), leads to a greater likelihood of emotional conflict stemming from divergent interests (ambivalence), and requires extensive practical strategies (behavioral complexity).[7]

It seems that instead of working hard to defuse, reduce, or redirect romantic attitudes and sexual desire for multiple people, as is the case in a monogamous framework, polyamorous people look to accommodate these attitudes and desires within their relationships. Polyamory can be perceived as complementing traditional romantic relationships, using a kind of outsourcing for some of your spouse's needs. However, it rejects the common romantic ideal that one person can fulfill all your romantic needs.

Polyamory replaces a flat notion of (predominantly sexual) fidelity with complex notions of emotional openness, sincerity, and explicitness as a romantic norm, and the ongoing manifestations of tenderness. Whereas monogamous relationships often resemble the rigid forms of an implicit contract, which are subsequently *defended* against encroaching sexual or romantic attitudes, polyamorous relationships can be understood as ongoing processes of negotiation and renegotiation aimed at *embracing* such feelings.

A prevailing way of dealing with romantic complexity in polyamory is indeed adopting the primary-secondary model. The difference between primary and secondary relationships refers to issues such as time spent together, physical cohabitation, child rearing, and finance. The secondary relation, which is more novel, often enjoys greater romantic intensity. The primary partner has more rights and obligations than those of the secondary one in these aspects— this is mainly due to the connection of the primary partner to the children. In a sense, the primary partner has more shares in the business. The secondary partner, who can be a primary partner in another relation, has the right to be treated with respect and attentiveness, though when conflicts arise, the primary partner usually has first priority, yet not an absolute one. Thus, it is possible that over time the secondary relation would evolve into a primary (or co-primary) form, and sometimes the primary-secondary is not present, or at least is unclear.

Another type of relation can be added: a tertiary type referring to mere sexual partners, such as one-night stands. The commitments and rights of such sexual partners are very minor, if they exist at all, and hence in some cases of polyamory one often does not have to report about them to one's primary or secondary partners. A polyamorous married woman said that she did not have a tertiary lover for almost a year—indicating thereby that the dry season is indeed long.

Polyamorous relationships enhance the personal capacities and social structures required to productively confront emotional complexity. This fact, coupled with the advantages of polyamorous framework concerning romantic intensity, ensures that polyamory is well placed to cope better with hedonic adaptation over time. However, while one might agree that polyamorous people can manage the emotional complexity of their lifestyle in a way that enables them to maintain romantic intensity, can such relationships be romantically profound?

Spreading Love Too Thin or Expanding
the Loving Heart

Thousands of candles can be lit from a single candle, and the life of the candle will not be shortened. *Happiness* is never reduced by being shared.
BUDDHA

The heart is not like a box that gets filled up; it expands in size the more you love.
SAMANTHA, in the movie *Her*

Ten men waiting for me at the door? Send one of them home, I'm tired.
MAE WEST

A major criticism of polyamory is that of spreading love too thin. In reply, one might compare love to happiness, which, as Buddha said, "is never reduced by being shared." In this sense, the heart can expand when you love more. Is spreading love around like spreading limited butter or like expanding happiness? The first option assumes a resources competition, or a contrast model, which essentially involves a zero-sum game, whereas the second option presupposes an expanding, additive resources model. It seems that both options have a valid point.

Does loving two (or more) people necessarily mean loving each of them "more thinly"? This would be the case, if love, like butter, is fixed in quantity—then, spreading your love between two lovers would inevitably reduce the amount each of them gets. Love requires lots of investment: of time, effort, financial resources, and emotional availability. All of these are limited, and some, such as time, are also fixed in quantity. In this sense, love is like butter; you cannot spread it too thin and expect to gain romantic profundity, which requires for its development time and other limited resources. Indeed, when thinking about loving two people at the same time, we typically assume shallowness: spreading your love over two lovers should result in less love to each. In this situation, the difficulty is not that we have too little butter or too little love, but that we have too much bread or too many lovers.

Here's where things get interesting. Love is not an entity with a fixed energy but a capacity that, when used, generates increasingly positive energy—in the sense of "using it or losing it." Hence, there is no point asking someone (as various love songs do) to save her love for the asking person by not using it. Although we may speak about a certain "saturation" of sexual desire, in the sense that we just do not want to (and actually cannot) have sex now, we can hardly speak about a "saturation" of love, in the sense that we cannot love now.

The main way to deal with the idea of decreasing love is to argue that unlike butter, romantic energy is not fixed in quantity but has the potential to grow. This is the case of shared happiness—a single candle can light thousands of wicks.

A few basic psychological capacities might be involved in expanding the heart: (1) the broadening capacity of positive emotions, (2) the expanding nature of the self, and (3) the ability to be generous.

In her influential broaden-and-build theory, Barbara Fredrickson claims that *positive emotions* such as happiness and love *broaden* people's momentary thought-action repertoire, which in turn serves to build their enduring personal resources, ranging from physical and intellectual strengths to social and psychological capabilities. Fredrickson further argues that positive emotions do not merely signal flourishing; they also produce flourishing. Positive emotions are valuable not just as ends in themselves but also as a means to enhance psychological growth and improve our well-being over time.[8]

Another capacity facilitating the growth of the heart is *self-expansion*. The "self-expansion model" holds that we are hard-wired to expand ourselves through relationships with other people. This is because relationships enable us to incorporate the resources and perspectives of others within ourselves. Over time, and because of their interpersonal relationships, people can "expand" by internalizing perspectives and resources that were previously unavailable to them.[9]

Both the broadening capacity of positive emotions and the expanding nature of the self are highly relevant for understanding how polyamory provides a context in which one's heart can expand by participating in a few loving relations. Polyamory is a form of romantic life that is maximally self-expansive.

One can further claims that the expanded nature of love may be due to the inclusive manner of certain romantic activities. Not all meaningful romantic activities should be done in the intimacy of merely two people; some, such as talking and walking, can be done with more than one person, thereby expanding the impact of such activities to other people.

Another capacity that expands our heart is that of generosity. Loving two people can be described as a kind of romantic generosity, which, like other types of generosity, increases the flourishing of the person. Generosity is an essential positive framework for prosperous marital relationships. Extending romantic generosity from one person to two people can in principle further enhance one's good feelings while expanding the heart.

To sum up, regarding a central criticism against polyamory—namely, the charge that it spreads love too thin—it seems that, in many circumstances, this charge is unfounded. This does not imply that polyamory is unequivocally suitable for all; it has, of course, its own difficulties.

The Quality of Polyamorous Relationships

I reserve the right to love many different people at once, and to change my prince often.
ANAÏS NIN

Polyamory is worse than open sexual relations. It is a pure greed—a permission to look for a better spouse.
A MARRIED WOMAN HAVING AN AFFAIR WITH A MARRIED MAN

Does polyamory increase the quality of the romantic relation? It is hard to measure the extent and depth of romantic love as it is determined by various factors, such as romantic intensity, romantic profundity, and length of relationship. I have called the combination of these factors "romantic robustness." Our question is whether polyamory enhances romantic robustness.

Loving two people at the same time clearly increases overall *romantic intensity*, which is highly dependent on change and novelty. The greater intensity, which is most evident when meeting a new partner, is described as the "new relationship energy" stage. This stage involves a kind of infatuation with the new partner, and everything seems wonderful, as if the world is opening for them. People feel more creative and energized about their projects and personal relationships.[10]

However, such additional new energy is divided unevenly: the new partner receives the lion's share of the individual's sexual energy in a way that
would even decrease the amount the current partner has received so far. Although we have more butter, the current partner may well get less of it. Moreover, as in the case of infatuation, the duration of the stage of new relationship
energy is relatively brief, after which the issue of limited romantic energy
becomes even more acute.

The relationship between polyamory and *romantic profundity* is multifaceted, mainly because profound love requires investing a lot of quality
time. Whereas time decreases emotional intensity, time enhances emotional
profundity. Accordingly, it is natural to assume that having a few romantic
partners considerably reduces the quality time available for each. Nonetheless, polyamory increases complexity, which underlies romantic profundity.
Living in complex circumstances requires a profound understanding of the
other partners. Hence, it would be a mistake to think of polyamory and emotional profundity as mutually exclusive. Polyamorous relationships can present people with ongoing opportunities for self-expansion through romantic
engagement with more than one person. However, sometimes such quantitative expansion runs the risk of reducing the quality of the present relation.

Empirical studies confirm the above considerations. Monogamous people
reported slightly lower sexual satisfaction and lower orgasm rates than those
who are in consensual nonmonogamy. This is true concerning all types of such
nonmonogamy: polyamory, swinging, and open sexual relations. Swingers,
in particular, reported better and more frequent sex than did monogamous
people, and the difference here is not minor, but considerable. Monogamous
people did not appear to be *dissatisfied* with their sexual relationships—they
just had slightly lower levels of sexual satisfaction. To be on the safe side, we
may say that there is no substantial empirical evidence for a significant difference between the various groups. It seems that relationship structure, in
itself, is not a powerful predictor of psychological and relational well-being.
It appears that consensual nonmonogamy is not significantly of a greater or
lesser quality than monogamy.[11]

Personal freedom seems to be the jewel in the crown of polyamory, as
polyamorous people can freely choose adding another partner(s) to enlarge
and spice up their dull romantic life. This freedom, however, comes with a
price tag: limiting our freedom in managing our primary and secondary relationships, which are now part of a greater net that has its own restrictions.
Such restrictions mainly concern taking account of the secondary partners,
which were not chosen by you. Similarly, when you live in a commune, the
commune determines some aspects of your life. The trade-off here is between

greater romantic freedom and lesser freedom in running your life, which becomes less private. When the romantic connection is of lesser depth—for example, when it is limited to the sexual domain, as in the case of open sexual marriages—the restrictions on one's personal life hardly exist.

The issue of privacy is also of some concern in polyamorous relationships, where openness and sincerity are very significant. The standard view often requires complete sharing and openness, leaving little personal space for privacy. A more sensible attitude taken by polyamorous people sees the value of privacy, and complete sharing and openness is not required, especially when it may hurt one of the lovers. Thus, one does not have to report all the details of one's sexual interactions with other partners. Similarly, one does not have to tell about all of one's fights with other partners—unless such fights would hurt the other relationships as well. Some may also withhold the identity of a new lover, though revealing, for example, that this person is not someone their primary partner knows. Some would not even report brief sexual encounters, such as one-night stands. As one married polyamorous woman said, "These experiences are brief and insignificant to me; hence, there is no reason for disturbing my husband concerning them."

The Length of Polyamorous Relationships

My fantasy is to have five lovers. However, I do not think that my husband will agree, and anyway, I will not have time for having them all. I believe that three is the limit.
A POLYAMOROUS MARRIED WOMAN

We have seen that the quality of polyamorous relationships is similar to, and sometimes even slightly higher than, that of monogamous relationships. Since relation satisfaction is associated with longer relationship longevity, it would be plausible to assume that polyamorous relationships will endure at least as long as monogamous ones. Is this indeed the case?

We should distinguish between the length of primary polyamorous relationships and the length of secondary ones. It is clear that the longevity of the secondary type is significantly briefer than the average longevity of monogamous relationships, as well as that of the primary polyamorous relation.

Polyamorous people testify that longevity is of lesser value to them than the relation quality. This somewhat negative attitude toward longevity is expressed in various attitudes of polyamorous people, like expecting the relation to end at some point in the future, living for the moment, taking breakups easily, and looking around for replacements. Such attitudes can easily become self-fulfilling prophecies. If indeed less value is placed on longevity, then the members of the relationship are going to be less inclined to stay in a relationship that is not satisfying.[12]

Polyamorous relations include further features that are negatively associated with enduring relationships. Two such features are having an existential dependency on someone you have not chosen (such as the partners of your primary and secondary partners) and the increased possibility of feeling that you are second-best.[13] Other problems include managing the great intensity associated with a new partner; the potential pitfalls of "choice fatigue" when faced with many potential partners; the dangers of "compassion fatigue" in a life with competing demands; social stigma; complications in family life; reduced privacy; and resisting the allure of unworkable polyamorous ideals, such as abolishing envy and jealousy.[14] It seems, indeed, that on average the longevity of poly relationships is briefer.

The briefer temporal dimension of a secondary relationship can be measured not merely by the period the two are dating (usually assessed in terms of years), but also by the frequency and length of their actual face-to-face meetings. Thus, it is customary to restrict the number and length of the meetings, to prohibit overnight or weekend meetings, and to require that they take place at the house of a primary relationship. Although such restrictions are stricter at the beginning of the secondary relationships, they still exist later on as well.

These restrictions make it harder for the secondary relationship to develop romantic profundity and intimacy. One may say that even with these restrictions, polyamorous people get more freedom than do most monogamous people. This may be true, but the insistence on such restrictions indicates the ongoing tension, insecurity, and jealousy that are present in polyamorous relationships.

Working on Your Relationship

I love you no matter what you do, but do you have to do so much of it?
JEAN ILLSLEY CLARKE

Falling in love is easier than staying in love, and we fall out of love more slowly than we fall in it. Staying in love—or more precisely, maintaining loving relationships—requires much conscious effort. While almost everyone should make a conscious effort to maintain their relationship, not everyone has to invest equally to keep their loving relationship alive. Furthermore, as Laura Kipnis tells us, "good relationships may take work, but unfortunately, when it comes to love, trying is always trying too hard; work doesn't work. Erotically speaking, play is what works." Kipnis mentions further that no one works at adultery.[15] If love seems like work, you are clearly not in the right work-place. Nowadays, many types of work are fulfilling and have an intrinsic value. These jobs can hardly be considered "work" in the traditional sense of being unpleasant, instrumental chores, such as cleaning the house or paying bills. We certainly do not want to make love that kind of unpleasant work. However, not all romantic relationships start with love at first sight, and meaningful (often, but not always, enjoyable) work is required.

Polyamorous relations are certainly not for everyone. However, for some people, currently about 5 percent of couples in the United States, polyamory is an optimal solution. This does not devalue monogamy; it just shows that monogamous relationships are not the only game in town.

Can You Be Happy with Your Partner's Affair?

She says it's really not very flattering to her that the women who fall in love with her husband are so uncommonly second-rate.
W. SOMERSET MAUGHAM, *The Painted Veil*

"Compersion" is a recently coined term that describes your happiness from your partner's happiness with another lover. Is such an emotional experience possible, and how deep is it?

Emotional Attitudes toward the Good
Fortune of Others

Sometimes, we evaluate someone's good fortune in a way that conflicts with our evaluation, and we end up with emotions like envy and jealousy. At other times, the two evaluations meet, and we wind up with the emotions of happy-for and admiration.

The root of envy lies in seeing ourselves in an undeserved position of inferiority. Since feeling this way hurts our self-esteem, we evaluate it negatively. Similarly, jealousy, which involves the fear of losing our partner to a lover, includes a negative evaluation of the partner's good fortune, as such a loss can be a mighty blow to the lover's self-esteem.

Unlike envy and jealousy, the emotions of "happy-for" and admiration involve a positive evaluation of the other's good fortune. Some people doubt that this is possible. Jean-Jacques Rousseau, for example, argued that nobody can share anyone's happiness—even one's best friend—without envy. Only the friend's neediness, which poses no threat to us, can bring out our generous emotions.[16] This idea, which seems to reflect reality well, may not apply when someone is so close to us that we consider her success our own, and hence, it poses no threat to our self-esteem. This is known as "basking in reflected glory"; the other's glory shines on us, enhancing our own self-esteem. We often see this in parental love and in the admiration of sport fans for their winning teams.[17]

Happy-For in the Romantic Realm

The emotional attitude described in compersion is then not a new emotion, but rather a kind of "happy-for." Such happiness is said to occur in polyamorous relationships.

There is no conceptual contradiction in being romantically happy for your partner's happiness with another lover; however, there are various emotional obstacles in experiencing such happiness. Polyamorous thinkers, and others, tend to identify such obstacles with prevailing arbitrary social conventions that we can and should replace. There is no doubt that society and culture influence our emotions. However, the fact that our emotional repertoire is stable across various periods and societies indicates that emotions are more profound than mere social constructs. I believe that the widespread emotions of envy and jealousy are not arbitrary social constructs; they are, rather, profound psychological attitudes.

The circumstances in which people are more likely to experience compersion than jealousy relate to the issue of self-esteem. Consider, for instance, the following reaction of a married polyamorous woman, upon realizing that her married lover, who did not see her for a few months, came back to her country to be with her, but also had sex with another woman: "I felt like I wanted to die—a kind of paralyzed fear and choking, the feeling of a knife in my heart." This woman felt all right when her lover had affairs with other women in his country, but now his behavior is much more hurtful to her, as he had come for just a few days, and chose to divide his precious little time in her country with another lover as well. After this heartbreak, this woman and her lover agreed upon the following rules: when the lover comes to her country, she is only his and he is only hers. When they are far away from each other, each can do whatever he or she wants to do.[18] The emergence of jealousy here has nothing to do with social artifacts, but rather with emotional damage to one's self-esteem. It is such relevancy to one's self-esteem that determines whether jealousy rather than compersion will prevail.

Similar considerations are evident in the testimony of polyamorous people that jealousy, rather than compersion, is more likely to emerge in the infatuation stage. Infatuation, as one polyamorous scholar writes, "is a pretty much a monogamous stage. The person with whom we are in love fulfills all good parts of us, and there is no wish or ability to share him with others."[19] Jealousy, rather than compersion, is also more likely to emerge toward a new partner. Indeed, a new partner for one's spouse poses the greatest risk of one losing one's uniqueness. Time, which enhances profundity and decreases intensity, is crucial here. This is one reason for the rigid temporal restrictions on meeting with the secondary partner.

Differences between the two partners reduce the comparative value and protect self-esteem in a way that makes compersion more likely. Indeed, it was found that jealousy is greater when the domain of a rival's achievements is also a domain of high self-relevance to one's self-esteem. Thus, women who consider external appearance to be of great relevance to their self-esteem are more jealous if their spouses have an affair with a good-looking woman than with a wise woman.[20] Having your own affair will also decrease jealousy toward your partner's affairs, as the risk of hurting your self-esteem is less.

We can distinguish three major attitudes toward the happiness of your partner when having an affair with another person: (1) jealousy, (2) nonemotional acceptance or rejection, and (3) compersion. Jealousy seems to be most common, while compersion can be found in some specific circumstances, which are more common in polyamory.

Consider the following honest claims made by a married woman in a traditional relationship: "I will be happy for my husband if he finds a lover; I will also be pleased if my young lover finds a woman his age. However, I want my profound lover only for myself completely. For whatever reason, I think he has been my only true love." This woman cares about her husband, but since there is no romance between them, she would be happy if he had a lover as well, for it would be easier for her to carry on her affairs. In a sense, she loves her young lover, but her love is no deeper than pleasurable sexual experiences, which often bore her. Hence, she encourages this lover to find a young woman his own age. Concerning her profound (married) lover, with whom she sees prospects for a deep future relationship, she vehemently rejects sharing him with anyone else (except, of course, his wife, who is a given fact of his life); she would be quite jealous if he had an affair with another woman.

Another real dilemma that is common in polyamorous relationships concerns the location of sexual activities in secondary relationships. One woman said that her husband does not want her and her lover to have sex in their house (even if no one else is at home), claiming that it will stain his house. The wife argues that it is her house too. The wife's request to have sex with her lover in their house seems reasonable, since the alternative is for them to have sex in a hotel room, which would accentuate the transient nature of the relation, the sense of being a guest. It would be more reasonable for the husband to require that the sexual encounters not be in the bed where he and his wife have sex. The above considerations, including the husband's harsh claim that his wife's sex with her lover may stain his house, clearly imply that although the husband accepts his wife's affairs, he is not happy about them. All these subtleties indicate that even if the husband accepts his wife's affairs, he is not happy about it, and is sometime jealous.

The case of the painter Frida Kahlo is a particularly interesting one. Frida and her husband, the painter Diego Rivera, believed that the many lovers each of them took did not affect the great love they felt for one another. When Rivera had an affair with his wife's younger sister, Christina, however, Frida was devastated and did not paint for a year. And, while Rivera expressed acceptance of Frida's affairs with other women, he was not okay with her sleeping with other men. Thus, while neither Rivera nor Kahlo upheld exclusivity norms, considering them social artifacts, they nevertheless experienced jealousy when the comparative concern was dominant enough to hurt their self-esteem.

Although polyamory requires the reduction of the comparative concern, this is often not the case, as comparison is quite natural in polyamorous relations. Such an enhanced comparative concern makes these relationships less likely to be calm, a trait that is quite valuable for long-term relationships. It is true that greater openness, sensitivity, reasoning, and self-awareness can help reduce the tension in polyamorous relations, but the tension is still emotionally genuine and not merely a social construct.

Jealousy and polyamory are a lethal mix. Eliminating, or at least reducing, jealousy is essential for polyamorous relations. It seems that even if jealousy is not completely absent, as is the case in many polyamorous relationships, its intensity is reduced—leading to behavior that is less hostile than that of a typical romantic jealousy. The fact that jealousy is not eliminated in polyamory indicates that the presence of compersion, in both polyamorous and monogamous relations, is due to the nature of jealousy and happy-for, rather than to the relational structure of the given relation.

To sum up, compersion can be a significant step in enabling the partner to cope with the basic difficulties of a dull relationship. One might say that in such a case one should enable, and even encourage, these experiences, provided that they are not harmful in other ways. Making our partner happy is, after all, what underlies profound love.[21]

Concluding Remarks

I think we can all agree that sleeping around is a great way to meet people.
CHELSEA HANDLER

No need for coffee; my lover keeps me awake all the time.
A MARRIED MAN

Today's abundance of romantic opportunities makes it difficult for people to be romantically happy with their lot, and they often envy those whose lot seems different from their own. In this regard, many married people envy singles for their romantic freedom. Most singles, however, are seeking serious relationships, while also being interested in romantic and sexual diversity.

As modern society's approach to love evolves, important questions are emerging about the scope of romantic exclusivity, including how to keep it usefully flexible but still practically limited. Social norms govern our understanding of romantic love as an emotion that ought to be directed toward one person at a time. However, loving more than one individual simultaneously is not a logical contradiction. It does, however, raise significant psychological difficulties.

In polyamory, this type of love is embraced, and instead of the typical notions of jealousy in response to a partner's love for other partners, some members of this community can appreciate any source of their lover's happiness and fulfillment, including other people. This can lessen the demand for romantic compromises, as different partners can adopt distinct romantic roles, depending on their preferences and the nature of their connection.

Adding a third person to an existing marriage (or other committed relationships) typically generates emotional discomfort that is expressed in jealousy, which is ignited by the fear of losing the partner to a third party. However, sometimes adding a third person to the relationship can help to better address the needs of the existing partners. This is true not merely in polyamorous relations, where such an addition is obvious, but also in extramarital affairs.

Open sexual marriages are similar to polyamory in being a consensual nonmonogamous relation. However, while open marriages focus on additional sexual experiences, polyamorous people seek an additional intimate, loving relation (to which sexual experiences can be added). Hence, polyamory is both more complex and more profound than open marriage. This does not imply that its impact upon the primary relation is more beneficial than that of open sexual marriage; often it is not.

Compersion, which refers to the case when a partner's happiness with another lover elicits happiness in the individual, is not a new emotion, but rather a type of the happy-for emotion. Its presence indicates the greater acceptance of polyamory these days.

A Balanced Diet Is the New Romantic Feast

I want to caution you against the idea that balance has to be a routine that looks the same week in and week out.

KEVIN THOMAN

I definitely need to date someone who is calm.

FREIDA PINTO

Alongside greater romantic diversity and flexibility, there has been another, somewhat surprising, development in romantic relationships: the increasing presence of romantic profundity. No doubt about it—tempestuous romantic experiences are certainly valuable. However, our high-paced society floods us with superficial excitement. Slow, profound, or older people often fall victim to this rapid pace; fast and superficial people have the edge. Social networks make connection between people faster and less profound, decreasing romantic profundity and increasing loneliness, which stems not from a lack of social connections, but from a lack of meaningful, profound connections. As we live longer and our society offers ever more superficial experiences, romantic profundity has taken on even greater value. These days, it is not more brief, exciting experiences that we need for a happiness upgrade but rather the ability to establish and enhance long-term robust romantic relationships.

In this chapter, we will consider some ideas that may help enduring profound love to flourish today. These ideas will modify the strict notions underlying romantic ideology. Although I believe that the traditional ideas still have a guiding value as ideals to which we can aspire, the emphasis should be on more moderating views that facilitate profound love.

Romantic love is often understood as an uncompromising, extreme attitude involving great sensitivity, significant closeness, and intense excitement. The main thrust here is protective (and preventive). I propose to supplement this with contextual moderation involving a limited, yet significant, amount of indifference; an appropriate amount of distance; and calmness. In this view, profound romantic love is essentially a nurturing attitude.

I am not suggesting that we toss out the traditional ideas in favor of new ones. What I am proposing is that we temper the old with a mix of the new in trying to achieve a more balanced diet, leading us to the new romantic feast.

Mild (Not Wild) Intensity Is the New Romantic Gratification

> Could I love less, I should be happier now.
> PHILIP JAMES BAILEY

> Idle youth, enslaved to everything; by being too sensitive I have wasted my life.
> ARTHUR RIMBAUD

In this section, I argue that although the occasional experience of wild, intense, romantic love is desirable and stimulating, this is not what enables romantic love to endure. Romantic profundity is not limited in this sense; increasing romantic profundity is always beneficial. Given that it is possible to enhance such profundity, the main task in seeking moderation here is the lover's ability to accept a good-enough partner, who offers the chance of a moderately profound relationship, although this lover might not be the hottest.

For Aristotle, it is the pursuit of excess—of too much—that is bad. Excess, which is typically associated with intense emotions, can be harmful. And it is not only emotional excess that is harmful, said Aristotle, but also emotional depletion. So, too much *and* too little are not good for a person. The ideal situation is that of emotional balance. Aristotle went on to explain that the real measure of something is if it is *appropriate*, that is, how suitable it is to the *given circumstances*. With younger people, the appropriate romantic attitudes might be those of greater intensity. Similarly, in moments of extreme danger, one's reactions need to be extreme. There are some activities in which the issue of being excessive hardly arises. The doctrine of the golden mean does not apply to intellectual virtues, but only to moral ones, in which appropriateness and balance take top priority.[1]

We have seen that while extreme romantic intensity often hinders the development of romantic profundity, there is hardly ever too much romantic profundity. However, since romantic profundity is a matter of degrees, and a high degree is hard to achieve, the lover's attitude can be moderate in the sense of considering the beloved to be (at least) a good-enough partner.

The advantages of long-term profound love are clear in terms of our romantic and personal flourishing. Aristotle's notion of *eudaimonia* is relevant here. He takes profound intrinsic activities to be the most important factor in human flourishing (*eudaimonia*), though he also acknowledges the importance of instrumental activities in such flourishing. Human flourishing is not a temporary state of superficial pleasure. Rather, it refers to a longer period involving the fulfillment of natural human capacities.

Can we then say, then, that in the long term, moderate romantic love is better for us than intense romantic love? I believe that although the occasional experience of wild, intense, romantic love is desirable and stimulating, this is not what enables romantic love to endure over time. The moderate type of romantic love, in which profundity, intrinsicality, and growth are combined, is what sustains long-term flourishing love. Profound love has many advantages, and we should try not to relinquish our search for such love. However, profound love does not mean giving up romantic intensity; on the contrary, such love maintains its intensity at a moderate level, which is higher than usual. Profound love limits extreme desire to occasional circumstances, but it does not eliminate such desire.

Moderate negative and positive emotions are essential for our well-being and for enduring love. There is nothing wrong with wishing to have wild, rather than mild, sexual activities. The problem with excessive intensity is that it goes haywire when it overshadows the romantic relationship as a whole.

Prudent Indifference Is the New Romantic Sensitivity

> We also often add to our pain and suffering by being overly sensitive, over-reacting to minor things, and sometimes taking things too personally.
> TENZIN GYATSO, the 14th Dalai Lama

> Do not give in too much to feelings. An overly sensitive heart is an unhappy possession on this shaky earth.
> JOHANN WOLFGANG VON GOETHE

Sensitivity has a good reputation in the romantic arena: it is often considered one of the most important pillars of a good romantic relationship. While this is certainly true, too much romantic sensitivity can overburden a relationship. A degree of indifference, which is valuable in any kind of relationship, is particularly valuable when coping with an abundance of enticing romantic options.

Elaine Aron discusses highly sensitive people, who constitute about 20 percent of the overall population. She characterizes these people as those who "pick up on subtleties, reflect deeply, and therefore are easily overwhelmed." So, when highly sensitive people are in love, "they will tend to demand more depth in their relationships in order to be satisfied; see more threatening consequences in their partners' flaws or behaviors; reflect more and, if the signs indicate it, worry about how things are going." Highly sensitive people are more sensitive than others to both positive and negative environmental influences; thus, they are more prone to stress, as well as to empathy.[2]

Romantic sensitivity can be expressed toward one's partner but also toward other possible romantic partners. Such sensitivity can lead the lover into a constant search for a better romantic option. As discussed above, this search, which is often futile, makes you dissatisfied with your own romantic lot and accordingly impedes the development of long-term robust love. Human curiosity makes us sensitive to every open romantic door, tempting us to enter, so as not to miss any option. Trying to enjoy all options runs the risk of losing the relationship you are presently in. Closing some open doors, which requires some kind of indifference toward these tempting doors, is difficult but necessary in a world of limited resources and conflicting values. Love requires great investment; being sensitive to all romantic options can spread the required investment too thin.

Dan Ariely argues that people have an irrational tendency to keep their options open for too long and hence wind up chasing down impractical roads. Given the greater freedom in modern society, people "are beset not by a lack of opportunity, but by a dizzying abundance of it." We want to taste and experience every aspect of life regardless of its price. In this sense, Ariely claims, we are spreading ourselves too thin. He notes that another risk in such behavior is that some options disappear if we do not invest enough resources to keep them alive. Their disappearance may occur too slowly for us to see them vanishing. He argues that we need to close some of our options; otherwise, the better options may not survive. There is a price for keeping so many options open, and sometimes this price is higher than any gain we could derive from doing so.[3]

From a simplistic point of view, cognitive sensitivity implies that the more sensitive you are, the more relevant information you will discover, and the better your romantic relationship will be. One difficulty with this view is that greater knowledge does not always increase the quality of a relationship. Sometime, romantic ignorance can be quite useful. Thus, La Rochefoucauld argues that "in friendships as well as love, ignorance very often contributes more to our happiness than knowledge." Romantic relationships require some balance of positive illusions, on the one hand, and accurate knowledge, on the other. However, romantic ignorance is valuable only in limited circumstances and only for some people. In general, profound love feeds on the idea that "to know you is to love you." This is because knowledge enables greater understanding and therefore deeper sensitivity toward the other. There are, however, personal and contextual variations in this regard. The value of greater knowledge does not imply the value of dwelling upon the unpleasant flaws of the beloved. Rumination on matters we cannot change does nothing but increase pain.

Romantic sensitivity works best within limits. Just as I cannot love everyone, I cannot be sensitive in the same degree and manner to all my beloved's characteristics and behaviors. Romantic sensitivity should focus on the most meaningful and relevant aspects involved in romantic thriving. Without such focus and prioritization, sensitivity can become toxic. If we deal with a penny as we would a million dollars, sensitivity overloads us with irrelevant and even destructive noise.

Why should you develop limited indifference to your partner's behavior? It's all about trust. If you trust your beloved, you will be less likely to worry endlessly about insignificant flaws or inappropriate deeds. Trust requires a degree of indifference—being certain that the other acts out of love and good intentions. Certainly, trust has to be gained. However, it ought not to be constantly inspected. We should not be blind, or at least not completely blind, to some of our partner's flaws, but we should also be less sensitive to them by according them minor weight. We cannot conduct our lives properly if we treat everything as equally important; we must have some order of priority. We must learn to be insensitive to some issues and more sensitive to others; otherwise, our mental system will become overwhelmed. Love involves being sensitive to the beloved. Too much sensitivity, however, can ruin love; indiscriminate sensitivity, like indiscriminate freedom, disrupts our order of priorities.

Research suggests that profound lovers do develop such prudent indifference. Garth Fletcher and colleagues argue that people in highly committed relationships tend to perceive attractive individuals as less appealing than those who are not committed or are single. To defuse the threat of a romantic alternative, individuals in more committed relationships downplay the attractiveness of other potential partners. The authors conclude that certain cognitive biases operate as effective strategies that suppress mate-search processes and strengthen established relationship bonds.[4]

A wonderful love song from the 1930s runs: "Millions of people go by, but they all disappear from view—because I only have eyes for you." These lyrics, written by Al Dubin, represent a great romantic ideal. Of course, committed lovers do not have a cognitive deficiency (lovers are not blind to other romantic options), but they do have an evaluative change of focus (lovers are less attracted to such options). Profound romantic love suppresses the search for mates but does not wholly eliminate the desire for other romantic options.

To sum up, sensitivity is indeed the hallmark of emotions, and its role in love is significant. Love involves being sensitive to the beloved. However, too much sensitivity, or indiscriminate sensitivity, can destroy love, as it disrupts our normative order of priorities. Adhering to that order requires not merely sensitivity, but also selective indifference. Notably, I am not suggesting apathy, which is lack of interest, enthusiasm, or concern, and hence not being willing to make any effort to change things. Prudent indifference is still sensitivity—but one that is shaped by our more profound value. Today, we are flooded with intense exciting options, making the maintenance of long-term relations difficult. A reasonable degree of indifference toward alluring options, as well as toward one's partner's flaws and mistakes, can go a long way toward the sustaining of these relations.

Restricted Distance Is the New Romantic Closeness

And stand together yet not too near together: For the pillars of the temple stand apart,
And the oak tree and the cypress grow not in each other's shadow.
KAHLIL GIBRAN

In true love the smallest distance is too great, and the greatest distance can be bridged.
HANS NOUWENS

Being temporally and geographically close to your partner is central to romantic love. This centrality is often associated with the idea that the two lovers, as soulmates, merge into one entity. However, we have seen that this false notion of fusion conflicts with the reality that each lover must enjoy a degree of autonomy. Thus, there must be some geographical and temporal distance in profound love. What is the nature of such distance, and is it truly intolerable?

Distance/closeness can be spoken of in a few different ways: temporal, geographical, and psychological. The relation between these types is complex. My main concern here is with the impact of the temporal and geographical distances on romantic closeness (which is one type of psychological closeness).

Temporal Distance: Do You Always Wish to Be
with the One You Love?

Only miss the sun when it starts to snow; only know you love her when you let her go.
PASSENGER

Can partners cope with temporal distance—that is, can they tolerate waiting? Patience involves being able to endure waiting, without becoming annoyed or upset, especially when encountering difficulties or frustration. Passion involves being excited or agitated, and the inclination to feel emotions intensely. Profound lovers are both patient and impatient, as profound love involves both the excitement of sexual desire and the calmness of profound love.

Love songs sing of the lover's wish to be with the beloved "always" and "all the time." This wish can express two different desires: (1) wanting to be with the beloved for the rest of one's life or (2) wanting to be with the beloved every day as much as possible. These two wishes are not identical: someone might wish to be with her partner for the rest of her life but prefer doing so only on weekends. What are the requirements underlying the two kinds of wishes?

The wish to be with another person for the rest of one's life does not necessarily express a profound love; it could merely imply a desire to share a comfortable life with a person who is a good father, a reasonable provider, or a great sexual partner. However, wishing to be with someone every day and as much as possible does denote a kind of profound love, in which the togetherness itself has an intrinsic value in being fulfilling and enjoyable. Couples in love can enjoy seeing a movie together regardless of its quality (unless they really hate that movie!). The wish to be together persists although the lovers are enjoying activities with other people. One type of activity does not get in the way of others, as our lives are full of intrinsic enjoyable activities, and it is unreasonable to expect that one person can fulfill all of our needs.

Although profound love involves the wish to be with each other as much as possible every day, it also requires a kind of limited distance that creates personal space, enabling a lasting togetherness.

Geographical Closeness

Relationship at a distance can do things for the heart that a closer, day-to-day companionship cannot.
THOMAS MOORE

Distance doesn't separate people . . . Silence does.
JEFF HOOD

We have seen that lovers can tolerate temporal distance, but can they tolerate geographical distance? Being physically close has been considered essential to romantic love, in part so partners can engage in sexual interaction. Moreover, in the past, the "one and only" was likely to be found not far from where potential partners lived, as this required fewer resources and less effort than long-distance relationships.

Increasing numbers of romantic couples today live at a geographical distance from each other. Take commuter marriage, for example. A commuter marriage is a relationship between people who are married and intend to remain so, but live apart, usually because of the locations of their jobs, educational demands, or dual-career pursuits. Technologies such as phone calls,

videos, instant messaging, texting, Skype, and emails enable direct and immediate communication that can sustain a continuous, meaningful romantic
relationship, despite the geographical distance.

A growing body of research indicates that long-distance relationships often
have equal or greater value than close-proximity relationships in promoting
and maintaining romantic connections. The couples in these relationships enjoy greater personal space, which enhances their personal flourishing, as well
as the flourishing of their togetherness. Several studies have shown that communication in long-distance dating is more intimate, more positive, and less
argumentative than in geographically close dating. Openness and positivity—
two strategies that involve intimate self-disclosure—are frequently observed
in the communication of couples in long-distance relationships, and these
add to relationship stability and satisfaction. Commitment and trust are important in all romantic relationships, but in long-distance relationships, they
have greater significance, as there are more opportunities for things to happen that will threaten the commitment. Indeed, the percentage of extramarital
affairs in these relationships is similar, or even lower, than that in standard
marriages. Divorce rates also appear to be similar. Whereas in geographically
close relationships, coresidence might be considered key to the romantic relationship, in commuter marriage, commitment outweighs coresidence in
importance.[5]

In our cyber society, geographical distance has lost some of its negative aspects. Sometimes, living apart is more conducive to profound long-term love
than living under the same roof; for a growing number of couples, geographical distance promotes emotional closeness. Can we say then that (geographical) distance is the new (romantic) closeness?

Long-distance relationships can suffer from a limited amount of interaction between the partners and from clashing schedules that often express
conflicting needs as well. When this happens, people in such relationships
sometimes feel distress, leading them to view the relationship as less than
fully satisfactory. Of particular significance is that such couples miss out on
daily interactions over trivial matters. Frequent telephone conversations or
online communications are valuable, but not sufficient to make the marital
relationship fully satisfactory or fulfilling.[6] Karla Mason Bergen argues that
many wives in commuter marriages describe their marriage as "the best of
all worlds"; others describe it as "torn between two worlds." It is the best of
all worlds because the wives are both independent and interdependent; they
take advantage of opportunities for personal fulfillment, while still keeping
their marriages intact. They feel torn between two worlds, because their life
unfolds in two different environments.[7]

As distance facilitates idealization, people in long-distance relationships tend toward higher levels of optimism and greater idealization of their partner. This could cause them to assess their relationship inaccurately. Thus, couples in commuter marriages consider the likelihood of breaking up within the next year lower than do individuals in close-proximity relationships. However, breakup rates turned out to be similar in the two groups. Idealization is often self-fulfilling, and this plays a positive role in enhancing marital quality, which might partly explain the higher marital quality in long-distance relationships. Indeed, some people who have maintained a long-distance relationship and then began to live geographically closer report that they now miss the feeling of missing each other ("I miss missing him," as one woman said) and the anticipation of seeing each other.[8]

Since more and more contemporary couples are entering commuting relationships because of work, the time apart might save as many marriages as it destroys. Finding the right physical and emotional distance for the partners is crucial for a satisfactory romantic relationship. Distance has its costs, but a mutually desired distance can minimize the impact of other costs. While many married couples are busy thinking about how to reduce distance, others would like to enlarge it in order to provide more personal space for activities of personal fulfillment. Determining appropriate distance is not easy, but doing so eases the enormous burden put on lovers in intimate relationships. Alas, there is no formula for love.

When circumstances impose such distance, it often turns out to have real benefits. It is usually counterproductive, however, to decide in advance to be further from your partner for the sake of the relationship. However, all relationships benefit when each partner has some type of personal space.

Long-distance relationships involving profound love are a growing phenomenon from which more and more people are benefiting. It seems then that (geographical) distance might, indeed, be the new (romantic) closeness, though this does not eliminate the value of other types of romantic closeness.

The Need for Romantic Cartilage

The closer you are to someone, the more intolerable is the distance between the two of you.
TEA

Do we need distance to get close?
SARAH JESSICA PARKER

Geographical proximity and frequent face-to-face interactions have long been considered crucial for promoting romantic relationships. However, too much closeness can be too much of a good thing. Since an essential aspect of love and lasting romantic togetherness is that of personal flourishing, and as we do many of our self-expressive activities on our own, the complete elimination of all types of temporal and geographical distance can be harmful.

Cartilage is the body's connective tissue. It provides support and protects bones from the friction that would otherwise result from bones rubbing against each other at the joints. Romantic distance can be seen as a kind of shock absorber that functions similarly to cartilage: it protects lovers from the friction that excessive proximity causes. People keep different kinds of distance to reduce such personal friction in their close intimate relationships.

In contrast to the romantic ideal of unity, marriage counselors warn that spending too much time with the beloved can decrease love.[9] Indeed, it seems that some degree of distance, which allows for personal space, is important for a personal relationship. Distance can focus the partners' attention on the profound aspects of their relationships and help them to disregard the superficial ones. Significant and temporally extended physical distance might harm relationships, but a more restricted distance can be beneficial.

Those in one's inner circle sometimes want a bit of distance. This can have to do with the feeling that someone's influence or demands are too strong. Debra Mashek and Michelle Sherman compiled a list of powerful terms that people who report a desire for less closeness use to describe their experience: "caged in," "controlled," "imbalanced," "locked down," "merged," "not being able to escape," "oppressed," "overwhelmed," "possessed," "imprisoned," "restricted," "suffocated," and "trapped." Such terms evoke a sense of extreme influence or control, as well as an impingement on freedom. Indeed, the major cause for desiring less closeness is a perceived threat to one's personal control and identify. Let's listen to one of Mashek and Sherman's interviewees: "For seven years, every decision, from what to eat for dinner to where to live, has been made by the two of us together. I want to make some decisions on my own; I don't want my life to be tied to my partner."[10] Without question, autonomy undergirds profound romantic love.

Does the Heart Grow Fonder with Distance?

Absence is to love what wind is to fire; it extinguishes the small, it kindles the great.
ROGER DE RABUTIN

Despite the popular phrase "Absence makes the heart grow fonder," *both* closeness *and* distance can make the heart grow fonder, as well as make it forget some types of love.

Distance (in the sense of absence) adds to our everyday perspective on our romantic relation. It can extinguish the weak flame of a romantic candle or stoke a strong romantic fire. Thus, distance is the best way to recover from a broken heart and at the same time a good way to reassure the hesitating heart. Along these lines, too much closeness can prevent you from seeing the virtues of your beloved, as when putting something over your eyes prevents you from seeing it. But closeness in the sense of closely interacting with each other is likely to increase romantic profundity.

Once again, it is balance—this time between distance and closeness—that is the burning bottom line.

Dynamic Calmness Is the New Romantic Excitement

I discovered the wonder of love (new, brand new) with the discovery of a wonderful peacefulness that is flowering in me. All is quiet, calm, without stress and the upheaval of fear.

YEHUDA BEN-ZE'EV

True love is not a strong, fiery, impetuous passion. It is, on the contrary, an element calm and deep. It looks beyond mere externals and is attracted by qualities alone. It is wise and discriminating, and its devotion is real and abiding.

ELLEN G. WHITE

My lover brings me tranquility. Not during our lovemaking, which is so exciting, but an overall peaceful feeling.

A MARRIED WOMAN

Because emotions are so deeply changeable, they are often compared to storms and fire. We have seen that emotions can be unstable, intense states that signify passionate excitement and agitation. And emotions tend to magnify situations and make them seem urgent—prompting us to quickly mobilize our resources. Romantic love has a strong resonance with this feeling. As Betsy Prioleau argues, "Love goes brackish in still waters. It needs to be stirred up with obstruction and difficulty and spiked with surprise." Hence, "What's granted is not wanted."[11]

I have argued that the above serves as a reasonable description of brief, tempestuous, loving relationships but not of relationships that involve long-term profound love, the basis of which is a calm, yet dynamic excitement. Is the latter combination possible to achieve?

Friedrich Kambartel suggests that calmness concerns not striving to control things that are beyond our control, such as, first, inalterable conditions of our life; second, other people; and third, ourselves. Calmness involves a trust that the course of events beyond our control does not affect the meaning of our life. Kambartel further argues that in practicing calmness, we are relieved of the endless, futile strain of trying to control the things that are beyond our control.[12]

In everyday terms, calmness refers to an absence of agitation or excitement. When we say that the weather is calm, we mean that we don't anticipate storms, high winds, or rough waves anytime soon. Yet, and this is my main point, while calmness is free of negative elements, such as tension, agitation, or distress, it can be full of positive excitement. As Julia Roberts said, "The kind of energy I attract is very calm." While calmness implies an absence of violent or confrontational activity, it does not imply an absence of profound, positive activities that enhance flourishing. Interestingly, precisely because profound calmness is linked to internal strength, it can be perceived, in certain circumstances, as a sort of internal weapon (think of Oscar Wilde's comment "Nothing is so aggravating as calmness").

In discussing emotions and moods, two basic continuums of the feeling dimension—the arousal continuum and the pleasantness continuum—are relevant. Robert Thayer suggests dividing the arousal continuum into two types: one that ranges from energy to tiredness, and the other from tense to calm. Doing so, we have four basic affective states: calm-energy, calm-tiredness, tense-energy, and tense-tiredness. Each of these states is related to a certain state on the pleasantness continuum. Thayer considers the state of calm-energy to be the most pleasant state, whereas tense-tiredness is the most unpleasant one.[13]

Thayer notes that many people fail to distinguish between calm-energy and tense-energy, since they believe that whenever they are energetic, there is a certain degree of tension in their situation. The idea of calm-energy, he says, is foreign to many Westerners, but it is quite familiar to people from other parts of the world. Thayer quotes the Zen master Shunryu Suzuki: "Calmness of mind does not mean you should stop your activity. Real calmness should be found in the activity itself. It is easy to have calmness in inactivity, but calmness in activity is true calmness."[14] This kind of dynamic calmness can be found in meaningful intrinsic activities, which promote balanced human flourishing.

Profound love is cultivated during meaningful intrinsic activities, which promote the flourishing of each lover, as well as their togetherness. Such love does not stem from subordinating one's activities to those of the beloved, but from considering the activities for and with the beloved as compatible with one's own profound intrinsic activities. Moreover, such activities need to be chosen with an eye to the flourishing of both partners. When love is profound, romantic activities can be calm and yet dynamic. Romantic calmness is associated with the profound trust prevailing in the loving relationship; the dynamism comes from the joint activities shared by the lovers.

Calm-energy love can solve the dilemma of romantic stability. This dilemma involves the common desire to have both an exciting and a stable romantic relationship. Couples want their romantic love to be exciting and dynamic; they want to feel fully alive. The motto of an online group that calls itself "Married and Flirting" is "Married, Not Dead"; the group promises that its members will "feel alive again." On the other hand, people also want their romantic relationships to be calm and stable while maintaining their initial high, intense level.

This dilemma is really about whether long-term stable romantic relationships can be exhilarating or whether they are doomed to "be dead." In other words, must romantic love be short and unstable in order to be stimulating? As I have suggested throughout the book, romantic intensity and profundity are the key issues here. As long as we consider romantic love to consist of merely, or even mainly, of intensity, romantic love cannot be both dynamic and calm. However, if we believe that profound intrinsic activities can be dynamic and exciting, and accompanied by moments of intense love, profound and enduring love can indeed be vibrant and stimulating. Although calmness does not scream to make itself heard, it certainly has something important to say for love and life. Sometimes, it is the still water that makes all the difference to the romantic heart.

Do You Take Your Lover for Granted? Congratulations!

Being taken for granted can be a compliment. It means that you've become a comfortable, trusted element in another person's life.

JOYCE BROTHERS

Marriage counselors have a favorite line: Do not take your partner for granted! And there is much wisdom in this advice—especially when it involves romantic intensity. Change and a bit of uncertainty can indeed fan the flames of a dying romance. Conversely, the status quo can fool us into thinking that we need not invest effort in the relationship. Yet there is an additional, deeper sense of taking for granted that surfaces when love is profound and trust prevails.

Let's recall that romantic intensity is marked by a certain superficiality and that change holds a privileged position in this kind of relationship. When romantic intensity and change are the stars of the show, lovers are always on the alert, looking for more and different external stimuli to fan the sexual flame. Relationships of romantic profundity, however, which promote the flourishing of each partner, require a deep trust. The hunt for verification and new stimuli eats away at this trust. And if you ask around, you'll find that many people connect the experience of "being in love" with being able to trust one's partner.

Let's clarify terms. When we speak of taking a partner for granted in profound love, we are not suggesting being insensitive. Instead, we are talking about not walking around worried about how to prevent your partner from leaving you. While the trust underlying profound love is not immune to risks, the baseline attitude is one of nonsuspicion. Taking your partner for granted also does not mean spending a great deal of time on repetitive and boring activities. Romantic relationships do need variation. But it is best if this dynamism comes from activities of flourishing that the lovers regularly share.

Although trust includes the risk of betrayal, its bedrock feeling is a positive attitude toward the partner and optimism concerning his or her trustworthiness.[15] As we have learned, when survival is at stake, noticing negative qualities is more important than noticing positive qualities. However, the active search for positive qualities is valuable as well, especially in the long term. In the short run, being on guard might prevent one's partner from doing some misdeeds, but in the long run, "on guard" turns the relationship into a competitive fencing match!

To sum up, calm-energy romantic experiences help to ensure that a stable romantic relationship is not a dull relationship. In enduring profound romantic relationships, stability goes hand in hand with dynamic and stimulating activities. In fact, it is only by partners engaging in profound intrinsic activities that promote calmness and foster the flourishing of each lover that romantic love can survive over time.

Nurturing Is the New Romantic Conduct

Too many lovers, Not enough love these days.
CRYSTAL GAYLE

Long-term robust love is based on mutual nurturance. Unlike romantic compromise, which shuts the door on potentially better opportunities, the nurturing approach increases lovers' horizons, involving opportunities that better suit their needs and abilities. Nurturing can be understood as helping a person to grow and develop. In raising our children, for example, we try to nurture their talents, tolerance, and friendships. We can also nurture our intimate partner and ourselves. Although romantic love entails a great deal of giving to others, such giving can best be done by a person who is flourishing within the relationship.

In the nurturing approach, "intrinsic activities," in which the value of the activity lies in the activity itself, take precedence over "extrinsic activities," which aim for a certain external goal. Intrinsic activities often involve complementary experiences, while extrinsic activities are more compatible with compromises. Satisfying lives include many intrinsic activities. While engaging in them, we are flourishing and have no active interest in getting more or changing our partner. As one's character remains rather stable over time, intrinsic activities are more likely to maintain their value over time, thus enhancing our long-term well-being.

Although modern society rewards extrinsic activities, which tend to be brief and efficient, intrinsic activities are not lacking. Thus, whether you like to read, dance, or do any highly fulfilling job, you can derive unending satisfaction and pleasure from such activities. Extrinsic or instrumental activities are more likely to become boring over time, as we do not value them for their own sake; we merely value the goal that we hope to achieve by performing them. It is essential for the quality of a romantic relationship that the value of mutual and individual intrinsic activities is recognized. Always adopting the other's interest is likely to end in dissatisfaction. Our partners should not feel "left out" when we are involved in intrinsic activities but rather should find their own intrinsic activities, and we should try to make sure that at least some of these are done together.

Instead of craving ready-made external products, profound love pursues ongoing, mutual intrinsic activities. The former, which is self-destructive, can provide immediate superficial pleasure, while the latter, which is self-perpetuating, offers ongoing profound satisfaction and hence generates less need to compromise. When our romantic relationship complements and nurtures us, we are not called upon to make compromises within the relationship—on the contrary, such a relationship improves the other's well-being. In such nurturing circumstances, there is more enabling than prohibiting. Similarly, in such relationships, uniqueness is more significant than exclusivity. The push for uniqueness foregrounds nurturing ourselves and others; exclusiveness, in contrast, seeks to prevent the other from engaging in particular behaviors.

Of course, we would all like to live in a world without compromises. In the romantic realm, this would mean that we find a profound romantic relationship involving intrinsic activities, passionate sex, reciprocity, respect, and caring. No one would argue with the idea that is better to be healthy, rich, and happy than to be sick, poor, and miserable. The issue is what to do when you do not get the perfect prince, or even someone close to it. Should we be looking for such a prince at all? Should we give up every activity in the romantic realm if we cannot get "the best"? Should we never fall in love if it will not last forever? And what kind of compromises are the least painful? These are hard questions with no ready-made answers—both the questions and the answers must be tailored to each person. Yet we know that, like too tight shoes, extremes should be avoided.

In our global and cyber society, more and more people are giving up the search for romantic profundity and settling for occasional, instantaneous sexual intensity. Most of us, however, still yearn for romantic profundity, which produces the sweet fruits of romantic serenity and trust. The task of combining romantic intensity with profundity, then, has never been so urgent. As the abundance of romantic opportunities is likely to reduce the number of people living without love, we may yet witness love's comeback.

Limited Flexibility Is the New Romantic Stability

Better bend than break.
SCOTTISH PROVERB

Sometimes I've lost you from my arms. Sure, we've had lovers in our beds . . . But in the end . . . Our only special skill was never growing up, just ageing.
JACQUES BREL

Early on in our journey toward profound love, we learned the crucial role of change in generating emotions; here, in the final stage of our trip, I discuss again the role of flexibility in the romantic realm. We can think of flexibility, which is the quality of bending without breaking, as the ability to make changes in a situation that is changing. Stability is highly valuable in romantic relations and in particular in achieving profundity. Interestingly, in our diverse and dynamic environment, it is through flexibility that our enduring romantic relationships remain stable. To understand this point, let us first consider the value of psychological flexibility in general health.

Todd Kashdan and Jonathan Rottenberg discuss the importance of psychological flexibility (and stability) for health. This flexibility spans a wide range of human abilities, such as adapting to situational demands, shifting behavioral priorities when needed, maintaining balance among important life areas, and being open and committed to behaviors that fit with deeply held values. These abilities capture the dynamic, fluctuating, and context-specific behaviors of people navigating the challenges of daily life. Rigidity, which indicates a lack of sensitivity to one's context, often points to psychopathology. Kashdan and Rottenberg claim that healthy people can manage themselves in the uncertain, unpredictable world around them, where novelty and change are the norm rather than the exception. With psychological flexibility, we can find ways to shape our automatic processes in better directions.[16]

Psychological flexibility, which is essential to a flourishing life, is also crucial in the romantic realm. In no small measure, this is so because romantic flourishing presupposes general flourishing. And romantic flexibility echoes psychological flexibility: adapting to situational demands, shifting priorities, and maintaining a delicate balance between life, love, and sexual needs. Regarding romantic stability as well, flexibility, which involves bending some rigid rules, can prevent romantic relationships from breaking.

It is easier to draw clear romantic (and other) boundaries than to keep them. Although normative boundaries are supposed to guide our behavior, reality is rather complicated. In this regard, the distinction between guiding and specific rules is relevant. Guiding principles provide general directions, such as "Drive safely," rather than specific rules, like "Don't exceed 100 miles per hour." What constitutes safe driving can vary considerably, depending on different factors, such as driver competence and road conditions.[17] Similarly, what constitutes romantic flourishing varies considerably, depending on personal and contextual features. People use specific rules to help them cope with their chaotic romantic environment, but there is no golden rule to tell us what constitutes a flourishing, lasting romantic relationship.

Our romantic life is made more complicated by the many alternatives available to us. As we have discussed, these alternatives concern not merely finding a new partner, but also reunion with a former one. This widespread state, which prevails more among young adults, can be described as not together, but not completely broken up; it reflects the presence of dynamic trajectories involving "a heterogeneous and multidirectional array of transitions."[18] Since ex-lovers have a privileged place in our heart, and as it has become simpler to find them, their contribution to the flexible nature of our romantic environment is significant.

Extreme romantic flexibility, in which we try every such alternative, is contrary to the values relating to who we are. However, extreme rigidity is likely to break us. Bending, which is a kind of compromise, is the flexibility that enables what is less than ideal to be maintained and enhanced for a long time. People who refuse to compromise their ideals often end up abandoning them. It is indeed better to bend than to break. But too much bending can break us as well.

Friendship and Love: Is the Difference Worth the Effort?

Strong-ties make the world smaller, weak-ties make it bigger.
MARK GRANOVETTER

Love degrades the world from significant people, while friendship can fill it with such people.
AVINOAM BEN-ZE'EV

Love is a friendship set to music.
JOSEPH CAMPBELL

No two ways about it: enduring romantic love is hard to achieve. This fact has resulted in the suggestion that friendship is more valuable than romantic love since (a) romantic love is more costly and risky than friendship, and (b) friendship is more profound than romantic love. Do we really want to "waste" our time and energy on uncertain and risky romantic love when we can more easily aim for profound friendship?

As we have seen, romantic love, as well as its basics, friendship and sexual interaction, contribute to our flourishing and happiness. Achieving friendship or sexual satisfaction is obviously easier than achieving lasting profound love, which depends upon a subtle balance between these relations and so much more. We might, indeed, have a greater chance of being happy if we seek merely friendship or sexual satisfaction rather than lasting romantic love. This would also allow us to avoid the frequent failures and unhappiness associated with attaining enduring romantic love.

It can also be argued that the major elements responsible for long-term love are those related to friendship and not to romantic love.[19] Moreover, exclusivity, which is central in romantic love (mainly because of its sexual aspect), but not in friendship, is a superficial demand, limiting our diversity and complexity.

There is a grain of truth in these ideas. Sometimes, we need to minimize losses and maximize sure gains. It is important to remember, though, that romantic love is one of the most sublime of human experiences. Moreover, others' success in achieving romantic love can create in us a yearning for it and sadness about lacking it. It is very difficult to exclude ourselves from the romantic realm, as the desire to achieve such love is built into the human system.

Sometimes, we are forced to give up certain precious experiences. However, we should not make our second-best our first choice. We should think hard before making such surrender permanent policy. Indeed, people who have given up romantic love would gladly embrace it if it walked through their door. While they have given up hope of achieving it, they have not abandoned it as an ideal. Nonetheless, these individuals may not actively search for this love, as such a search has a price and risks they are not willing to take.

There is also some truth to the idea that exclusivity is superficial in nature, as it prevents diversity and decreases the level of complexity. Once again, the dilemma boils down to the issue of optimal balance. No doubt, romantic profundity requires a certain preferential attitude. Like other emotions, romantic love is by nature discriminative; hence, we need to restrict our flexibility. This is also the case in friendship—we cannot have, as people claim concerning Facebook, thousands of close friends. Some sense of restriction applies here as well. Since romantic love is a more comprehensive and complex attitude than friendship, involving a greater investment of effort, time, and other resources, exclusiveness should be even more restricted.

We do not have to choose between love and friendship. Rather, we should choose between the mere experience of friendship and an experience that includes both friendship and romance. Love is indeed the music, or the dance, added to profound friendship.

Is achieving profound love worth the heartache? Well, since it can make life more meaningful, and often more blissful, the answer is yes. Giving up music is a too painful surrender. As Nietzsche said, "Without music life would be a mistake." So, I believe, with love.

Concluding Remarks

True happiness consists in decreasing the difference between our desires and our powers, in establishing a perfect equilibrium between the power and the will. Then only, when all its forces are employed, will the soul be at rest and man will find himself in his true position.

JEAN-JACQUES ROUSSEAU, *Emile, or On Education*

We have reached our destination: we have arrived at long-term profound love. And, as any traveler will tell you, the glance backward makes everything clearer. In our own trip, we saw many phenomena whose coexistence in romantic relationships seems nothing short of paradoxical: mild *and* wild intensity, sensitivity *and* indifference, distance *and* closeness, calmness *and* excitement, nurturing *and* preventing, as well as flexibility *and* stability. These apparent paradoxes stem from our desire to draw one comprehensive, consistent, intellectual picture for all people, all of the time. However, we now know better: the dynamism and partiality of the emotional and romantic realms mean that emotional and romantic experiences can be radically mixed. And, along with Joni Mitchell, we can "look at love from both sides now," and profound love can look like passion over time.

To flourish in life, we need to know what we are dealing with. Flourishing in love is no different. Intense love expresses the passion and excitement that we find at the beginning of romantic relationships, but it is time that ultimately allows for the blossoming of profound love. Over time, we can cultivate our romantic responsivity and make space in the garden for romantic compromise, which tends to feel less compromising as profound love grows.

Identity fusion in the context of love is courting disaster. Healthy romantic relationships leave lots of room for growth. Intrinsic activities are essential to the good life, and it is important to find a partner who supports your personal fulfillment. Excitement feels fabulous, but to focus only on excitement is to lose out on the benefits of a deeper, dynamic calmness that lends itself to profound love.

As we have learned, the "ideal" romantic relationship is one that helps both partners flourish. Different people and different circumstances call for different decisions to make that happen. If there is any recipe at all, it would start with an optimal balance. Today's romantic reality combines great diversity and restricted flexibility. While we cannot romantically indulge in everything we want and still stay healthy, we also do not need to go on a hunger strike. Adopting a moderate diet never killed anyone.

Afterword: Fresh Eggs, Aging Wine, and Profound Love

> I will raise a glass to both fresh and profound love tonight!
>
> A MARRIED WOMAN

> Wine comes in at the mouth and love comes in at the eye; that's all we shall know for truth before we grow old and die.
>
> WILLIAM BUTLER YEATS

The beneficial role of wine in creating romantic atmosphere is obvious. Does this make aging wine and aging love similar?

Aging Wine and Aging Love

> While I want to have wine in small doses, leaving the yearning for more, in love I am more demanding, wishing for it in big doses.
>
> A DIVORCED WOMAN

> My heart says chocolate and wine, but my jeans say, for the love of God, woman, eat a salad.
>
> UNKNOWN

Love and wine. That sounds better than love and eggs, right? Especially considering the common notion that wine gets better with time. The reader will not be surprised, having by now come full circle in our trek, that things are just not that simple.

I believe that love and wine have a similar potential to get better over time. Unlike most other consumable goods, wine has the potential to improve in quality over time. The ratio of sugars, acids, and phenolics (most notably tannins) to water is pivotal to how well a wine will age. The less water in the grapes prior to harvesting, the more likely the resulting wine will have some aging potential. Grape variety, climate, vintage, viticultural practice, storage, and bottling factors are relevant as well.[1]

So many variables go into wine improving with age. Likewise, and more so, many variables go into love improving with age. Lasting, enduring love is forged and shaped by personal and contextual factors, and especially those relating to the interactions between the lovers. We have learned that neither wine nor romance is a closed system: both are influenced by a multitude of factors that can either enhance or degrade their quality. In the case of love, greater weight is attributed to factors that are under the individual's control; hence, time can be kinder to love than to wine. Thus, while experts estimate that merely 5–10 percent of wine improves after one year, and only 1 percent improves after five to ten years, the success rate of romantic aging is much higher—according to one study, about one-third of married couples are still in love after thirty years.[2] It seems that wine, more than profound love, is susceptible to the polluting impact of external factors—a major reason being our ability to develop intrinsically meaningful activities, which decrease the weight of external polluting factors.

Wine and romantic love might well go together like the "horse and carriage" of song fame. Thus, Madeline Puckette suggests that we love wine because it's an acquired taste, it has zillions of aromas and flavors, and no matter how deep you go, there's more to know.[3] These claims are even truer in the case of romantic love: we love loving because it provides an extra, acquired taste, it has zillions of aromas and flavors, and no matter how deep you go, there's more to experience and acquire. And as life is too short to drink bad wine (it is said), so too is life too short to waste on meaningless, bad romantic relationships.

To paraphrase Napoleon Bonaparte, who said that "nothing makes the future look so rosy as to contemplate it through a glass of Chambertin," we can say that nothing makes the future look so rosy as to contemplate it through profound love.

If You Like Piña Coladas

Wine, love, and sex are natural bedfellows. The offer of a glass of wine is frequently a prologue to a sexual or romantic relationship that can break everyday boredom. In the amusing song "Escape," by Rupert Holmes, the protagonist says that he was tired of his long-beloved lady; together they both were like a worn-out recording of a favorite song. One night he saw in the personal column of a newspaper a letter from a woman inviting a man who likes Piña Coladas, getting caught in the rain, and making love at midnight in the dunes of the cape to meet her.[4] The man replies to the ad, sets up a meeting place, and prepares to escape. And . . . lo and behold! Who should enter the bar but his very own lady, who seeks just what he desires—to make love at midnight in the dunes of the cape.

This wonderful song perfectly expresses the message of this book—we tire of our beloved partner, been together too long, like a worn-out recording, of a favorite song; however, it is still our favorite song, which we are ready to listen to again and again. True, the song is not as thrilling as it was on first hearing. But this doesn't mean that we don't want to make love with her or him at midnight in the dunes of the cape. And making such an escape with your very own partner can yield a surprisingly rich bouquet of romantic fragrance.

Back to Eggs

Love and eggs taste best when they are fresh.
RUSSIAN PROVERB (REVISED)

When it comes to eggs, we look for two things—taste and nutritional value. And it is when eggs are fresh that these are at their peak. Life gets more complicated when love is at stake. The intensity of excitement (the "taste") is strongest when love is fresh, but the profundity of the connection (the "nutritional value") is often best when love is mature. While the old saying has it that "revenge is a dish best served cold," I believe that romantic love should never be cold. It does not need to be served at the boiling point, however; warm is very good as well.

In this book, we have traversed the highways and byways of love. The journey has cast doubt on the prevailing popular attempts to make love as fresh as it was at its very beginning. When freshness is foremost, we are setting ourselves up to lose the battle for long-lasting profound love before the war has begun, as there will always be fresher and tastier occasional romantic affairs than the present one.

I am not the kind of romantic nutritionist who advises giving up enjoyable but non-nutritious food while promising that, ultimately, we will feel better without it. I do not recommend giving up intense, wild love—on the contrary, in my view, we are witnessing a renaissance of romantic intensity and excitement, and this is a positive development. However, these new circumstances have disturbed the balance between intensity and profundity to the extent that romantic profundity is becoming harder and harder to achieve.

When the bond between partners is nourishing, and lovers bring out the best in each other, they become calmer, happier, and healthier. In this way, they discover new tastes in their ongoing romantic relationships. People who live in a romantic environment that helps them flourish continue to surprise themselves and their partners, making each other the sunshine of their life.

Acknowledgments

Many people helped to bring this book to its present form. I am profoundly grateful to each of them. Naturally, I can mention here only a few of them. For her profound insights, I am especially thankful to Angelika Krebs, with whom I coauthored an article on the role of time in love that laid the groundwork for this book. I am also thankful to Luke Brunning, with whom I wrote an article on emotional complexity, a section of which is featured in this book. Mollie Teitelbaum, Talia Morag, and Daniel Arel read the whole manuscript and raised many thought-provoking issues, which considerably improved the book's quality. Glendyr Sacks, Sara Tropper, and Marian Rogers, my superb linguistic editors, transformed my thoughts not merely into proper English but into powerful and elegant prose. I am also grateful to Elizabeth Branch Dyson, my editor at the University of Chicago Press, for continuous support and advice. I had conversations that significantly advanced my ideas with Tom Angier, Ruth Ben-Ze'ev, Dikla Falk, Rick Furtak, Inbar Gazit, Amihud Gilead, Jacob Gray, Lirit Gruber, Masha Halevi, Avraham Kenan, Iddo Landau, Shira Lightsdorf- Shkedy, Ariel Meirav, Sonja Rinofner-Kreidl, Orit Shavit, Saul Smilansky, and Daniel Statman, to note a few among many. Two anonymous reviewers of University of Chicago Press provided exceptionally helpful comments. Last, but by no means least, I wish to thank the many individuals who have generously shared with me their own personal romantic experiences. Excerpts from some of these conversations are included in this book.

Some discussions in the book were previously published in a somewhat different manner in my blog on love in *Psychology Today*.

All of the stories, anecdotes, and quotations from anonymous people are genuine; I did not invent any of them (of course, some of these individuals have received fictional names). While I tend to use heteronormative language out of convention, I believe that important components of romantic relationships are universal. Understanding what is essential for love to flourish is relevant for any couple. I sometimes discuss perspectives in love that are more common for men, or for women, so in relation to these aspects, I expect that there are some unique considerations for lesbian, gay, and queer relationships that I do not cover in this book. However, I mostly consider the complexity and uniqueness of human beings and the profound, loving connections they can develop together. Specific sexual orientation is not at the center of this endeavor.

The reader will note that I feature more anonymous quotations from women than from men. This is nothing more than a reflection of who tends to approach me to discuss these issues—women, it seems, are more likely than men to discuss matters of the heart with me.

I dedicate the book to my beloved wife of more than thirty years, Ruth. Whenever she hears people introducing me as an expert on love, she nods in agreement and says, "Yes, he is indeed very good in theory." Ruth also likes to tell the story that after her parents met me for the first time, they offered to sponsor a lengthy trip abroad for her—alone. I am forever grateful to Ruth for rejecting her parents' generous offer and for her endless support and love.

My late brothers Avinoam and Yehuda had a tremendous impact on my personal behavior and my views concerning emotions and love. In its own way, this book constitutes a memorial candle for them.

Notes

Chapter One

1. The quotation from Tom Robbins is cited in Solomon 1988, 13.

2. Ben-Ze'ev and Goussinsky 2008.

3. Jeffrey Jensen Arnett, The Clark University Poll of Emerging Adults, December, 2012, http://www2.clarku.edu/clark-poll-emerging-adults/pdfs/clark-university-poll-emerging -adults-findings.pdf.

4. Baumeister and Bratslavsky 1999; Berscheid 2010; Brewis and Meyer 2005; Buss 1994; Call et al. 1995; Finkel et al. 2015.

5. O'Leary et al. 2012.

6. Acevedo et al. 2012.

7. Finkel et al. 2015. See also Perel 2007.

8. Proulx et al. 2017; Lorber et al. 2015; Birditt et al. 2012.

9. Ben-Ze'ev 2000, 2017b.

10. Spinoza (1677) 1985, IIIp6; IIIdef.aff.; Vp39s. The above characterization refers merely to what Spinoza terms "passive emotions"; it does not refer, for example, to the intellectual love of God.

11. See, e.g., Nussbaum 2001, 42.

12. Amodio and Showers 2005; Finkel et al. 2015; Watson et al. 2004.

13. McNulty et al. 2008.

14. Gilbert and Wilson 2007; Roese and Olson 2014.

15. Gilovich and Medvec 1995.

16. Roese and Summerville 2005.

17. Carstensen 2006.

18. See, e.g., Esch and Stefano 2005; Kansky 2018.

19. Myers 2000.

20. Lawrence et al. 2018.

21. Sprecher 1999, 51.

22. Mogilner et al. 2011.

Chapter Two

1. Frijda 2007, chap. 5; Helm (2009) 2017; Nussbaum 2001; Taylor (1985) 2017.
2. Kahneman and Miller 1986.
3. Ben-Ze' ev 2000, 23–31; Oatley 2018, 47–51.
4. Ben-Ze' ev 2004; Yee 2014.
5. Solomon 1988, 262–71.
6. Frijda et al. 1991.
7. Ben-Ze' ev 2017a; Ben-Ze' ev and Krebs 2018; Frijda 1994; Frijda et al. 1991.
8. Beedie et al. 2005; Ben-Ze' ev 2017a; Krebs 2015, 2017a, 2017b; Parkinson et al. 1996.
9. Furtak 2018, 103–21.
10. Parts of this section were written together with Luke Brunning; see Ben-Ze' ev and Brunning 2018.
11. Gaver and Mandler 1987.
12. Quoidbach et al. 2014.
13. Ortega y Gasset 1941, 43, 76–77.
14. Grossmann et al. 2016.
15. Ajzen 2001; de Sousa (2007) 2017; Greenspan (1980) 2017.
16. See, e.g., Frijda 2007.
17. Ben-Ze' ev and Goussinsky 2008.
18. Baumeister et al. 2013.
19. Ben-Ze' ev 2017a.
20. Frederick and Loewenstein 1999; Frijda 2007; Lyubomirsky 2011.
21. Diener et al. 2015.
22. Gilbert and Wilson 2000; Irvine 2006.
23. See Russell 1930, 15; Kenny 1965, 102.
24. Del Mar Salinas-Jiménez 2011.

Chapter Three

1. Fugère et al. 2017; Meltzer et al. 2014; McGee and Shevlin 2009.
2. Etcoff 1999, chap. 1.
3. Jollimore 2018.
4. I am grateful to Sonja Rinofner-Kreidl for bringing this song to my attention.
5. Berggren et al. 2017; Peterson and Palmer 2017.
6. Scruton 2011, 164, 57.
7. Scruton 2011, 44.
8. Helm 2010.
9. Krebs 2015.
10. Baumeister and Bratslavsky 1999; Cacioppo et al. 2012; Meyers and Berscheid 1997.
11. Martin 2018, intro.
12. Kashdan et al. 2018.
13. McNulty et al. 2016.
14. Sudo 2000, 66–69.
15. Ben-Ze' ev and Krebs 2018.
16. Birnbaum 2017.
17. Birnbaum 2017; Birnbaum et al. 2016.

18. Elster 1999, 91.
19. Brogaard 2015, 83; de Sousa 2015, chap. 4; Morag 2016, 2017.
20. See, e.g., Frankfurt 1999; Helm 2010; LaFollette 1996; Sobel 1990.
21. Fromm 1956, 26.
22. Levinas 1998, 105, 228–29.
23. Buber (1923) 1937; Krebs 2015.
24. Krebs 2002, 2009, 2014a, 2015, 2017a, 2017b; see also Sherman 1993.
25. Nozick 1991, 418, 421.
26. Girme et al. 2014; Määttä and Uusiautti 2013.
27. Ellison et al. 2010.
28. Dwyer et al. 2018.
29. See, e.g., Fredrickson 2013a; Helm 2010, chap. 8.

Chapter Four

1. Higgins 1997.
2. Girme et al. 2014.
3. Baumeister et al. 2001.
4. Baumeister et al. 2001; Ben-Ze' ev 2000, 99–103.
5. Gottman 1995; Saad and Gill 2014.
6. Jonason et al. 2015.
7. See, e.g., Aristotle, *Metaphysics* 1048b18ff., 1050a23ff.; *Nicomachean Ethics* 1174a14ff.
8. Krebs 2015; Rosa 2013, 141–44.
9. Nussbaum 1986, 326–27.
10. Csikszentmihalyi 1990, 53.
11. Ben-Ze' ev and Krebs 2018; Ben-Ze' ev 2017a.
12. Kahneman 2011; Sloman 1996; see also Oatley (2010) 2017.
13. Scitovsky 1976.
14. Armenta et al. 2017.
15. Drigotas 2002; Drigotas et al. 1999.
16. Finkel et al. 2014.
17. Rinofner-Kreidl 2017.
18. Valdesolo et al. 2010; see also Reddish et al. 2013; Valdesolo and DeSteno 2011; Wiltermuth and Heath 2009.
19. Reis and Clark 2013, 400.
20. Birnbaum et al. 2016.
21. Birnbaum et al. 2016.
22. Birnbaum et al. 2016.
23. Reis and Clark 2013.
24. See, e.g., Coburn 2001; Fredrickson 2013b; Krebs 2014a, 2014b, 2015; Mühlhoff 2019; Rosa 2016.
25. *Oxford English Dictionary*, online ed., s.v. "resonance."
26. Mühlhoff 2019.
27. Scruton 1997, 357–59.
28. Krebs 2009.
29. Aristotle, *Nicomachean Ethics* 1157b10–13.

30. May 2011, 154.
31. Ben-Ze'ev and Krebs 2015.
32. McNulty et al. 2013.
33. Rosa 2016.
34. Ben-Ze'ev and Goussinsky 2008.
35. Neff and Karney 2005.

Chapter Five

1. Rinofner-Kreidl 2018.
2. Karney and Coombs 2000.
3. Ben-Ze'ev 2000, 21–23; Kahneman and Miller 1986.
4. Ben-Ze'ev 2000, chap. 5.
5. Papp 2009.
6. Halpern-Meekin et al. 2013.
7. Binstock and Thornton 2003; Halpern-Meekin et al. 2013.
8. Byrne and Murnen 1988.
9. Bauman 2003.

Chapter Six

1. Baumeister and Leary 1995.
2. Baumeister and Leary 1995; see also Lambert et al. 2013
3. Baumeister and Leary 1995.
4. Krebs 2014a, 2015.
5. Coontz 2005, 15, 18.
6. Bruckner 2013, 27.
7. Finkel 2017; Finkel et al. 2014.
8. Finkel 2017.
9. Proulx et al. 2017; see also Anderson et al. 2010; Birditt et al. 2012; Gray and Ozer 2018.
10. Proulx et al. 2017; see also Birditt et al. 2012; Lavner et al. 2012; Lorber et al. 2015.
11. Finkel 2017.
12. Ben-Ze'ev and Goussinsky 2008.
13. Landau 2017.
14. Helm (2009) 2017; Kolodny 2003; Velleman 1999.
15. Landau 2017.
16. Jollimore 2011; Nozick 1991.
17. Ben-Ze'ev 2000, 61–62.
18. Buss et al. 2017.
19. Buss et al. 2017.
20. Ben-Ze'ev 1993, chap. 4; Ben-Ze'ev 2000, 57–59; Ben-Ze'ev and Krebs 2015; Gigerenzer 2007; Kahneman 2011.
21. Russell 1968, 195–96; cited in Irvine 2006, 14–15.
22. Ben-Ze'ev and Krebs 2015.
23. Benjamin and Agnew 2003.
24. Stanley et al. 2006; Rhoades et al. 2012.

25. Binstock and Thornton 2003.

26. Kulu and Boyle 2010; Lillard et al. 1995.

27. Rosenfeld and Roesler 2018.

28. Ben-Ze' ev 2000, chap. 10; Ben-Ze' ev 2016.

29. Ben-Ze' ev 1992, 2016; Gressel 2016. The dictionary definition of "inequality" comes from *Merriam-Webster Dictionary*, s.v. "inequality."

30. Prins et al. 1993.

31. Bruch and Newman 2018; Smith and Kim 2007; Whelan 2006.

32. Sprecher et al. 2006.

Chapter Seven

1. Ben-Ze' ev 2011.

2. Mitchell 2002, 39, 41; Perel 2007.

3. Bauman 2003; Rosa 2013.

4. Baker et al. 2017.

5. Grossmann et al. 2010.

6. Halbertal 2012.

7. See, e.g., Impett and Gordon 2008; Whillans et al. 2016.

8. Shulman et al. 2006; Gottman and Levenson 2000.

9. Goodin 2012. In contrast to his highly positive characterization of settling, Goodin's description of compromises is negative. I disagree with Goodin's assumption that every compromise is compromising oneself, since every compromise deals with principled concerns. As we have seen, compromises admit of degrees, and their evaluation differs in different contexts.

10. Solomon 1990, 150.

11. Gutmann and Thompson 2012.

12. For more details of this story, see my post in *Psychology Today*, "My husband was not the most romantic of my loves," March 3, 2013.

13. Galinsky et al. 2002.

14. Yougov study in the UK, 2014; https://yougov.co.uk/news/2014/09/29/marriage-first-love-deepest/.

15. Forste and Tanfer 1996.

16. Simon 1979.

17. Frankfurt 1987, 39–41; see also Frankfurt 2004.

18. The survey was done by the site Make Friends Online, and was published November 27, 2007.

Chapter Eight

1. Frank 2006.

2. Gottman 1995.

3. Brown 1987, 24–30; Frankfurt 1987.

4. Eastwick and Hunt 2014, 729.

5. Page 2017.

6. Gigerenzer 2007.

7. Sunnafrank and Ramirez 2004.

8. Barelds and Barelds-Dijkstra 2007.

9. Ben-Ze' ev 2004.

10. Kraus 2017.

11. Gottlieb 2010, 245–48.

12. McNulty et al. 2008.

13. Finkel 2017.

14. Finkel et al. 2012.

15. Rosenfeld and Thomas 2012.

16. Finkel et al. 2012.

17. Korey Lane, "Help, I can't stop hooking up with Trump supporters," *Glamour*, September, 8, 2017.

Chapter Nine

1. Greene 2001.

2. Clanton 1984, 15.

3. Ben-Ze' ev 2004.

4. Fisher 2004, 8; see also Fisher 2010.

5. See, e.g., Becker 1973; Heino et al. 2010.

6. Lindquist and Kaufman-Scarborough 2004.

7. *Merriam-Webster Dictionary*, s.v. "obsession."

8. Muise et al. 2016.

9. Schwartz 2004, 93.

10. Schwartz 2004.

11. Thaler and Sunstein 2009.

12. Lyubomirsky et al. 2005.

13. Oishi et al. 2009.

14. Peele and Brodsky 1975

15. Ackerman et al. 2011; Harrison and Shortall 2011; the survey was conducted by YouGov for eHarmony, 2013.

Chapter Ten

1. Both quotations used here as section epigraphs are from Marta Meana's research and are cited in Martin 2018.

2. Wentland and Reissing 2011.

3. Deitz 2016.

4. Muise et al. 2013; Day et al. 2015.

5. See, e.g., Whillans et al. 2016.

6. Dew and Wilcox 2013.

7. Brogaard 2017, 56.

8. Portmann 2013.

9. Portmann 2013 On generosity and generosity to oneself, see also Nussbaum 2016.

10. Dutton and Aron 1974.

11. Hakim 2012.

12. Scruton 1986, 78–82.

13. Diener and Chan 2011.
14. Diamond and Huebner 2012.
15. Meltzer et al. 2017.
16. Muise et al. 2014; Floyd et al. 2009.
17. Muise et al. 2014; Danovich 2017.
18. Hahn et al. 2012.
19. Ben-Ze'ev 2004.
20. Toulmin (1981) 2017, 89–90.
21. Schneider et al. 2012.
22. Sumter et al. 2017, 67.
23. Cacioppo et al. 2013.
24. Hakim 2012.
25. Deresiewicz (2009) 2017.
26. Amichai-Hamburger and Schneider 2014.

Chapter Eleven

1. Lyubomirsky 2013.
2. Carmichael et al. 2015.
3. Carstensen 2006.
4. Carstensen 2006.
5. Charles and Carstensen 2002.
6. Charles and Carstensen 2010; Birditt et al. 2018.
7. Ben-Ze'ev and Goussinsky 2008.
8. Bar-Nadav and Rubin 2016.
9. Rubin et al. 2012.
10. "How soon is too soon to find love after being widowed?," *Mail Online*, July 10, 2010.
11. Shavit et al. 2017.

Chapter Twelve

1. Proulx et al. 2017.
2. Kipnis 2003, 12.
3. Ben-Ze'ev and Goussinsky 2008.
4. Shaw 1952.
5. Hakim 2012, 3.
6. Parts of this section were written together with Luke Brunning; see Ben-Ze'ev and Brunning 2018.
7. Anapol 2010; Perel 2017; Deri 2015.
8. Fredrickson 2001.
9. Aron et al. 2013, 95–98.
10. Barker 2018.
11. See, e.g., Conley et al. 2018; Rubel and Bogaert 2015; Wood et al. 2018.
12. I owe this point to Jacob Gray.
13. I owe this point, as so many others, to Angelika Krebs.
14. Brunning 2018; Brunning 2019; Sheff 2014.

15. Kipnis 2003, 18, 45.

16. Rousseau 1979, 221.

17. Cialdini et al. 1976.

18. Halevi 2018, 229–30.

19. Halevi 2018, 240.

20. DeSteno and Salovey 1996.

21. De Sousa 2018.

Chapter Thirteen

1. See, e.g., Aristotle, *Nicomachean Ethics*, Book II; see also Angier 2010.

2. Aron 2001.

3. Ariely 2008.

4. Fletcher et al. 2015.

5. Bergen 2006; Jiang and Hancock 2013; Kelmer et al. 2013; Stafford 2005.

6. Baumeister and Leary 1995; Gerstel and Gross 1984.

7. Bergen 2006.

8. Stafford 2005.

9. Kipnis 2003, 60.

10. Mashek and Sherman 2004, 344.

11. Prioleau 2003, 14.

12. Kambartel (1989) 2017.

13. Thayer 1996.

14. Suzuki 1970, 46; cited in Thayer 1996, 14.

15. Indeed, attachment theory considers trust to be the most important feature in long-term, secured romantic relationships; see, e.g., Hazan and Shaver 1987.

16. Kashdan and Rottenberg 2010.

17. Averill et al. 1990, 34.

18. Binstock and Thornton 2003, 441.

19. Reis and Aron 2008.

Chapter Fourteen

1. Wikipedia, https://en.wikipedia.org/wiki/Aging_of_wine.

2. O'Leary et al. 2012; see also Wikipedia, https://en.wikipedia.org/wiki/Aging_of_wine.

3. https://medium.com/wine-folly/why-love-wine-447de95a6e4d.

4. I am grateful to Adin Tropper-Wachtel for bringing this song to my attention.

References

Acevedo, B. P., A. Aron, H. Fisher, and L. L. Brown. 2012. Neural correlates of long-term intense romantic love. *Social Cognition and Affective Neuroscience* 7:145–59.

Ackerman, J. M., V. Griskevicius, and N. Li. 2011. Let's get serious: Communicating commitment in romantic relationships. *Journal of Personality and Social Psychology* 100:1079–94.

Ajzen, I. 2001. Nature and operation of attitudes. *Annual Review of Psychology* 52:27–58.

Amichai-Hamburger, Y., and B. H. Schneider. 2014. Loneliness and internet use. In R. J. Coplan and J. C. Bowker (eds.), *The handbook of solitude*, 317–34. Chichester: Wiley-Blackwell.

Amodio, D. M., and C. J. Showers. 2005. "Similarity breeds liking" revisited: The moderating role of commitment. *Journal of Social and Personal Relationships* 22:817–36.

Anapol, D. 2010. *Polyamory in the 21st century*. Lanham, MD: Rowman & Littlefield.

Anderson, J. R., M. J. Van Ryzin, and W. J. Doherty. 2010. Developmental trajectories of marital happiness in continuously married individuals: A group-based modeling approach. *Journal of Family Psychology* 24:587–96.

Angier, T. 2010. *Techné in Aristotle's ethics: Crafting the moral life*. London: A&C Black.

Ariely, D. 2008. *Predictably irrational*. New York: HarperCollins.

Aristotle. 1984. *The complete works of Aristotle: The revised Oxford translation*. Ed. J. Barnes. Princeton: Princeton University Press.

Armenta, C. N., M. M. Fritz, and S. Lyubomirsky. 2017. Functions of positive emotions: Gratitude as a motivator of self-improvement and positive change. *Emotion Review* 9:183–90.

Aron, A., G. W. Lewandowski Jr., D. Mashek, and E. N. Aron. 2013. The self-expansion model of motivation and cognition in close relationships. In J. A. Simpson and L. Campbell (eds.), *The Oxford handbook of close relationships*, 90–115. Oxford: Oxford University Press.

Aron, E. 2001. *The highly sensitive person in love*. New York: Harmony.

Averill, J. R., G. Catlin, and K. K. Chon. 1990. *Rules of hope*. New York: Springer.

Baker, L. R., J. K. McNulty, and L. E. VanderDrift. 2017. Expectations for future relationship satisfaction: Unique sources and critical implications for commitment. *Journal of Experimental Psychology: General* 146:700–721.

Barelds, D., and P. Barelds-Dijkstra. 2007. Love at first sight or friends first? *Journal of Social and Personal Relationships* 24:479–96.

Barker, M. J. 2018. Using New Relationship Energy (NRE) to open up rather than close down. *Rewriting the Rules* (blog), March 28. www.rewriting-the-rules.com/love-commitment /using-new-relationship-energy-nre-to-open-up-rather-than-close-down/

Bar-Nadav, O., and S. S. Rubin. 2016. Love and bereavement. *OMEGA—Journal of Death and Dying* 74:62–79.

Bauman, Z. 2003. *Liquid love.* Cambridge: Polity Press.

Baumeister, R. F., and E. Bratslavsky. 1999. Passion, intimacy, and time: Passionate love as a function of change in intimacy. *Personality and Social Psychology Review* 3:49–67.

Baumeister, R. F., E. Bratslavsky, C. Finkenauer, and K. D. Vohs. 2001. Bad is stronger than good. *Review of General Psychology* 5:323–70.

Baumeister R. F., and M. R. Leary. 1995. The need to belong: Desire for interpersonal attachments as a fundamental human motivation. *Psychological Bulletin* 117:497–529.

Baumeister, R. F., K. D. Vohs, J. L. Aker, and E. N. Garbinsky. 2013. Some key differences between a happy life and a meaningful life. *Journal of Positive Psychology* 8:505–16.

Becker, G. S. 1973. A theory of marriage: Part I. *Journal of Political Economy* 81:813–46.

Beedie, C., P. Terry, and A. Lane. 2005. Distinctions between emotion and mood. *Cognition & Emotion* 19:847–78.

Benjamin, L., and C. Agnew. 2003. Commitment and its theorized determinants: A meta-analysis of the investment model. *Personal Relationships* 10:37–57.

Ben-Ze' ev, A. 1992. Envy and inequality. *Journal of Philosophy* 89:551–81.

———. 1993. *The perceptual system.* New York: Peter Lang.

———. 2000. *The subtlety of emotions.* Cambridge, MA: MIT Press.

———. 2004. *Love online.* Cambridge: Cambridge University Press.

———. 2010. Jealousy and romantic love. In S. Hart and M. Legerstee (eds.), *Handbook of jealousy,* 40–54. New York: Wiley-Blackwell.

———. 2011. The nature and morality of romantic compromises. In C. Bagnoli (ed.), *Morality and the emotions,* 95–114. Oxford: Oxford University Press.

———. 2016. Envy and inequality in romantic relationships. In R. Smith, U. Merlone, and M. Duffy (eds.), *Envy at work and in organizations,* 429–54. New York: Oxford University Press.

———. 2017a. Does loving longer mean loving more? On the nature of enduring affective attitudes. *Philosophia* 45:1541–62.

———. 2017b. The thing called emotion: A subtle perspective. In Ben-Ze' ev and Krebs 2017, 1:112–37.

Ben-Ze' ev, A., and L. Brunning. 2018. How complex is your love? The case of romantic compromises and polyamory. *Journal for the Theory of Social Behaviour* 48:98–116.

Ben-Ze' ev, A., and R. Goussinsky. 2008. *In the name of love.* Oxford: Oxford University Press.

Ben-Ze' ev, A., and A. Krebs. 2015. Do only dead fish swim with the stream? The role of intuition, emotion, and deliberation in love and work. In M. W. Fröse, S. Kaudela-Baum, and E. P. F. Dievernich (eds.), *Emotionen und Intuitionen in Führung und Organisation,* 43–64. Wiesbaden: Springer Gabler.

——— (eds.). 2017. *Philosophy of emotion.* 4 vols. London: Routledge.

———. 2018. Love in time: Is love best when it is fresh? In C. Grau and A. Smuts (eds.), *Oxford handbook of philosophy of love.* Oxford: Oxford University Press.

Bergen, K. M. 2006. Women's narratives about commuter marriage. PhD dissertation, University of Nebraska-Lincoln.

Berggren, N., H. Jordahl, and P. Poutvaara. 2017. The right look: Conservative politicians look better and voters reward it. *Journal of Public Economics* 146:79–86.

Berscheid, E. 2010. Love in the fourth dimension. *Annual Review of Psychology* 61:1–25.

Binstock, G., and A. Thornton. 2003. Separations, reconciliations, and living apart in cohabiting and marital unions. *Journal of Marriage and Family* 65:432–43.

Birditt, K. S., S. Hope, E. Brown, and T. Orbuch. 2012. Developmental trajectories of marital happiness over 16 years. *Research in Human Development* 9:126–44.

Birditt, K. S., C. W. Sherman, C. A. Polenick, L. Becker, N. J. Webster, K. J. Ajrouch, and T. C. Antonucci. 2018. So close and yet so irritating: Negative relations and implications for well-being by age and closeness. *Journals of Gerontology: Series B*: gby038.

Birnbaum, G. E. 2017. The fragile spell of desire: A functional perspective on changes in sexual desire across relationship development. *Personality and Social Psychology Review* 22:101–27.

Birnbaum, G. E., H. T. Reis, M. Mizrahi, Y. Kanat-Maymon, O. Sass, and C. Granovski-Milner. 2016. Intimately connected: The importance of partner responsiveness for experiencing sexual desire. *Journal of Personality and Social Psychology* 111:530–46.

Brewis, A., and M. Meyer. 2005. Marital coitus across the life course. *Journal of Biosocial Science* 37:499–518.

Brogaard, B. 2015. *On romantic love.* Oxford: Oxford University Press.

———. 2017. The rise and fall of the romantic ideal. In R. Grossi and D. West (eds.), *The radicalism of romantic love,* 47–63. London: Routledge.

Brown, R. 1987. *Analyzing love.* Cambridge: Cambridge University Press.

Bruch, E. E., and M. E. J. Newman. 2018. Aspirational pursuit of mates in online dating markets. *Science Advances* 4(8):eaap9815. https://doi.org/10.1126/sciadv.aap9815.

Bruckner, P. 2013. *Has marriage for love failed?* Cambridge: Polity.

Brunning, L. 2018. The distinctiveness of polyamory. *Journal of Applied Philosophy* 35:513–31.

———. 2019. Imagine there's no jealousy. *Aeon.*

Buber, M. (1923) 1937. *I and thou.* New York: Scribner.

Buss, D. M. 1994. *The evolution of desire.* New York: Basic Books.

Buss, D. M., C. Goetz, J. D. Duntley, K. Asao, and D. Conroy-Beam. 2017. The mate-switching hypothesis. *Personality and Individual Differences* 104:143–49.

Byrne, D., and S. K. Murnen. 1988. Maintaining loving relationships. In R. J. Sternberg and M. L. Barnes (eds.), *The psychology of love,* 293–310. New Haven: Yale University Press.

Cacioppo, S., F. Bianchi-Demicheli, C. Frum, J. G. Pfaus, and J. W. Lewis. 2012. The common neural bases between sexual desire and love: A multilevel kernel density fMRI analysis. *Journal of Sexual Medicine* 9:947–1232.

Cacioppo, J. T., S. Cacioppo, G. C. Gonzaga, E. L. Ogburn, and T. J. VanderWeele. 2013. Marital satisfaction and break-ups differ across on-line and off-line meeting venues. *Proceedings of the Academy of Sciences* 110:1–6.

Call, V., S. Sprecher, and P. Schwartz. 1995. The incidence and frequency of marital sex in a national sample. *Journal of Marriage and the Family* 57:639–52.

Carmichael, C. L., H. T. Reis, and P. R. Duberstein. 2015. In your 20s it's quantity, in your 30s it's quality: The prognostic value of social activity across 30 years of adulthood. *Psychology and Aging* 30:95–105.

Carstensen, L. L. 2006. The influence of a sense of time on human development. *Science* 312 (5782): 1913–15.

Charles, S. T., and L. L. Carstensen. 2002. Marriage in old age. In M. Yalom, L. L. Carstensen, E. Freedman, and B. Gelpi (eds.), *American Couple*, 236–54. Berkeley: University of California Press.

———. 2010. Social and emotional aging. *Annual Review of Psychology* 61:383–409.

Cialdini, R. B., R. J. Borden, A. Thorne, and L. R. Sloan. 1976. Basking in reflected glory: Three (football) field studies. *Journal of Personality and Social Psychology* 34:366–75.

Clanton, G. 1984. Social forces and the changing family. In L. A. Kirkendall and A. E. Gravatt (eds.), *Marriage and the family in the year 2020*, 13–46. Buffalo: Prometheus Books.

Coburn, W. J. 2001. Subjectivity, emotional resonance, and the sense of the real. *Psychoanalytic Psychology* 18:303–19.

Conley, T. D., J. L. Piemonte, S. Gusakova, and J. D. Rubin. 2018. Sexual satisfaction among individuals in monogamous and consensually non-monogamous relationships. *Journal of Social and Personal Relationships* 35:509–31.

Coontz, S. 2005. *Marriage, a history*. New York: Viking.

Csikszentmihalyi, M. 1990. *Flow*. New York: Harper Perennial.

Danovich, T. 2017. Afterglow: Is what happens after sex more important than foreplay or the orgasm? *Aeon*, November 21, 2017.

Day, L. C., A. Muise, S. Joel, and E. A. Impett. 2015. To do it or not to do it? How communally motivated people navigate sexual interdependence dilemmas. *Personality and Social Psychology Bulletin* 41:791–804.

Deitz, B. 2016. 9 things you should never rush in a relationship. *Bustle*, April 5, 2016, https://www.bustle.com/articles/152029-9-things-you-should-never-rush-in-a-relationship.

del Mar Salinas-Jiménez, M., J. Artés, and J. Salinas-Jiménez. 2011. Education as a positional good: A life satisfaction approach. *Social Indicators Research* 103:409–26.

Deresiewicz, W. (2009) 2017. Faux friendship. In Ben-Ze' ev and Krebs 2017, 4:72–81.

Deri, J. 2015. *Love's refraction: Jealousy and compersion in queer women's polyamorous relationships*. Toronto: University of Toronto Press.

de Sousa, R. (2007) 2017. Truth, authenticity, and rationality of emotions. In Ben-Ze' ev and Krebs 2017, 3:251–72.

———. 2015. *Love: A very short introduction*. Oxford: Oxford University Press.

———. 2018. Love, jealousy, and compersion. In C. Grau and A. Smuts (eds.), *Oxford handbook of philosophy of love*. Oxford: Oxford University Press.

DeSteno, D. A., and P. Salovey. 1996. Jealousy and the characteristics of one's rival: A self-evaluation maintenance perspective. *Personality and Social Psychology Bulletin* 22:920–32.

Dew, J., and W. Wilcox. 2013. Generosity and the maintenance of marital quality. *Journal of Marriage and Family* 75:1218–28.

Diamond, L. M., and D. M. Huebner. 2012. Is good sex good for you? Rethinking sexuality and health. *Social and Personality Psychology Compass* 6:54–69.

Diener, E., and M. Y. Chan. 2011. Happy people live longer: Subjective well-being contributes to health and longevity. *Applied Psychology: Health and Well-Being* 3:1–43.

Diener, E., S. Kanazawa, E. M. Suh, and S. Oishi. 2015. Why people are in a generally good mood. *Personality and Social Psychology Review* 19:235–56.

Drigotas, S. M. 2002. The Michelangelo phenomenon and personal well-being. *Journal of Personality* 70:59–77.

Drigotas, S. M., C. E. Rusbult, J. Wieselquist, and S. Whitton. 1999. Close partner as sculptor of the ideal self: Behavioral affirmation and the Michelangelo phenomenon. *Journal of Personality and Social Psychology* 77:293–323.

Dutton, D. G., and A. P. Aron. 1974. Some evidence for heightened sexual attraction under conditions of high anxiety. *Journal of Personality and Social Psychology* 30:510–17.

Dwyer, R. J., K. Kushlev, and E. W. Dunn. 2018. Smartphone use undermines enjoyment of face-to-face social interactions. *Journal of Experimental Social Psychology* 78:233–39.

Eastwick, P. W., and L. L. Hunt. 2014. Relational mate value: Consensus and uniqueness in romantic evaluations. *Journal of Personality and Social Psychology* 106:728–51.

Ellison, C. G., A. M. Burdette, and W. Bradford Wilcox. 2010. The couple that prays together: Race and ethnicity, religion, and relationship quality among working-age adults. *Journal of Marriage and Family* 72:963–75.

Elster, J. 1999. *Alchemies of the mind.* Cambridge: Cambridge University Press.

Esch, T., and G. B. Stefano. 2005. Love promotes health. *Neuroendocrinology Letters* 26:264–67.

Etcoff, N. 1999. *Survival of the prettiest.* New York: Doubleday.

Finkel, E. J. 2017. *The all-or-nothing marriage.* New York: Penguin.

Finkel, E. J., P. W. Eastwick, B. R. Karney, H. T. Reis, and S. Sprecher. 2012. Online dating: A critical analysis from the perspective of psychological science. *Psychology Science in the Public Interest* 13:3–66.

Finkel, E. J., C. M. Hui, K. L. Carswell, and G. M. Larson. 2014. The suffocation of marriage: Climbing Mount Maslow without enough oxygen. *Psychological Inquiry* 25:1–41.

Finkel, E. J., M. I. Norton, H. T. Reis, D. Ariely, P. A. Caprariello, P. W. Eastwick, J. H. Frost, and M. R. Maniaci. 2015. When does familiarity promote versus undermine interpersonal attraction? A proposed integrative model from erstwhile adversaries. *Perspectives on Psychological Science* 10:3–19.

Fisher, H. 2004. *Why we love.* New York: Holt.

———. 2010. *Why him? Why her? How to find and keep lasting love.* New York: Henry Holt.

Fletcher, G. J., J. A. Simpson, L. Campbell, and N. C. Overall. 2015. Pair-bonding, romantic love, and evolution: The curious case of homo sapiens. *Perspectives on Psychological Science* 10:20–36.

Floyd, K., J. P. Boren, A. F. Hannawa, C. Hesse, B. McEwan, and A. E. Veksler. 2009. Kissing in marital and cohabiting relationships: Effects on blood lipids, stress, and relationship satisfaction. *Western Journal of Communication* 73:113–33.

Forste, R., and K. Tanfer. 1996. Sexual exclusivity among dating, cohabiting, and married women. *Journal of Marriage and the Family* 56:33–47.

Frank, R. H. 2006. When it comes to a search for a spouse, supply and demand is only the start. *New York Times,* December 21, 2006.

Frankfurt, H. G. 1987. Equality as a moral ideal. *Ethics* 98:21–43.

———. 1999. Autonomy, necessity, and love. In *Necessity, Volition, and Love,* 129–41. Cambridge: Cambridge University Press.

———. 2004. *The reasons for love.* Princeton: Princeton University Press.

Frederick, S., and G. Loewenstein. 1999. Hedonic adaptation. In D. Kahneman, E. Diener, and N. Schwarz (eds.), *Well-Being,* 302–29. New York: Russell Sage Foundation.

Fredrickson, B. L. 2001. The role of positive emotions in positive psychology: The broaden-and-build theory of positive emotions. *American Psychologist* 56:218–26.

———. 2013a. *Love 2.0.* New York: Plume.

———. 2013b. Positive emotions broaden and build. *Advances in Experimental Social Psychology* 47:1–53.

Frijda, N. H. 1994. Varieties of affect: Emotions and episodes, moods, and sentiments. In P. Ekman and R. J. Davidson, (eds.), *The nature of emotion,* 59–67. New York: Oxford University Press.

———. 2007. *The laws of emotion.* Mahwah, NJ: Lawrence Erlbaum.

Frijda, N. H., B. Mesquita, J. Sonnemans, and S. Van Goozen. 1991. The duration of affective phenomena or emotions, sentiments, and passions. *International Review of Studies on Emotion* 1:187–225.

Fromm, E. 1956. *The art of loving.* New York: HarperCollins.

Fugère, M. A., C. Chabot, K. Doucette, and A. J. Cousins. 2017. The importance of physical attractiveness to the mate choices of women and their mothers. *Evolutionary Psychological Science* 3:243–52.

Furtak, R. A. 2018. *Knowing emotions.* New York: Oxford University Press.

Galinsky, A. D., V. L. Seiden, P. H. Kim, and V. H. Medvec. 2002. The dissatisfaction of having your first offer accepted: The role of counterfactual thinking in negotiations. *Personality and Social Psychology Bulletin* 28:271–83.

Gaver, W. W., and G. Mandler. 1987. Play it again, Sam: On liking music. *Cognition and Emotion* 3:259–82.

Gerstel, N., and H. Gross. 1984. *Commuter marriage.* New York: Guilford Press.

Gigerenzer, G. 2007. *Gut feelings.* New York: Viking.

Gilbert, D. T., and T. D. Wilson. 2000. Miswanting: Some problems in the forecasting of future affective states. In J. Forgas (ed.), *Thinking and feeling,* 178–97. Cambridge: Cambridge University Press.

———. 2007. Prospection: Experiencing the future. *Science* 317:1351–54.

Gilovich, T., and V. H. Medvec. 1995. The experience of regret: What, when, and why. *Psychological Review* 102:379–95.

Girme, Y. U., N. C. Overall, and S. Faingataa. 2014. "Date nights" take two: The maintenance function of shared relationship activities. *Personal Relationships* 21:125–49.

Goodin, R. 2012. *On settling.* Princeton: Princeton University Press.

Gottlieb, L. 2010. *Marry him: The case for settling for Mr. Good Enough.* New York: New American Library.

Gottman, J. 1995. *Why marriages succeed or fail.* London: Bloomsbury.

Gottman, J. M., and R. W. Levenson. 2000. The timing of divorce: Predicting when a couple will divorce over a 14-year period. *Journal of Marriage and Family* 62:737–45.

Gray, J. S., and D. J. Ozer. 2018. Comparing two models of dyadic change: Correlated growth versus common fate. *Social Psychological and Personality Science.*

Greene, R. 2001. *The art of seduction.* New York: Penguin.

Greenspan, P. (1980) 2017. A case of mixed feelings: Ambivalence and the logic of emotion. In Ben-Ze'ev and Krebs 2017, 3:273–95.

Gressel, J. 2016. Disposable diapers, envy and the kibbutz. In R. Smith, U. Merlone, and M. Duffy, (eds.), *Envy in work and organizations.* 399–427. Oxford: Oxford University Press.

Grossmann, I., A. C. Huynh, and P. C. Ellsworth. 2016. Emotional complexity: Clarifying definitions and cultural correlates. *Journal of Personality and Social Psychology* 111:895–916.

Grossmann, I., J. Na, M. E. W. Varnum, D. C. Park, S. Kitayama, and R. E. Nisbett. 2010. Reasoning about social conflicts improves into old age. *Proceedings of the National Academy of Sciences of the United States of America* 107:7246–50.

Gutmann, A., and D. Thompson. 2012. *The spirit of compromise.* Princeton: Princeton University Press.

Hahn, A. C., R. D. Whitehead, M. Albrecht, C. E. Lefevre, and D. I. Perrett. 2012. Hot or not? Thermal reactions to social contact. *Biology Letters* 8:864–67.

Hakim, C. 2012. *The new rules.* London: Gibson Square.

Halbertal, M. 2012. *On sacrifice*. Princeton: Princeton University Press.

Halevi, M. 2018. *The freedom to choose*. Modi'in: Kinneret, Zmora-Bitan, Dvir (Hebrew).

Halpern-Meekin, S., W. D. Manning, P. C. Giordano, and M. A. Longmore. 2013. Relationship churning in emerging adulthood: On/Off relationships and sex with an ex. *Journal of Adolescent Research* 28:166–88.

Harrison, M. A., and J. C. Shortall. 2011. Women and men in love: Who really feels it and says it first? *Journal of Social Psychology* 151:727–36.

Hazan, C., and P. Shaver. 1987. Romantic love conceptualized as an attachment process. *Journal of Personality and Social Psychology* 52:511–24.

Heino, R. D., N. B. Ellison, and J. L. Gibbs. 2010. Relationshopping: Investigating the market metaphor in online dating. *Journal of Social and Personal Relationships* 27:427–47.

Helm, B. W. (2009) 2017. Emotions as evaluative feelings. In Ben-Ze'ev and Krebs 2017, 1:174–88.

———. 2010. *Love, friendship, and the self*. Oxford: Oxford University Press.

Higgins, E. T. 1997. Beyond pleasure and pain. *American Psychologist* 52:1280–1300.

Impett, E. A., and A. Gordon. 2008. For the good of others: Toward a positive psychology of sacrifice. In S. J. Lopez (ed.), *Positive psychology: Exploring the best in people*, 79–100. Westport, CT: Greenwood.

Irvine, W. B. 2006. *On desire*. New York: Oxford University Press.

Jiang, L. C., and J. T. Hancock. 2013. Absence makes the communication grow fonder: Geographic separation, interpersonal media, and intimacy in dating relationships. *Journal of Communication* 63:556–77.

Jollimore, T. 2011. *Love's vision*. Princeton: Princeton University Press.

———. 2018. Love as "something in between." In C. Grau and A. Smuts (eds.), *Oxford handbook of philosophy of love*. Oxford: Oxford University Press.

Jonason, P. K., J. R. Garcia, G. D. Webster, N. P. Li, and H. E. Fisher. 2015. Relationship dealbreakers: Traits people avoid in potential mates. *Personality and Social Psychology Bulletin* 41:1697–1711.

Kahneman, D. 2011. *Thinking, fast and slow*. London: Penguin.

Kahneman, D., and D. T. Miller. 1986. Norm theory: Comparing reality to its alternatives. *Psychological Review* 93:136–53.

Kambartel, F. (1989) 2017. On calmness: Dealing rationality with what is beyond our control. In Ben-Ze'ev and Krebs 2017, 2:51–57.

Kansky, J. 2018. What's love got to do with it? Romantic relationships and well-being. In E. Diener, S. Oishi, and L. Tay (eds.), *Handbook of well-being*, 1–24. Salt Lake City: DEF Publishers.

Karney, B. R., and R. H. Coombs. 2000. Memory bias in long-term close relationships: Consistency or improvement? *Personality and Social Psychology Bulletin* 26:959–70.

Kashdan, T. B., F. R. Goodman, C. Stiksma, C. R. Milius, and P. E. McKnight. 2018. Sexuality leads to boosts in mood and meaning in life with no evidence for the reverse direction: A daily diary investigation. *Emotion* 18:563–76.

Kashdan, T. B., and J. Rottenberg. 2010. Psychological flexibility as a fundamental aspect of health. *Clinical Psychology Review* 30:865–78.

Kelmer, G., G. K. Rhoades, S. M. Stanley, and H. J. Markman. 2013. Relationship quality, commitment, and stability in long-distance relationships. *Family Process* 52:257–70.

Kenny, A. 1965. Happiness. *Proceedings of the Aristotelian Society* 66:93–102.

Kim, J., A. Muise, and E. A. Impett. 2018. The relationship implications of rejecting a partner for sex kindly versus having sex reluctantly. *Journal of Social and Personal Relationships* 35:485–508.

Kipnis, L. 2003. *Against love*. New York: Pantheon.

Kolodny, N. 2003. Love as valuing a relationship. *Philosophical Review* 112:135–89.

Kraus, M. W. 2017. Voice-only communication enhances empathic accuracy. *American Psychologist* 72:644–54.

Krebs, A. 2002. *Arbeit und Liebe*. Frankfurt: Suhrkamp.

———. 2009. "Wie ein Bogenstrich, der aus zwei Saiten eine Stimme zieht": Eine dialogische Philosophie der Liebe. *Deutsche Zeitschrift für Philosophie* 57:729–43.

———. 2014a. Between I and Thou—On the dialogical nature of love. In C. Maurer, T. Milligan, and K. Pacovská (eds.), *Love and its objects*, 7–24. London: Palgrave Macmillan.

———. 2014b. Why landscape beauty matters. *Land* 3:1251–69.

———. 2015. *Zwischen Ich und Du: Eine dialogische Philosophie der Liebe*. Frankfurt: Suhrkamp.

———. 2017a. As if the earth has long stopped speaking to us: Resonance with nature and its loss. In Ben-Ze' ev and Krebs 2017, 3:231–66.

———. 2017b. Stimmung: From mood to atmosphere. *Philosophia* 45:1419–36.

Kulu, H., and P. J. Boyle. 2010. Premarital cohabitation and divorce: Support for the "trial marriage" theory? *Demographic Research* 23:879–904.

LaFollette, H. 1996. *Personal relationships*. Oxford: Blackwell.

Lambert, N, T. F. Stillman, J. A. Hicks, S. Kamble, R. F. Baumeiter, and F. D. Fincham. 2013. Belong is to matter: Sense of belonging enhances meaning in life. *Personality and Social Psychology Bulletin* 39:1418–27.

Landau, I. 2017. *Finding meaning in an imperfect world*. Oxford: Oxford University Press.

Lavner, J. A., T. N. Bradbury, and B. R. Karney. 2012. Incremental change or initial differences? Testing two models of marital deterioration. *Journal of Family Psychology* 26:606–16.

Lawrence, E. M., R. G. Rogers, A. Zajacova, and T. Wadsworth. 2018. Marital happiness, marital status, health, and longevity. *Journal of Happiness Studies*, 1–23.

Levinas, E. 1998. *On thinking-of-the-other: Entre nous*. New York: Columbia University Press.

Lillard, L.A., M. J. Brien, and L. J. Waite. 1995. Premarital cohabitation and subsequent marital dissolution: A matter of self-selection? *Demography* 32:437–57.

Lindquist, J. D., and C. F. Kaufman-Scarborough. 2004. Polychronic tendency analysis: A new approach to understanding women's shopping behaviors. *Journal of Consumer Marketing* 21:332–42.

Lorber, M. F., A. C. E. Erlanger, R. E. Heyman, and K. D. O'Leary. 2015. The honeymoon effect: Does it exist and can it be predicted? *Prevention Science* 16:550–59.

Lyubomirsky, S. 2011. Hedonic adaptation to positive and negative experiences. In S. Folkman (ed.), *Oxford handbook of stress, health, and coping*, 200–24. New York: Oxford University Press.

———. 2013. *The myths of happiness*. New York: Penguin.

Lyubomirsky, S., L. King, and E. Diener. 2005. The benefits of frequent positive affect: Does happiness lead to success? *Psychological Bulletin* 131:803–55.

Määttä, K., and S. Uusiautti. 2013. Silence is not golden. *Communication Studies* 64:33–48.

Marino, P. 2018. Love and economics. In C. Grau and A. Smuts (eds.), The *Oxford handbook of philosophy of love*. Oxford: Oxford University Press.

Martin, W. 2018. *Untrue: Why nearly everything we believe about women, lust, and infidelity is wrong*. Boston: Little, Brown and Company.

Mashek, D. J., and M. D. Sherman. 2004. Desiring less closeness with intimate others. In *Handbook of closeness and intimacy*, 343–56. Mahwah, NJ: Lawrence Erlbaum.

May, S. 2011. *Love: A history*. New Haven: Yale University Press.

McGee, E., and M. Shevlin. 2009. Effect of humor on interpersonal attraction and mate selection. *Journal of Psychology* 143:67–77.

McNulty, J. K., L. A. Neff, and B. R. Karney. 2008. Beyond initial attraction: Physical attractiveness in newlywed marriage. *Journal of Family Psychology* 22:135–43.

McNulty, J. K., M. A. Olson, A. L. Meltzer, and M. J. Shaffer. 2013. Though they may be unaware, newlyweds implicitly know whether their marriage will be satisfying. *Science* 342 (6162):1119–20.

McNulty, J. K., C. A. Wenner, and T. D. Fisher. 2016. Longitudinal associations among relationship satisfaction, sexual satisfaction, and frequency of sex in early marriage. *Archives of Sexual Behavior* 45:85–97.

Meltzer, A. L., A. Makhanova, L. L. Hicks, J. E. French, J. K. McNulty, and T. N. Bradbury. 2017. Quantifying the sexual afterglow: The lingering benefits of sex and their implications for pair-bonded relationships. *Psychological Science* 28:587–98.

Meltzer, A. L., J. K. McNulty, G. L. Jackson, and B. R. Karney. 2014. Sex differences in the implications of partner physical attractiveness for the trajectory of marital satisfaction. *Journal of Personality and Social Psychology* 106:418–28.

Meyers, S. A., and E. Berscheid. 1997. The language of love: The difference a preposition makes. *Personality and Social Psychology Bulletin* 23:347–62.

Mitchell, S. A. 2002. *Can love last?* New York: Norton.

Mogilner, C., S. D. Kamvar, and J. Aaker. 2011. The shifting meaning of happiness. *Social Psychological and Personality Science* 2:395–402.

Morag, T. 2016. *Emotion, imagination, and the limits of reason*. London: Routledge.

———. 2017. The tracking dogma in the philosophy of emotion. *Argumenta* 2:343–63.

Mühlhoff, R. 2019. Affective resonance. In J. Slaby and C. von Scheve (eds.), *Affective societies*. London: Routledge.

Muise, A., E. Giang, and E. A. Impett. 2014. Post-sex affectionate exchanges promote sexual and relationship satisfaction. *Archives of Sexual Behavior* 43:1391–1402.

Muise, A., E. A. Impett, A. Kogan, and S. Desmarais. 2013. Keeping the spark alive: Being motivated to meet a partner's sexual needs sustains sexual desire in long-term romantic relationships. *Social Psychological and Personality Science* 4:267–73.

Muise, A., U. Schimmack, and E. A. Impett. 2016. Sexual frequency predicts greater well-being, but more is not always better. *Social Psychological and Personality Science* 7:295–302.

Myers, D. G. 2000. The funds, friends, and faith of happy people. *American Psychologist* 55: 56–67.

Neff, L. A., and B. R. Karney. 2005. To know you is to love you: The implications of global adoration and specific accuracy for marital relationships. *Journal of Personality and Social Psychology* 88:480–97.

Nozick, R. 1991. Love's bond. In R. C. Solomon and K. M. Higgins (eds.), *The philosophy of (erotic) love*, 417–32. Lawrence: University Press of Kansas.

Nussbaum, M. C. 1986. *The fragility of goodness*. Cambridge: Cambridge University Press.

———. 2001. *Upheavals of thought*. Cambridge: Cambridge University Press.

———. 2016. *Anger and forgiveness: Resentment, generosity, justice*. New York: Oxford University Press.

Oatley, K. (2010) 2017. Two movements in emotions: Communication and reflection. In Ben-Ze'ev and Krebs 2017, 1:209–23.

———. 2018. *Our minds, our selves: A brief history of psychology*. Princeton: Princeton University Press.

Oishi, S., E. Diener, and R. E. Lucas 2009. The optimum level of well-being: Can people be too happy? *Perspectives on Psychological Science* 2:346–60.

O'Leary, K. D., B. P. Acevedo, A. Aron, L. Huddy, and D. Mashek. 2012. Is long-term love more than a rare phenomenon? If so, what are its correlates? *Social Psychological and Personality Science* 3:241–49.

Ortega y Gasset, J. 1941. *On love*. London: Jonathan Cape, 1967.

Page, S. E. 2017. *The diversity bonus*. Princeton: Princeton University Press.

Papp, S. M. 2009. *Outcasts: A love story*. Toronto: Dundurn.

Parkinson, B., P. Totterdell, R. B. Briner, and S. Reynolds. 1996. *Changing moods*. Harlow: Longman.

Peele, S., and A. Brodsky. 1975. *Love and addiction*. New York: Taplinger.

Perel, E. 2007. *Mating in captivity*. New York: Harper.

———. 2017. *The state of affairs*. London: Yellow Kite.

Peterson, R. D., and C. L. Palmer. 2017. Effects of physical attractiveness on political beliefs. *Politics and the Life Sciences* 36:3–16.

Portmann, J. 2013. *The ethics of sex and Alzheimer's*. London: Routledge.

Prins, K. S., B. P. Buunk, and N. W. Van Yperen. 1993. Equity, normative disapproval, and extramarital relationships. *Journal of Social and Personal Relationships* 10:39–53.

Prioleau, B. 2003. *Seductress*. New York: Viking.

Proulx, C. M., A. E. Ermer, and J. B. Kanter. 2017. Group-based trajectory modeling of marital quality: A critical review. *Journal of Family Theory and Review* 9:307–27.

Proulx, C. M., H. M. Helms, and C. Buehler. 2007. Marital quality and personal well-being: A meta-analysis. *Journal of Marriage and Family* 69:576–93.

Quoidbach, J., J. Gruber, M. Mikolajczak, A. Kogan, I. Kotsou, and M. I. Norton. 2014. Emodiversity and the emotional ecosystem. *Journal of Experimental Psychology: General* 143:2057–66.

Reddish, P., R. Fischer, and J. Bulbulia. 2013. Let's dance together: Synchrony, shared intentionality, and cooperation. *PLoS One* 8(8):e71182. https://doi.org/10.1371/journal.pone.00 71182.

Reis, H. T., and A. Aron. 2008. Love: What is it, why does it matter, and how does it operate? *Perspectives on Psychological Science* 3:80–86.

Reis, H. T., and M. S. Clark. 2013. Responsiveness. In J. A. Simpson and L. Campbell (eds.), *The Oxford handbook of close relationships*, 400–423. New York: Oxford University Press.

Rhoades, G. K., S. M. Stanley, and H. J. Markman. 2012. A longitudinal investigation of commitment dynamics in cohabiting relationships. *Journal of Family Issues* 33:369–90.

Rinofner-Kreidl, S. 2017. Grief: Loss and self-loss. In J. J. Drummond and S. Rinofner-Kreidl (eds.), *Emotional experiences: Ethical and social significance*, 91–120. London: Rowman & Littlefield.

———. 2018. Gratitude. In H. Landweer and T. Szanto (eds.), *Handbook of phenomenology of emotions*. London: Routledge.

Roese, N. J., and J. M. Olson. 2014. *What might have been*. London: Psychology Press.

Roese, N. J., and A. Summerville. 2005. What we regret most . . . and why. *Personality and Social Psychology Bulletin* 31:1273–85.

Rosa, H. 2013. *Social acceleration*. New York: Columbia University Press.

———. 2016. *Resonanz*. Frankfurt: Suhrkamp.

Rosenfeld, M. J., and K. Roesler. 2018. Cohabitation experience and cohabitation's association with marital dissolution. *Journal of Marriage and Family*.

Rosenfeld, M. J., and R. J. Thomas. 2012. Searching for a mate: The rise of the internet as a social intermediary. *American Sociological Review* 77:523–47.

Rousseau, J. J. 1979. *Emile: or on education*. New York: Basic Books.

Rubel, A. N., and A. F. Bogaert. 2015. Consensual nonmonogamy: Psychological well-being and relationship quality correlates. *Journal of Sex Research* 52:961–82.

Rubin, S. S., R. Malkinson, and E. Witztum. 2012. *Working with the bereaved*. New York: Routledge.

Russell, B. 1930. *The conquest of happiness*. London: Routledge, 2006.

———. 1968. *Autobiography of Bertrand Russell: 1872–World War I*. New York: Bantam.

Saad, G., and T. Gill. 2014. The framing effect when evaluating prospective mates: An adaptationist perspective. *Evolution and Human Behavior* 35:184–92.

Schneider, J. P., R. Weiss, and C. Samenow. 2012. Is it really cheating? Understanding the emotional reactions and clinical treatment of spouses and partners affected by cybersex infidelity. *Sexual Addiction & Compulsivity* 19:123–39.

Schwartz, B. 2004. *The paradox of choice*. New York: HarperCollins.

Scitovsky, T. 1976. *The joyless economy*. New York: Oxford University Press.

Scruton, R. 1986. *Sexual desire*. London: Weidenfeld and Nicolson.

———. 1997. *The aesthetics of music*. Oxford: Oxford University Press.

———. 2011. *Beauty: A very short introduction*. Oxford: Oxford University Press.

Shavit, O., A. Ben-Zeev, and I. Doron. 2017. Love between couples living with Alzheimer's disease: Narratives of spouse care-givers, *Ageing & Society*, 1–30.

Shaw, G. B. 1952. *Don Juan in hell*. New York: Dodd, Mead.

Sheff, E. 2014. *The polyamorists next door*. Lanham, MD: Rowman & Littlefield.

Sherman, N. 1993. The virtues of common pursuit. *Philosophy and Phenomenological Research* 53:277–99.

Shulman, S., R. Tuval-Mashiach, E. Levran, and S. Anbar. 2006. Conflict resolution patterns and longevity of adolescent romantic couples: A 2-year follow-up study. *Journal of Adolescence* 29:575–88.

Simon, H. A. 1979. Rational decision making in business organizations. *American Economic Review* 69:493–513.

Sloman, S. A. 1996. The empirical case for two systems of reasoning. *Psychological Bulletin* 119:3–22.

Smith, R. H., and S. H. Kim. 2007. Comprehending envy. *Psychological Bulletin* 133:46–64.

Sobel, A. 1990. *The structure of love*. New Haven: Yale University Press.

Solomon, R. 1988. *About love*. New York: Simon and Schuster.

———. 1990. *Love*. New York: Prometheus Books.

Spinoza, B. (1677) 1985. *Ethics*. In E. Curley (ed.), *The collected works of Spinoza*. Princeton: Princeton University Press.

Sprecher, S. 1999. "I love you more today than yesterday": Romantic partners' perceptions of changes in love and related affect over time. *Journal of Personality and Social Psychology* 76:46–53.

Sprecher, S., M. Schmeeckle, and D. Felmlee. 2006. The principle of least interest: Inequality in emotional involvement. *Journal of Family Issues* 27:1255–80.

Stafford, L. 2005. *Maintaining long-distance and cross-residential relationships*. Mahwah, NJ: Lawrence Erlbaum.

Stanley, S. M., G. K. Rhoades, and H. J. Markman. 2006. Sliding vs. deciding: Inertia and the premarital cohabitation effect. *Family Relations* 55:499–509.

Sudo, P. T. 2000. *Zen sex: The way of making love*. San Francisco: Harper.

Sumter, S. R., L. Vandenbosch, and L. Ligtenberg. 2017. Love me Tinder: Untangling emerging adults' motivations for using the dating application Tinder. *Telematics and Informatics* 34:67–78.

Sunnafrank, M., and A. Ramirez. 2004. At first sight: Persistent relational effects of get-acquainted conversations, *Journal of Social and Personal Relationships* 21:361–79.

Suzuki, S. 1970. *Zen mind, beginner's mind*. New York: Weatherhill.

Taylor, C. (1985) 2017. The concept of a person. In Ben-Ze'ev and Krebs 2017, 1:42–56.

Thaler, R. H., and C. R. Sunstein. 2009. *Nudge*. Penguin Books.

Thayer, R. E. 1996. *The origin of everyday moods*. New York: Oxford University Press.

Thomas, M. L., et al. 2016. Paradoxical trend for improvement in mental health with aging. *Journal of Clinical Psychiatry* 77:e1019–e1025.

Toulmin, S. (1981) 2017. The tyranny of principles. In Ben-Ze'ev and Krebs 2017, 3:76–92.

Valdesolo, P., and D. DeSteno. 2011. Synchrony and the social tuning of compassion. *Emotion* 11:262–66.

Valdesolo, P., J. Ouyang, and D. DeSteno. 2010. The rhythm of joint action: Synchrony promotes cooperative ability. *Journal of Experimental Social Psychology* 46:693–95.

Velleman, J. D. 1999. Love as a moral emotion. *Ethics* 109:338–74.

Watson, D., E. C. Klohnen, A. Casillas, E. Nus Simms, J. Haig, and D. S. Berry. 2004. Match makers and deal breakers: Analyses of assortative mating in newlywed couples. *Journal of Personality* 72:1029–68.

Wentland, J. J., and E. D. Reissing. 2011. Taking casual sex not too casually: Exploring definitions of casual sexual relationships. *Canadian Journal of Human Sexuality* 20:75–91.

Whelan, C. B. 2006. *Why smart men marry smart women*. New York: Simon & Schuster.

Whillans, A. V., E. W. Dunn, G. M. Sandstrom, S. S. Dickerson, and K. M. Madden. 2016. Is spending money on others good for your heart? *Health Psychology* 35:574–83.

Wiltermuth, S. S., and C. Heath. 2009. Synchrony and cooperation. *Psychological Science* 20:1–5.

Wood, J., S. Desmarais, T. Burleigh, and R. Milhausen. 2018. Reasons for sex and relational outcomes in consensually nonmonogamous and monogamous relationships: A self-determination theory approach. *Journal of Social and Personal Relationships* 35:632–54.

Yee, N. 2014. *The Proteus paradox*. New Haven: Yale University Press.

Index